net niet nat

Bies van Ede
tekeningen van Marjolein Krijger

loes en mik

dit is mik.
loes is zijn kat.
zij is dik.
zij likt uit haar kom.
wat zit daar in?
geen sap en ook geen bier.
wat is het wel?
mik weet het.
weet jij het ook?

zeg maar:

ik weet het.

of

nee, ik weet het niet.

en wat is het dan?

loes is lui.
zij ligt vaak in de tuin.
als er zon is.
niet als het nat is.
dan ligt loes in huis.
loes wil niet nat zijn.
nat is naar voor een kat.
mik wist dat wel.
wist jij het ook?

zeg maar:

ik wist het.

of

nee, ik wist het niet.

en hoe wist jij het?

een poes houdt niet van nat.
maar wel van nat uit haar kom.
gek is dat.
'mauw,' zegt loes.
'het is niet gek.
mijn bek mag nat zijn,
maar mijn vel niet.
net als bij jou, mik.'
is dat waar?

in de tuin van man buur

loes gaat door het hek.
daar is ook een tuin.
de tuin van man buur.
ze maakt er een gat.
fijn is dat.
loes doet dat niet in de tuin van mik.
het gat dekt ze af.
maar man buur ziet het.
het maakt hem boos.
'ik wll geen kat in de tuin.'
man buur pakt een kan.
wat doet hij er in?
loes weet het niet.
weet jij het?

zeg maar:

ik weet het.

of

nee, ik weet het niet.

wat is het dan?

daar komt man buur.
loes ziet hem niet.
ze hoort hem ook niet.
man buur mikt met de kan.
'dat is raak, vies dier!'
maar hij heeft het mis.
'ha ha!' roept loes.
'het was mis.
ik ben net niet nat!'
dan is ze weg.
hup, weer naar de tuin van mik.
loes is niet nat.
en man buur is boos.
boos...

7

een dier dat jeukt

loes ligt in de tuin.
wat is er, loes?
je doet zo raar.
'mauw,' zegt loes.
en weer: 'mauw.'
een kat zegt dat vaak.
loes heeft jeuk!
jeuk is naar.
net zo naar als nat zijn.
loes bijt.
ze doet haar poot heen en weer.
de jeuk gaat niet weg.
mik kijk in haar vel.
daar zit een dier.
kijk maar.
mik weet de naam van het dier.
weet jij hem ook?

zeg maar:

ik weet hem.

of

nee, ik weet hem niet.

wat is het dan?

8

mik tilt loes op.
'jij moet in de teil,' zegt hij.
'er zit een dier in je vel.
een dier dat jeukt.
we doen de teil vol.
ik doe je er in.
dan gaat het dier wel weg.
en je jeuk ook.'

9

mik neemt loes mee in huis.
loes wil niet in de teil.
'nee,' roept ze, 'nee.'
'laat me los.'
mik laat niet los.
maar loes is leep.
ze mept!
en weg is ze.
'au!' roept mik.
'naar dier.'

'ha! ha!' mauwt loes.
'net niet nat.'
'loes, kom nou hier,' roept mik.
'je moet van je jeuk af!'
loes doet het niet.
'ik hou niet van nat,' zegt ze.
ik hou mijn jeuk wel.

man buur is nog boos

mik zoekt loes.
loes zit bij het hek.
dan kan ze gauw weg.
ze wil niet met mik mee.
ze heeft nog jeuk.
het is niet fijn.
'maar het geeft niet,' zegt loes.
'jeuk is niet leuk.
maar nat, dat is pas naar.'
ze bijt op haar rug.
ze bijt in haar buik.
het dier gaat niet weg.

loes tilt haar kop op.
ze hoort mik.
'loes!' roept hij.
'kom nou!'
maar loes komt niet.

loes gaat door het hek.
wie ziet ze daar?
man buur!
wat heeft hij?
weet jij het?

zeg maar:

of

ik weet het.

nee, ik weet het niet.

zeg, wat is het dan?

man buur heeft zijn kan.
de kan is vol.
en wat doet hij?
hij kiept de kan.

hij is net te laat.
loes is weer rap.
'ha ha, buur!
net niet nat.'
loes wil weg.
maar dat gaat fout.
man buur rent naar loes toe.
wat moet loes doen?
door man buur heen?
dat gaat niet.
ze komt op zijn voet.
man buur tilt zijn voet op.
en loes?
loes zoeft.
'au au!' roept ze.
'dit wil ik niet.
een poes zoeft niet.'

zeg maar:

dat kan ik ook.

of

nee, dat kan ik niet.

zeg, hoe kon dat nou?

man buur heeft jeuk

loes ligt in de tuin.
ze is niet nat.
dat is fijn.
maar ze heeft wel wat pijn.
ze heeft pijn en jeuk.
of nee...
de jeuk is weg.
ze voelt het dier niet meer.
waar is het heen?

mik holt de tuin in.
'loes, doet het pijn?'
'nee,' mauwt loes.
'de pijn is al weg.
en de jeuk ook.
waar zou het dier zijn?'
mik kijkt om.
en dan ziet hij het.
het dier is...
weet jij het?

zeg maar: ik weet het al.
    of
    nee, ik weet het niet.

zeg, waar is het dan?

het dier is bij man buur.
dat zie je wel.
man buur doet raar.
hij bijt in zijn voet.
zijn been gaat heen en weer.
hij is net een kat.
'ha! ha!' roept loes.
'ik was net niet nat.
maar man buur moet in de teil.
wat is jeuk leuk!'

een muur in de tuin

loes doet een dut.
man buur is in de tuin.
man buur is boos.
te boos om in de teil te gaan.
man buur maakt een muur.
de muur is hoog.
wat wil hij met die muur?
weet jij het?

zeg maar:

ik weet het wel.

of

nee, ik weet het niet.

wat wil man buur?

net niet nat?

loes ligt lui in de tuin.
dan tilt ze haar kop op.
ze rekt haar poot.
ze kijkt naar de muur.
veel te hoog.
dan moet het maar hier.
loes maakt een kuil in de tuin van mik.
maar ze let niet op...
'nee, loes!' zegt mik.
'dat wil ik niet.
ga maar op de bak.
ik wil geen kuil in mijn tuin.'
mik pakt een kan.
wat gaat hij doen?
weet jij het?

zeg maar:

ik weet het wel.

of

nee, ik weet het niet.

loes wil weg.
maar waar naar toe?
het hek is weg.
ze kan niet door de muur.
de muur is hoog.
loes kan er ook niet op.
waar moet ze heen?
en daar komt mik.
mik mikt met de kan...
mikt hij raak?
of mikt hij mis?
wie weet het?

zeg maar:

loes is nat.

of

net niet nat.

dat is nat!

Spetter

Serie 1, na 4 maanden leesonderwijs, sluit aan bij *Veilig leren lezen* kern 7.
Serie 2, na 5 maanden leesonderwijs, sluit aan bij *Veilig leren lezen* kern 8.
Serie 3, na 6 maanden leesonderwijs, sluit aan bij *Veilig leren lezen* kern 9.
Serie 4, na 7 maanden leesonderwijs, sluit aan bij *Veilig leren lezen* kern 10.
Serie 5, na 8 maanden leesonderwijs, sluit aan bij *Veilig leren lezen* kern 11.
Serie 6, na 9 maanden leesonderwijs, sluit aan bij *Veilig leren lezen* kern 12.

In Spetter serie 1 zijn verschenen:

Lieneke Dijkzeul: naar zee, naar zee!
Bies van Ede: net niet nat
Vivian den Hollander: die zit!
Rindert Kromhout: een dief in huis
Elle van Lieshout en Erik van Os: dag schat
Koos Meinderts: man lief en heer loos
Anke de Vries: jaap is een aap
Truus van de Waarsenburg: weer te laat?

Spetter is er ook voor kinderen van 7 en 8 jaar.

AVI 1

Boeken met dit vignet zijn op niveaubepaling geregistreerd en gecontroleerd door KPC Onderwijs Adviseurs te 's-Hertogenbosch.

6 7 8 / 06 05 04

ISBN 90.276.3971.x • NUGI **260**/220

Vormgeving: Rob Galema (studio Zwijsen)
Logo Spetter en schutbladen: Joyce van Oorschot

© 1998 Tekst: Bies van Ede
Illustraties: Marjolein Krijger
Uitgeverij Zwijsen Algemeen B.V. Tilburg

Voor België:
Uitgeverij Infoboek N.V. Meerhout
D/1998/1919/203

PANIC ATTACKS

PANIC ATTACKS

MEDIA MANIPULATION AND MASS DELUSION

ROBERT E. BARTHOLOMEW
HILARY EVANS

SUTTON PUBLISHING

First published in the United Kingdom in 2004 by
Sutton Publishing Limited · Phoenix Mill
Thrupp · Stroud · Gloucestershire · GL5 2BU

British Library Cataloguing in Publication Data
A catalogue record for this book is available from the British
Library.

ISBN 0-7509-3785-8

Typeset in 11/14.5 pt Sabon.
Typesetting and origination by
Sutton Publishing Limited.
Printed and bound in England by
J.H. Haynes & Co. Ltd, Sparkford.

Contents

You can fool too many of the people too much of the time.

James Thurber

Introduction

Knowledge is power.

Francis Bacon

Without a doubt, the mass media – newspapers, magazines, books, radio, television, the internet – have great potential to effect positive change in society. In today's information age, we depend on some aspect of the media every day of our lives: politics, economic news, foreign events, natural disasters, weather and traffic reports, stock quotations, sports scores, car accidents, obituaries. Yet, for all of the potential good, there is a dark side. We have reached a point where we are so reliant on the media and it is so taken for granted that we are more susceptible than ever before to mass deception. Never before have so many been so literate, so educated and had so much access to so much information. Yet, never before has so much information been controlled by so few and travelled so fast to so many. Never has the potential for mass manipulation been greater.

We truly live in a global village. This is especially so with the growing trend of newspaper, radio and television syndication whereby the same article or programme can be read, watched or heard by hundreds of millions of people. The problem is, media outlets do not simply report, they filter, interpret, editorialize. Sometimes the 'spin' is deliberate and political such as the conservative bias of the Fox TV News Channel which touts itself as 'Fair and Balanced'. This is nothing more than a hollow advertising slogan. At other times the reporting bias is subtle, subconsciously reflecting core cultural values and beliefs such as predictable rah-rah war stories whereby everyone on 'our side' is a hero while those on the 'other side' are portrayed as ignorant, misguided, evil. To a certain extent the media must reflect society's core beliefs on certain emotional issues or lose its audience and advertising sponsorship. Either way, truth is the casualty. There is no impartiality. Yet we are presented with the illusion of impartiality.

This book examines cases of media deception and manipulation – both famous and obscure. Each example highlights our vulnerability to believing myths and poppycock that are presented as gospel and accepted as reality. We can learn from past mistakes, not to grow overly complacent or trusting of what we read, watch and hear, and to ask questions and challenge claims. We can learn to step back from the rat maze and see the bigger picture. History is a valuable tool in examining these events, distancing us from their emotional impact, affording a better vantage point from which to glean insights.

Chapter one examines the birth of tabloid journalism. Today's flashy headlines of celebrity scandal and shock can be traced back to the summer of 1835, with a series of reports appearing in a New York City newspaper. The stories in the *Sun* caused a worldwide sensation. Created by journalist Richard Adams Locke and *Sun* publisher Benjamin Day, the paper claimed that British astronomer Sir John Herschel had perfected the world's strongest telescope in a South African observatory and could actually see living creatures on the moon. Why was the 'Great Moon Hoax' so successful, making the *Sun* the world's best-selling newspaper? Why were even many scientists fooled? How could people believe such wild descriptions of beaver people and bat-men? How did Locke manage to embarrass rival papers who unscrupulously reported the story as their own? Why did Edgar Allen Poe stop writing his story of Hans Pfaall when he read the bogus accounts? Why did Herschel laugh upon learning of the hoax, only to grow resentful?

In chapter two, we discuss the Halley's Comet Scare. In May 1910, many people became terror-stricken after the publication of a sensational report on the front page of the *New York Times*. The alarming article warned of the possible extinction of human life when the tail of Halley's Comet was projected to pass through the Earth's atmosphere on the night of 18 May. A series of chance events, combined with newspaper sensationalism, fostered the scare. The relatively recent discovery of deadly cyanogen gas in the tail, and news that its tail would take an unusual course, culminated in worldwide fear. Many newspapers and magazines across the United States and Europe speculated about possible doomsday scenarios. When the appointed hour arrived some people went so far as to stuff rags in doorways, while opportunists sold masks and 'comet pills' to counter the effects of the gas. Some sealed up their homes and stayed inside with oxygen cylinders to wait out the night. Many workers in the southern United States refused to work and left their jobs, choosing instead to attend all-night church vigils, believing that the end of the world was at hand. Others made light of the concern, whooping it up with rooftop comet parties. Similar scenes occurred around the world. In Bermuda, upon the report of the death of King Edward VII, some citizens said the comet turned red. Many dock workers 'fell on their knees and began to pray. They thought that the end of the world was surely coming' and refused to work. The workers were adamant that the observation was a portent that war would occur during the reign of the new king, George. They were also convinced that a great disaster would strike Earth. In San Juan, Puerto Rico, hundreds marched in a candlelight parade through the streets and sang religious songs.

In 1997, a similar media-driven scare surrounded the appearance of another comet: Hale-Bopp was blamed for over three dozen deaths when the California-based 'Heaven's Gate' committed mass suicide. After examining the notes they left behind, it is clear the members were convinced that by killing themselves they would be beamed aboard a spaceship hiding behind the comet. The publication of books, magazines and documentaries promoting the reality of UFOs, and discussion of the comet–spaceship theory on a popular American radio talk show, combined to trigger the event.

Chapter three describes the infamous Martian invasion scare of Halloween Eve in 1938, when over a million people became frightened after listening to a realistic radio drama produced by

Orson Welles' CBS Mercury Theatre. Based on the book *The War of the Worlds*, the play spooked a nation and is a vivid reminder of the potential power of the media. Several issues are examined: why couldn't the Federal Communications Commission take any action against Welles, CBS or the Mercury Theatre? Why did newspaper editors deliberately exaggerate the broadcast's impact? Why was the drama so believable? How did the script get by CBS censors? How did Welles ingeniously 'snare' listeners to other programmes? How did people's minds play tricks on them, experiencing things described on the radio – things that weren't real? How did events in Europe render the play more believable? Why are we destined to have similar scares in the future? What was the reaction near ground zero – Grovers Mill, New Jersey – the reported crash site of the Martians? How did this hoax come back to haunt Welles during the 1941 attack on Pearl Harbor?

In chapter four, we analyse six other radio panics that were triggered by adaptations of the *War of the Worlds* script. What do these scripts have in common? Why were they so successful? Why do these episodes keep occurring? In 1944, terrified residents in parts of Chile ran into the streets; others hid in their homes after a localized version of the Welles drama. In one province, military units were mobilized to repel the Martian invaders. Five years later, a similar episode occurred in Ecuador, resulting in pandemonium. The realistic broadcast included impersonations of leaders, reporters, vivid eyewitness accounts and real names of local places. In Quito a riot broke out. An angry mob torched the building housing the radio station which broadcast the play, killing several occupants including its mastermind.

Regional adaptations of the Orson Welles play have triggered localized scares in the United States. In 1968 at Buffalo, New York, a play on radio station WKBW fostered widespread anxiety, even prompting the mobilization of the Canadian National Guard. Three years later, after a broadcast on WPRO in Providence, Rhode Island, residents flooded police with phone calls after listening to a report that a meteorite had fallen in nearby Jamestown, Rhode Island, followed by accounts of invading Martians. The incident was serious enough for the Federal Communications Commission (FCC) to reprimand the station and rewrite the law on broadcasting such potentially deceptive programmes. The most recent 'war of the worlds' panic occurred on 30 October 1998 in northern Portugal. Broadcast on Radio Antena 3, news bulletins claimed that Martians were heading towards the capital of Lisbon, panicking hundreds.

Chapter five scrutinizes four media-created social delusions involving real or imaginary creatures, and why they were successful. The 'Central Park Zoo Hoax' of 1874 was perpetrated by the *New York Herald*, resulting in many residents refusing to go to work or leave their dwellings for fear of being eaten by ferocious animals that were supposedly loose in the city. What made the story so plausible to New York City dwellers? What was the motivation of the writer? Why did some animal morality advocates applaud the scare?

During the summer of 1899, James McElhone of the *Washington Post* unwittingly created an epidemic of 'kissing bug' bites across the country. McElhone erroneously reported on what he thought was an impending plague of 'kissing bugs' that were said to be biting people's lips while they slept, in the Washington, DC, area. The 'wounds' were said to be serious and cause great swelling. The report was quickly picked up by other papers and spread across the country as jittery citizens rushed to emergency rooms and doctors' offices for treatment of what they feared were potentially fatal bites. Bug experts examining 'kissing bugs' collected by so-called bite victims identified a variety of mundane insects – beetles, houseflies, bees, mosquitoes, but not a solitary kissing bug! What are the parallels with medieval episodes of hysteria involving tarantism whereby peasants in southern Italy would begin to dance uncontrollably after supposedly being bitten by the tarantula spider?

On Halloween night 1992 the BBC aired a bogus 'live' documentary during which it created a malicious ghost named 'Pipes'. The show frightened many viewers around Great Britain, and was blamed for cases of post-traumatic stress disorder in children, and at least one suicide. Why was the show's host, Michael Parkinson, unrepentant, even defiant at critics?

Introduction

The 'Texas Earthworm Hoax' occurred in 1993, when the *Morning Times* of Laredo published an account of a giant 300lb earthworm supposedly draped across Interstate 35. Many residents believed the story and flocked to the site despite claims that the worm was 79ft long! How could so many people believe such an absurd claim? Why was south Texas one of the few places in the United States where the story seemed plausible?

Chapter six explores two events during the 1990s that shook European confidence: the mass poisoning of nearly a thousand citizens by contaminated Coca-Cola products, and a belief that the dreaded mad cow disease was spreading to humans from contaminated beef. Both fears were unfounded. Yet, driven by media sensationalism and speculation, Europeans suffered with needless anxiety and worry as their fears were blown up beyond all proportion to the real threat.

In chapter seven the media's role in creating two separate witch-hunts, hundreds of years apart, is examined. The barbarity of the medieval European witch-hunts and the Salem witch trials of 1692 seem like ancient history. The stark contrast with today's modern, sophisticated, tolerant society could seemingly not be greater. Today's superior education and legal and judicial systems would seem to render us immune from any semblance of such cruelty and injustice. Yet a witch-hunt on a similar scale began to take shape in the United States during the late 1970s and did not abate until the early 1990s. An 'epidemic' of child sexual abuse swept across America, triggered by a new fad in psychotherapy involving the search for 'hidden memories'. Soon overzealous therapists were seeking to find the causes of various problems and disorders as stemming from childhood molestation. It didn't matter that the patient had no initial recall of such crimes. Vague feelings and faint inklings were sufficient to justify the use of dubious techniques intended to reveal these truths: hypnotic regression, dream interpretation, journaling, imaging. On such subjective evidence thousands were imprisoned, their reputations forever tarnished, haunted for the rest of their lives by the spectre of such heinous accusations. They may as well have had the words 'sex offender' branded on their foreheads. This chapter compares the role of the book *The Courage to Heal* in fostering the 'hidden memory' movement, with the impact of the notorious *Malleus Maleficarum* which is responsible for sending more witches to their death than any other publication in history.

In chapter eight, several examples of chemical or biological terrorism scares are presented. In each case, the mass media was influential in either creating or spreading fear that was either entirely imaginary or greatly exaggerated. Such scares are not new. We begin with the 1630 'Bubonic Plague Scare' in Milan, Italy, which was fostered by the printing and posting of public proclamations. This episode is followed by the case of the 'mad gasser' of Mattoon, Illinois, during the Second World War, involving reports of a crazed gasser spraying residents in their homes with a noxious chemical. Many 'victims' reported getting sick; some even caught fleeting glimpses of the imaginary gasser. The two-week episode and dozens of reported attacks and related illness were the creation of the local newspaper, the *Mattoon Daily Journal-Gazette*. Other Illinois papers quickly followed suit and within days the entire nation was reading of the gasser's exploits until authorities determined the fictitious nature of the malady.

In 1983, a mysterious illness was reported among a relatively small number of Arab students at a school in the disputed Israeli-occupied territories. Unfounded press reports began to appear stating that the girls had been poisoned by Jews, triggering a wave of psychosomatic illness reports in nearly a thousand Arab students in schools throughout the Jordan West Bank. The attacks on America on 11 September 2001, and subsequent media anticipation and exaggeration of the threat from imminent attacks using chemical or biological weapons, triggered a flurry of mass hysterical illness reports ranging from 'anthrax cough' to the 'Bin Laden Itch'. Studying these events can help us better deal with future terror scares which seem inevitable given the level of American social paranoia at the dawn of the twenty-first century.

Chapter nine examines media complicity in promoting myths and stereotypes about the capabilities and intelligence of 'primitive' peoples that are depicted on a simplistic continuum of two extremes: irrational natives or 'noble savages'. The first part of the chapter discusses the President Johnson cult of the 1960s. In February of 1963, the world first learned of a small, bizarre group of natives on tiny New Hanover island in the South Pacific. We were led to believe that, upon hearing stories of American wealth and power, many of the inhabitants stopped paying taxes and began collecting money in order to 'buy' the then president, Lyndon Johnson – the leader of these great people – in hopes that he would use the money to fly to their island and guide them to prosperity. Media reports portrayed the natives as 'Johnson cultists' who were confused and irrational; ignorant yahoos, incapable of even the simplest use of logic and reasoning. Yet a closer scrutiny of these events, based on an interview with the anthropologist who lived with them, reveals the cult as a sophisticated tax protest movement that had no intention of 'buying' Johnson. The natives have a long history of using theatrics and bluffing as a way to negotiate. The real purpose of the cult was to embarrass their unpopular Australian rulers – embarrass them into a better deal as their island had been neglected for years. Australian authorities refused to allow independent reporters or anthropologists onto the island for fear of learning the truth, instead issuing media reports about a strange cult of irrational natives. The Western media simply parroted the story that the Australians wanted the world to believe. The Johnson cult continues to be the brunt of Western jokes to this day, yet any joke is on them.

The second part of chapter nine recounts another media-created myth. In 1971, it was reported that a Stone Age tribe was discovered in the Philippines. Despite limited access and 'red flags' galore, the media accepted the story at face value, reporting it to the world as fact. The media fell in love with the Tasaday people who were compared to living in a Biblical Eden – 'noble savages' who didn't even have a translatable word for war, living in physical and moral isolation from the world. Their pictures graced the pages of *Time, US News & World Report* and the cover of *National Geographic*. There was only one problem – it was a hoax perpetrated by the Ferdinand Marcos government. How were so many people fooled for so long? Hints and clues were everywhere but journalists, intoxicated at being part of such a discovery, could not see the clear signposts.

Awareness and knowledge are critical lines of defence against future media-made deceptions. There is every indication that during the twenty-first century we will continue to grow more reliant on the mass media. With this dependency comes a responsibility to thoroughly understand this medium and its potential for good and bad. To fully reach our potential, we must heed the lessons of the past. This book is a starting point in that learning process.

ROBERT E. BARTHOLOMEW   HILARY EVANS
Whitehall, New York   London, England

ONE

The Great Moon Hoax of 1835: Tabloid Journalism is Born

What ardently we wish, we soon believe.[1]

Edward Young (*Night Thoughts*)

The modern era of tabloid journalism began with a whopper created in the New York city offices of Benjamin H. Day, owner of the *Sun*. It was the summer of 1835, when Day and his cohort pulled off what is arguably the most successful hoax in newspaper history. They claimed to have indisputable proof that the Moon was inhabited by an array of strange creatures including beings resembling bat-men and two-legged beavers. The hoax was the brainchild of the paper's star reporter, Richard Adams Locke (1800–71), a Cambridge-educated amateur astronomer, who at the relatively tender age of thirty-five, had been recently lured to the two-year-old penny daily for the then substantial wage of $12 per week. Edgar Allan Poe describes Locke as a literary genius: 'Everything he writes is a model in its peculiar way, serving just the purposes intended and nothing to spare.'[2] Locke was gifted with a fantastic imagination and a knack for making his stories seem believable. A masterful blend of fact and fiction, the writing of the Moon hoax was spellbinding; science fiction at its vivid and plausible best. The public was also strung along brilliantly. Like a hungry school of fish patiently coaxed by a veteran fisherman to nibble, many New Yorkers and others across the country soon took the bait, gobbling it down hook, line and sinker. The *Sun*'s 'fishy story' began modestly, rendering it all the more believable. It quickly grew in proportion, turning into one of the greatest hoaxes of all time.

1

Our story begins in November 1833, when the eminent British astronomer Sir John Frederick William Herschel (1792–1871), son of the equally renowned astronomer Sir William Herschel, discoverer of the planet Uranus, made an historic voyage. He and his family boarded a ship in Portsmouth, England, bound for the Cape of Good Hope in South Africa, intent on observing the heavens in order to map out portions of the southern sky not visible north of the equator. Stored in the ship's cargo hold were two of the most powerful telescopes of the period, though modest by modern standards. On 16 January, Herschel's party went ashore at Claremont and soon took up residence there on the grounds of Feldhausen, just south of Cape Town. The location was ideal for setting up the telescopes, and the spacious nineteen-room mansion was equally suited for Herschel's large family. This would be the location from which Herschel would make many important discoveries. But it was his planned observation of the Moon which was highly anticipated and caught the popular interest. Thanks to the promise offered by Herschel's remarkable new equipment, there were high expectations that he would add substantially to our knowledge of the Moon, and perhaps learn whether or not it was inhabited.[3]

Herschel's expedition would be the inspiration for one of the greatest hoaxes of all time, and the first known case of modern tabloid journalism. It was against this backdrop that, during the summer of 1835, a series of newspaper reports appeared in the *Sun*, causing a worldwide sensation. It was reported that Herschel could see living creatures on the Moon! While the claim was outrageous, it was also plausible in its time. Speculation as to whether the Moon might possess inhabitants had exercised the human imagination since the earliest times. Many writers had conceived voyages to the Moon, notably the seventeenth-century French writer, Cyrano de Bergerac, whose character was carried there propelled by flasks of water heated by the Sun. But when it came to fact, the existence of life of any kind on the Moon, let alone human life similar to ours, remained as doubtful as the existence of the peoples that Swift's Lemuel Gulliver had encountered in the course of his travels.

The twisted saga of what would eventually become known as the 'Great Moon Hoax' first came to the public's attention on Friday 21 August 1835. On that day, the *New York Sun* reprinted an announcement that was supposedly taken from the *Edinburgh Courant*: 'We have just learnt from an eminent publisher in this city that Sir John Herschel, at the Cape of Good Hope, has made some astronomical discoveries of the most wonderful description, by means of an entirely new principle.' Four days later on Tuesday 25 August came a front-page article headlined 'Great Astronomical Discoveries', which the *Sun* had supposedly extracted from the supplement to the respectable periodical, the *Edinburgh Journal of Science*. This was the first of six articles that were supposedly excerpted from the *Journal*, in which a detailed account of Herschel's discoveries was given to the reading public.[4]

By the early 1800s most American newspapers were weeklies, often selling for several cents a copy – 6 cents was perhaps the most common price – and targeting one of two elite audiences: commercial or political. The so-called 'party press' was funded by political groups intent on getting their partisan message across; commercial papers were dominated by advertisements and shipping news, being 'little more than bulletin boards for the business community'.[5] At the time, the *Sun*'s publisher was determined to market his paper to the working class. When the *Sun* first hit the news-stands on 3 September 1833, it was a revolutionary concept in journalism. It was the beginning of a new breed of paper called 'the penny press'. Until this time, newspapers tended to be dull and stuffy, catering to the upper class, featuring erudite viewpoints, and most were sold in advance through annual subscriptions. The *Sun*'s aim was achieved, in part, by undercutting the major New York papers. A prospectus from the day touted that the paper's aim was 'supplying the public with the news of the day at so cheap a rate as to lie within the means of all'. The other strategy was to print sensational stories that seemed plausible; to appeal to emotions, not intellect; and to sell each four-page issue for only one cent. The Editor made sure to include an array of short but spicy stories from local courts on such hot topics as prostitution, theft and public intoxication. The public, especially the common man, couldn't get enough of this new breed of journalism. Sales soared. Soon circulation topped 5,000 papers a day. Newspaper historian Andie Tucher notes that this 'was the first paper that was going to support itself by marketing to a mass audience'.[6] The *Sun* was not the first penny paper. That distinction goes to the *New York Morning Post*, established on 1 January 1833. But the new business of sensational tabloid journalism was a tricky one; the paper folded in just two and a half weeks. The *Sun*'s place in history is that it was the first *successful* attempt at tabloid journalism.

The first article appearing on Tuesday 25 August 1835 was full of minute detail, telling the *Sun*'s readers about the construction of Herschel's large telescope. The account goes into great technical detail to explain how far the younger Herschel had improved on his father's instrument. That had been remarkable enough, giving observers the illusion of being a mere forty miles from the Moon: but his son's new telescope offered observers a magnification of 42,000, enabling them to obtain 'a distinct view of objects in the moon, fully equal to that which the unaided view commands of terrestrial objects at a distance of a hundred yards; and has affirmatively settled the question whether this satellite be inhabited'.[7]

If this wasn't spectacular enough, it was revealed that the image received on the telescope could be transferred to a cloth screen, 50ft wide, enabling observers to see scenes in much the same way as we today watch a widescreen motion picture. Yet even this fell short of the astronomer's ambitions, for he predicted that before long he would be able to improve on this present device to such a degree as would enable him 'to study even the entomology of the moon in case she contained insects upon her surface'!

BEAVER PEOPLE AND BAT-MEN

This first article under the headline: 'GREAT ASTRONOMICAL DISCOVERIES LATELY MADE BY SIR JOHN HERSCHEL, L.L.D., F.R.S., &c. at the Cape of Good Hope', took up three columns on the front page. It was dry and academic, describing the telescope with a wealth of technical information which even professional astronomers might find hard to follow. Mixing in odd details and uneven numbers can do wonders to enhance credibility, and Locke was a master at sounding plausible. The telescope was said to weigh 14,826lb and have the capacity to magnify objects 42,000 times.[8] In the article, Herschel supposedly says that he is excited to be on the verge of knowing unequivocally, once and for all, whether or not the Moon is inhabited. While the article generated curiosity on the streets of New York, there was only muted excitement owing to the stuffiness of the writing and its tedious detail.[9] But the foundation for the grand deception had been laid. Locke had succeeded on two vital fronts: capturing attention and establishing credibility. Even if most readers could not understand the scientific mumbo-jumbo, it certainly sounded as if he was quoting from a science journal, and he was able to get his main point across – that readers could expect an unprecedented survey of the lunar surface in the near future.

Locke's knowledge of astronomy and inclusion of great detail only lent further credence to the article's reality. For instance, in describing the construction of the telescope, he writes that through experimentation, 'the amalgam would as completely triumph over every impediment, both from refrangibility and discoloration, as the separate lenses. Five furnaces of the metal, carefully collected from productions of the manufactory, in both the kinds of glass, and known to be respectively of nearly perfect homogenous quality, were united, by one grand conductor, to the mold; and on the third of January, 1833, the first cast was effected.' Just as in the real world, we are told that when the mould was opened after eight days, it had an 18in flaw and had to be discarded. Then, 'a new glass was more carefully cast on the 27th of the same month, which upon being opened during the first week of February, was found to be immaculately perfect, with the exception of two slight flaws so near the line of its circumference that they would be covered by the copper ring in which it was designed to be enclosed'. While this is pure fiction, it was eloquently written gobbledygook, written by someone with an obvious knowledge of science and astronomy.

But the second instalment on Wednesday 26 August began to describe the observations which had begun on 10 January, when the observers had their first close-up sight of the satellite. Readers were treated to the revelation that there was life on the Moon! The writer first describes lush vegetation and rocks of great beauty. They saw 'a beach of brilliant white sand, girt with wild castellated rocks, apparently of green marble, varied by chasms occurring every two or three hundred feet, with grotesque blocks of chalk or gypsum, and feathered or festooned at the summit with the clustering foliage of unknown trees. . . . The water was nearly as blue as that of the deep ocean, and broke in large white billows upon the strand.'

This breathtaking description was followed by an even more fantastic claim – the discovery of various life forms on the Moon including a bluish-grey creature the size of a goat, a powerful looking bison-like mammal, and an array of colourful birds. 'In the shade of the woods on the south-eastern side, we beheld continuous herds of brown quadrupeds, having all the external characteristics of the bison, but more diminutive than any species of the *bos genus* in our natural history. Its tail is like that of our *bos grunniens*; but in its semi-circular horns, the hump on its shoulders, and the depth of its dewlap, and the length of its shaggy hair . . .'[10] Then came water birds – pelicans and cranes – and they had a tantalizing glimpse of 'a strange amphibious creature which rolled with great velocity across the pebbly beach'.

On the following night came a greater marvel: 'four successive flocks of large winged creatures, wholly unlike any kind of birds', which slowly descended from the cliffs to the plain and folded their wings on their backs and walked like men. Seen from a distance of 80yd, they seemed to be about 4ft tall, and were covered with copper-coloured hair. 'The face was a slight improvement upon that of the large *orang outang*, being more open and intelligent in its expression.' They were evidently engaged in conversation. Later they saw more human-like creatures, taller and seemingly superior. 'They were chiefly engaged in eating a large yellow fruit, like a gourd, sections of which they divided with their fingers, and ate with rather uncouth voracity, throwing away the rind. They seemed eminently happy. . . .' A stag was seen trotting up to the semi-humans without the least manifestation of fear. 'This universal state of amity among all classes of lunar creatures, and the apparent absence of every carnivorous or ferocious species, gave us the most refined pleasure and doubly endeared to us this lovely nocturnal companion of our larger, but less favored world.'

With each passing day, Locke's 'fish' story gradually grew bigger and bigger, and crowds began to form each day as excited citizens waited to read the latest reports. On 27 August, Herschel reportedly classified nine separate types of mammals including creatures resembling a horned bear, an elk and moose. But the most startling observation was yet to come – the discovery of a community of creatures resembling two-legged beavers without the tail. 'It carries its young in its arms like a human being, and moves with an easy gliding motion. Its huts are constructed better and higher than those of many tribes of human savages, and from the appearance of smoke in nearly all of them, there is no doubt of its being acquainted with the use of fire. Still its head and body differ only in the points stated from that of the beaver, and it was never seen except on the borders of lakes and rivers . . . [where it] has been seen to immerse for a period of several seconds.'[11]

His most astonishing observation came in the fourth article on Friday the 28th, when it was reported that flocks of human-like forms could be seen flying about with bat-like wings. The creatures were given the scientific name of 'Vespertilio-homo' meaning bat-man. These beings were described with angelic innocence, peacefully coexisting with their fellow creatures in an environment apparently free from carnivores. The highly pretentious yet plausible scientific description of these strange creatures continued: 'We could then perceive that they possessed wings of great expansion, and were similar in structure to this of the bat, being a semi-transparent membrane expanded in curvilineal divisions by means of straight radii, united at the back by the dorsal integuments.'[12]

Like a good spy novel, Locke even manages to slip in intrigue and sex. In describing these male and female bat-creatures, he notes how they were seemingly innocent and content, 'notwithstanding that some of their amusements would but ill-comport with our terrestrial notions of decorum'. It soon becomes obvious that Locke is referring to their sexual conduct, which he was not at liberty to describe for the *Sun's* readers. 'We have, of course, faithfully obeyed Dr Grant's private injunction to omit those highly curious passages in his correspondence which he wished us to suppress. . . . From these . . . and other prohibited passages, which will be published by Dr Herschel, with the certificates of the civil and military authorities of the colony, and of several Episcopal, Wesleyan, and other ministers . . .'[13]

Locke went on to describe great oceans and land masses,[14] providing his final instalment on Monday 31 August.[15] Here we are treated to a description of angelic creatures sporting wings, who seemed to live a utopian existence. 'They seemed eminently happy, and even polite, for we saw, in many instances, individuals sitting nearest these piles of fruit, select the largest and brightest specimens, and throw them archwise across the circle to some opposite friend or associate who extracted the nutriment from those scattered around him, and which were frequently not a few. While thus engaged in their rural banquets, or in social converse, they were always seated with their knees flat upon the turf, and their feet brought evenly together in the form of a triangle.' We are also treated to a description of a glistening lunar temple made of sapphire, with a yellow, metallic roof, held up by huge columns towering 70ft into the sky.

The Moon hoax was to end as subtly and cleverly as it began. We are told that Herschel and his colleagues suffered an unexpected setback: one night the telescope, though lowered, had been left in a perpendicular position facing east – and the sunrise. The next morning, the astronomers were awakened by the natives who told them the 'Big house' was on fire. The observatory was enveloped in a cloud of smoke. We are told that the rays of the rising Sun, concentrated by the lenses, had burned a hole 15ft wide through the reflecting chamber and the screen on which the observations were projected. Though the plaster walls of the observatory were vitrified to blue glaze, the damage was not crucial: but it meant that observations had to be suspended. 'This concludes the Supplement, with the exception of forty pages of illustrative and mathematical notes . . . Ed. *Sun*.'[16] And with these words, the series was over.

As the spectacular events unfolded, two Yale professors – Elias Loomis and Denison Olmstead – failing to find the original articles in the Yale library, took a steamship to New York in order to view the supplement at first hand and verify its contents. One day these gentlemen showed up at Benjamin Day's office asking to see the mathematical notes and unpublished technical details that were deemed too tedious and erudite for the *Sun*'s readers. Locke came to his rescue, giving the address of a printer on William Street. As the two learned gentlemen set off, Locke cut through alleyways and side streets to get there ahead of them to prompt the employees on what to say. When they got there, the professors were told that the pamphlet had just gone to another shop for proof-reading. In this manner they were given the runaround. Needless to say, they were unable to track down the journal by the end of the day when they had to return to Yale, disappointed and highly suspicious.[17]

As word of the great discoveries quickly spread through the city, soon Herschel's revelations dominated all conversation, and sent the paper's circulation skyrocketing. Even rival newspapers had to applaud the remarkable news. During the affair, newspaper editors, frantically trying to confirm the claims, were faced with the dilemma of possibly missing out on one of the greatest stories in recorded history – or being monumentally embarrassed if it proved untrue. This must have irked them no end, as many New York papers were bitter rivals – to the extent that some editors and reporters were known to get into fist fights when chancing to meet on the street. Newspaper editors could not wait the several weeks it would have taken to contact Herschel who was incommunicado in South Africa, so many took the gamble and reprinted the *Sun*'s story on their front pages.[18] Some gave no credit to the *Sun*, instead attributing the source as the *Edinburgh Journal of Science*. Copyright law was not what it is today, and this was accepted practice even though Day complained. In fact, Day was notorious for engaging in the same practice himself.

Even the prestigious *New York Times* was hoodwinked, declaring that the writer 'displays the most extensive and accurate knowledge of astronomy, and the description of Sir John's recently improved instruments . . . [and] the account of the wonderful discoveries on the moon, &c., are all probable and plausible, and have an air of intense verisimilitude'.[19] Interest in the fantastic discoveries quickly spread round the world: three journals translated it in France, and three more in Italy. Locke also published the articles in a pamphlet and sold 60,000 copies within a month to meet the public's insatiable appetite for the story.[20]

A student of astronomy and mechanics, Edgar Allan Poe said he had stopped work on the second part of *The Strange Adventures of Hans Pfaall* because Herschel's 'discoveries' outdid anything he would dare include in a work of fiction. Poe's story describes a trip to the Moon that was full of plausible details and consistent with known science. A well-known English writer, Harriet Martineau, was travelling in New England at the time, and recorded in her book *Retrospect of Western Travel* the effect of the articles:

> I happened to be going the round of several Massachusetts villages when the marvellous account of Sir John Herschel's discoveries in the moon was sent abroad. The sensation it excited was wonderful. . . . A story is going about, told by some friends of Sir John Herschel (but whether in earnest or in the spirit of the moon story I cannot tell) that the astronomer has received at the Cape a letter from a large number of Baptist clergymen of the United States congratulating him on his discovery, informing him that it had been the occasion of much edifying preaching and of prayer meetings for the benefit of brethren in the newly explored regions; and beseeching him to inform his correspondents whether science affords any prospects of a method of conveying the Gospel to residents in the moon. . . .[21]

Poe later said that 'Not one person in ten discredited it; and it is especially noticeable that the doubters were, for the most part, those who doubted without being able to say why – the ignorant – those uninformed in astronomy, people who would not believe merely because the thing was so novel – so entirely "out of the usual way".'[22] When he wrote a critical article on the claims shortly after they had appeared in the *Sun*, Poe said that he was surprised by the response: 'I . . . pointed out distinctly its fictitious character, but was astonished at finding that I could obtain few listeners, so really eager were all to be deceived, so magical were the charms. . . .'[23]

A writer for the *Southern Quarterly Review*, in New Haven, Connecticut, at the time of the *Sun's* revelations, reports that the Moon story elicited widespread excitement across the campus of Yale college. 'Have you read the Sun?' and 'Have you heard the news?' replaced the customary 'Hello.' 'The literati – students and professors, doctors in divinity and law – and all the rest of the reading community, looked daily for the arrival of the New York mail. . . .' News of the reported discovery of life on the Moon dominated conversation. According to the writer, 'Nobody expressed or entertained a doubt as to the truth of the story.'[24]

The *New York Sunday News* urged its readers to exercise patience: 'Our doubts and incredulity may be a wrong to the learned astronomer, and the circumstances of this wonderful discovery may be correct.' The *Mercantile Advertiser* was one of several newspapers to reprint the articles and endorse their authenticity, though it refused to identify the *Sun* as its source by name, instead referring to a 'journal of this city'. The *Advertiser* states: 'It appears to carry intrinsic evidence of being an authentic document.' The *Daily Advertiser* was similarly enthusiastic: 'No article, we believe, has appeared for years, that will command so general a perusal and publication. Sir John has added a stock of knowledge to the present age that will immortalize his name, and place it high on the page of science.' Even the stolid *New Yorker* seemed 'over the Moon' at the reports: 'Great Astronomical Discoveries! – By the late arrivals from England there has been received in this country a supplement to the *Edinburgh Journal of Science* containing intelligence of the most astounding interest from Prof. Herschel's Observatory at the Cape of Good Hope. . . .' These 'discoveries' were said to usher in 'a new era in astronomy and science generally'.[25]

11

Some sceptical voices were also raised, though they were in the minority. The *New York Commercial Advertiser*, on 29 August (the fifth day of the articles), wrote in patronizing tone:

It is well done, and makes a pleasant piece of reading enough, especially for such as have a sufficient stock of available credulity; but we can hardly understand how any man of common sense should read it without at once perceiving the deception. Without referring to the monstrosities of the story itself, can any one suppose for a moment that such preparations as are described, should have been made without a word of notice in the English papers? Preparations going on for years – an object of glass of twenty-four feet in diameter – a donation of ten thousand pounds by the King – consultations with Sir David Brewster – and other extravagances not less preposterous![26]

The *New York Evening Post*, edited by two eminent literary personalities, William Cullen Bryant and Fitz-Greene Halleck, observed that 'It is quite proper that the *Sun* should be the means of shedding so much light on the Moon' and went on to liken the articles to the eighteenth-century fantasy voyages of Peter Wilkins, indicating that the *Evening Post*, at least, was not to be spoofed. Wilkins was the heroic character of Robert Paltock's 1750 novel, *The Life and Adventures of Peter Wilkins, a Cornish Man*. Like Locke, Paltock had an extraordinary imagination, including a description of a group of winged Indians who flew in a similar manner to the 'bat-men'. Also, like Locke, he managed to bring sex into the picture, as Wilkins was able to learn his intimate details of the strange tribe through sexual relations with one of its females.[27]

Shortly after the last of the six articles appeared in the *Sun*, the *Journal of Commerce* requested permission to publish them in pamphlet form. A reporter named Finn visited the *Sun* to discuss the proposal: he was a friend of Richard Locke. But Locke discouraged him from reprinting the articles for, as he now admitted, he himself was their author. This was revealed by the *Journal* the following day. The *Sun*'s rival, the *New York Herald*, whose proprietor was James

Gordon Bennett, known for his sponsorship of motor racing, also proclaimed the hoax and named Locke as its author. The *Herald* pointed out that Locke was British, a Cambridge graduate, and had an interest in astronomy and optics; also that the article contained numerous errors. Bennett invited Locke to tell the story of the hoax in his columns.

Locke replied in a letter to the *Herald*, insisting that the suggestion that he had anything to do with the hoax was 'too ridiculous to receive any further notice'. As for any errors, he, having no expertise in astronomy or optics, was not qualified to judge: if any there were, no one but Herschel himself could be held responsible for them.

So far, the story had been one of bluff and counter-bluff, with everyone concerned hoping to outmanoeuvre the other. But at this point, the plot thickens. What seemed to be a simple hoax was now generating its own clouds of mystification. Some historians assert that Locke never admitted to being the author of the articles[28] and if that is the case, then the story of his confession to Finn from the *Journal of Commerce* is nothing but a fiction.

While Locke is supposed, by almost all commentators, to be the sole author, the detailed knowledge of astronomy evinced in the technical portions of the narrative showed that a more expert person had surely been consulted. Indeed the *Sun* admitted its debt to Dr Andrew Grant, who had been a pupil of the elder Herschel, and 'the inseparable coadjutor' of the younger, accompanying him to South Africa and bringing back a great deal of material to the *Edinburgh Journal*, including fine engravings representing what the astronomers had seen. All of which sounds plausible enough – except that no trace of this individual could be found, and it seems evident that he was a fictitious character.

If, as the paper claimed, the articles were extracted from the reputable academic publication, the *Edinburgh Journal of Science*, all might be explained: but this journal, though real enough, had ceased publication two years previously. So, with a journal that no longer existed and Dr Grant who had never existed, whence did the *Sun* derive its astronomical know-how? Locke, though accused by

Bennett of being an expert in astronomy and optics, insisted that he had no special knowledge of those subjects. Yet the articles, bogus though they might be, displayed a considerable familiarity with the technology of astronomical equipment.

The prime candidate is Jean Nicolas Nicollet, a noted French astronomer who had emigrated to the United States, perhaps for political reasons concerned with the 1830 Revolution, perhaps for more disreputable reasons involving missing money. Apart from the fact that he was one of the few people qualified to write with such knowledge, there is the circumstantial fact that he was the author of a paper, *Sur la Libration de la Lune* and that the technical term 'libration' appears frequently in the *Sun* articles. But even that does not mean much, for any well-written paper on the Moon might indeed be concerned with its libration, which relates to its oscillation. As to why such a man should allow his writings to be published under another man's name, this could be accounted for by the fact that Nicollet left France under somewhat suspicious circumstances, also, as a fugitive in America, he may have been short of money. At the time of the articles' publication, he was in Mississippi, and although perhaps he could have supplied material to Locke earlier, there is not a scrap of evidence to support this suggestion.

The hoax also generated conspiracy theories. For instance, in 1853, one observer notes that belief in the discovery of 'Moonlings' still persisted in some quarters, prompting one writer to exclaim: 'It is hardly possible to name a popular folly which has been so general and has endured so long.'[29] Locke, for one, is said to have had a hidden agenda: according to this view, he wrote the articles neither as a simple prank nor as a circulation-booster. Rather, he intended them, proposes Michael J. Crowe,[30] as a satire on a well-known astronomical author of the day, Dr Thomas Dick, who, writing in the *Edinburgh New Philosophical Journal* (the successor to the defunct *Edinburgh Journal of Science*) in 1826, had published a paper suggesting a scheme of communication between Earth and Moon. However, Dick himself had been writing with tongue in cheek, having a go at the extravagances of certain German astronomers.[31]

This theory is supported by a statement by Locke to the effect that, as a satire, his articles had failed. 'It is quite evident that it is an abortive satire; and I am the best self-hoaxed man in the entire community'[32] – which is only just short of an outright confession. Nor was Locke the only one credited with a personal motivation: if Nicollet was the technical consultant for the articles, it has been suggested that this was because he hoped to entrap his rival, the eminent French astronomer Arago. If so, he succeeded, for Arago appears to have swallowed the Herschel revelations until the hoax was revealed.

Further mystification surrounds the question of whether the *Sun* ever confessed to the hoax. It is often stated that on 16 September the paper published a confession, but in fact it did nothing of the sort. What it said was: 'Certain correspondents have been urging us to come out and confess the whole to be a hoax; but this we can by no means do, until we have the testimony of the English or Scotch papers to corroborate such a declaration.'[33]

With the publication of the Moon hoax, the *Sun* enjoyed a meteoric rise in circulation. Even on the first day over 15,000 copies were sold, and by 28 August, Benjamin Day, the paper's proprietor, reported a sale of 19,360 copies; 15,440 were regular subscribers, 2,000 were sold on street corners, and 1,220 were sent out of town. In its brief two-year existence, the *Sun* had become the world's most widely read newspaper, eclipsing the previous record-holder, the highly respected London *Times*, with a circulation of 17,000. All told, the circulation of the *Sun* was multiplied by five, and had the effect of establishing the newspaper, which had been struggling hitherto, on a permanent basis. The *Sun*'s Napier double cylinder printing press was pushed to the limit having all it could do to keep up with demand, and during this period was operating ten hours per day.

Finally, tribute must be paid to the perpetrators of the hoax, be they who they may. The wealth of plausible detail, in which the authentic and the spurious is indissolubly mixed: the splendidly pompous prose, a fine piece of writing by any standard; the artful ingenuity of the narrative, in which the discoveries gradually escalate from topographical description to simple fauna and flora and finally to intelligent humanoids who can be compared to angels; along with such convincing touches as the accident which brought the researches to a temporary close, something which could happen to anybody: all these speak of inventiveness of the highest order. The Moon hoax was not the first press hoax, and was far from the last: but for sheer panache it remains without rival.

When word of the episode finally reached Herschel by letter, he reportedly erupted with laughter, regretting only that his actual discoveries, published twelve years later in 1847, would be far less sensational.[34] His amusement soon wore off after being mercilessly pestered with questions about the hoax from journalists across America and Europe.

WRITING ON THE WALL

The notion that the Moon is inhabited with intelligent life seems ridiculous today but the idea has been the subject of widespread speculation for centuries. While in 1835 most astronomers pooh-poohed the idea, science fiction writers had long used this theme, and it seemed plausible to the common man and woman on the street. Many of the *Sun*'s readers were poorly educated, first-generation working-class immigrants with a knowledge of the English language that was minimal at best. Many had only recently stepped off ships from Europe, understanding just enough English to function in their new world. They were ignorant and gullible. Yet, many of the well-educated were also taken in, most notably scientists and newspaper editors. While they should have known better, they wanted to believe, and believe they did, turning a blind eye to some conspicuous details which with hindsight must have stuck out like a sore thumb. For as eloquently as it is written, the lunar descriptions contain fatal flaws.

In the *Sun* articles, it is claimed that the Earth is thirteen times bigger than the Moon. In fact, it is forty-nine times bigger. This should have made any astronomer worth his salt, suspicious, though such learned men of science were few and far between. The reference to the *Edinburgh Journal of Science* was clearly incorrect as it was no longer published. This should have set off alarm bells for anyone who had been familiar with the journal and knew it was defunct. Herschel's description of the Moon's topography was inconsistent with known period charts of the Moon's landscape. Scientists of the era were already able to determine that the Moon was devoid of air and water, and hence, the notion of lush vegetation or creatures was ludicrous and bat-men could not fly without air. The accounts also seemed too good to be true – observations of angelic beings co-existing in harmony; descriptions of mythical unicorns; and an abundance of gold. Despite claims that the telescope could magnify objects 42,000 times, it still would not be sufficient to reveal some of the minute objects described, such as birds' eyes and tiny flowers. The Moon's distance of roughly 240,000 miles, divided by the telescope's supposed magnifying power of 42,000 times, yields an observing distance of over five miles. From this distance, it would not be possible to discern even large animals, to say nothing about their eyes! The description of the bat wings appears to have been borrowed from the writings of Peter Wilkins. Further, Herschel's supposed description of the use of artificial light to enhance the great telescope's magnification made no sense. As Poe observed: 'It could not possibly work.'[35]

Poe believed the hoax was successful not because of the seemingly scientific accuracy of the descriptions including intimate details about the construction and use of the telescope, but *in spite of* its inaccuracy. Poe felt that the real reason for its success was the novelty: 'It took the people by surprise, and there was no good reason (apart from internal evidence) for disbelief. It was therefore believed, although abounding in gross errors, which should have caused it to be discredited at once.'[36]

All good journalists possess two qualities that no amount of money can buy. Reputation and credibility. When you have been discredited and your reputation tainted, the damage is irreparable. Locke learned this lesson the hard way. In the autumn of 1836 he left the *Sun* and tried to start a new penny paper, the *New Era*. In an effort to boost readership, he began to write a series of sensational adventures in Africa by a Scottish explorer. He was up to his old tricks again as 'The Lost Manuscript of Mungo Park' was entirely fictional yet it was presented as fact. When readers saw his name associated with such a remarkable story, few believed it and there was a cry of 'Hoax!' Locke's reputation was tainted. He would live the rest of his days under a veil of suspicion, dying on Staten Island, New York, on 16 February 1871, his credibility forever in question; his legacy to be forever remembered as the father of tabloid journalism.

TWO

'We're All Going to Die!'
The Halley's Comet Scare of 1910

If men define situations as real, they are real in their consequences.
William Isaac Thomas[1]

Every social delusion is an unpredictable confluence of circumstances and events that are framed in a unique context. Like baking, each ingredient must be added in a particular sequence, or the final product may be unrecognizable – and inedible. Even bread dough requires a receptive atmosphere in which to ferment and rise. History is replete with episodes of human behaviour that for one reason or another were culinary flops, so to speak, failing to reach their potential and culminate into a fully fledged scare or panic. The seeds of potential mass delusions lie dormant everywhere, awaiting the right conditions under which to bloom.

Such was the case in 1910, when as a result of newspaper irresponsibility and sensation-mongering, many feared that poison gas from the tail of Halley's Comet would extinguish human life. The first ingredient materialized in 1705, when British astronomer and mathematician Edmond Halley (1656–1742) published *A Synopsis of the Astronomy of Comets*, in which he boldly predicted the return of the comet that now bears his name. While confident of its reappearance in 1758, Halley never lived to see his theory confirmed. Sixteen years earlier, after complaining of fatigue, he tipped back a glass of wine and quietly slumped in his chair, dying in Greenwich, England, on 14 January 1742, at the ripe old age of eighty-six.[2] Halley's successful prediction of the periodic passage of his comet roughly every seventy-six years was a major scientific milestone, and ever since, the return of Halley's Comet has become an eagerly anticipated social event and a rite of passage for each succeeding generation.[3]

When Halley's Comet reappeared in 1835, global interest was subdued. But before its next predicted show in 1910, more ingredients were added to the mix that would eventually give rise to fears of an impending apocalypse. In 1881, British astronomer Sir William Huggins was analysing light spectra from comets in order to determine their composition, when he discovered the presence of the lethal gas cyanogen (C_2N_2) – a form of the deadly substance cyanide.[4] At the time, this obscure discovery went virtually unnoticed by anyone other than astronomers and chemists, but would subsequently become the basis of the 1910 scare. In 1908, Comet Morehouse passed in view of Earth and analysis of the light, using spectroscopes, confirmed the presence of cyanogen. This news, coupled with new calculations of Halley's orbit, began to cause concern. Astronomers were realizing that the comet would take the unusual course of passing between the Sun and the Earth.[5] Just as Earth would be closest to Halley, the comet was due to pass in front of the Sun, sending its tail spraying outward in the opposite direction, enveloping Earth. No one was panicking yet and most astronomers were dismissing any notion of Earth being affected. While the idea of the comet's tail grazing Earth sounds dramatic, in reality its nucleus was a comfortable 23 million kilometres away, and gasses in the tail were so minute as to be inconsequential.[6] By some estimates, they comprised about one in every trillion air molecules.[7]

By the time of Halley's Comet's fly-by in 1910, mass communications were considerably more evolved than they had been in 1835, with the invention of the telegraph in 1837, the laying of the first transatlantic cable in 1866, and the invention of the telephone in 1876. Ten years later publishers celebrated the invention of Linotype or mechanical typesetting which revolutionized the newspaper industry. For the first time, journalists could write lengthy stories that were quickly disseminated to large readerships. Linotype led to the rapid proliferation of dailies. By 1900, about 2,200 dailies were circulating in the United States alone.[8] By the early 1900s, some presses could produce up to 144,000 papers per hour to meet demand.[9] Owing to a combination of technological advancement and timing, Robert Burnham describes the 1910 news coverage of Halley's Comet as 'the world's first international media event'.[10] Halley's Comet was a truly global affair, and highly personal, being visible to the naked eye from many parts of the world.

When the Great Comet of 1860 had unexpectedly blazed across the southern hemisphere and was first spotted in Australia, the only way to convey the news was by ship. By the time cargo and passenger vessels had reached their destinations, the comet was already visible in Europe and North America. In 1860, the world was a much bigger place as news travelled slowly.[11] But by 1910 the world had taken a giant step towards becoming a global village. The rapid proliferation of and advances in telegraphy served as the lifeblood for syndicated wire services which fed newspapers a never-ending stream of information.

The first visual sighting of Halley's Comet was recorded by Sherburne W. Burnham on 15 September 1909. As the comet gradually waxed throughout the autumn, so did press interest. By early 1910, when public excitement for the return of Halley's Comet was growing daily, a second comet suddenly burst onto the scene on 12 January, stealing the show and grabbing international headlines. Dubbed the 'Great Daylight Comet' or 'Great January Comet', its initial appearance was brilliant, and could even be clearly seen in broad daylight near the Sun. This dazzling new comet also sported an exceptionally long tail, but was a 'flash in the pan', quickly fading from view and public interest, and by the end of the month, people were again focused on Halley's Comet.[12] However, the unexpected appearance of the 'Great Daylight Comet' served to underscore the inexact state of astronomy. Here was a comet that no one had predicted. As one astronomer notes: 'Vivid and totally unexpected, the Great January Comet made a strong impression on a public already well primed for comets.'[13] Humans are creatures of routine and habit who have difficulty with the unpredictable. The appearance of this new comet seemed to make many uneasy.

DEBACLE AT THE *NEW YORK TIMES*

In 1910, the *New York Times* was already a press legend, one of the world's leading newspapers, well known for its journalistic integrity and attacks on sensational 'yellow' journalism, which it helped send into serious decline. The paper oozed credibility. It also exchanged news with the authoritative London *Times*. This is why, in retrospect, the events of early February 1910 are so surprising and out of character. The Halley's Comet scare can be traced to the publication of a single *New York Times* article on 7 February. On that fateful day, the *Times* editors published a speculative, jaw-dropping, front-page story that astronomers at the University of Chicago's Yerkes Observatory in Williams Bay, Wisconsin, had identified bands of poison gas in the comet.[14] Adding further credibility to the account, the dateline was Boston, Massachusetts, and astronomers at the prestigious Harvard Observatory reported receiving the Yerkes dispatch. The article's tone was chilling, stating that cyanogen was deadly, and noting that if 'a grain of its potassium salt touched to the tongue . . . [it was] sufficient to cause instant death'. The article went on to portray an image of growing concern by astronomers around the world. 'The fact that cyanogen is present in the comet has been communicated to Camille Flammarion [a highly respected French astronomer] and many other astronomers, and is causing much discussion as to the probable effect on the earth should it pass through the comet's tail. Prof. Flammarion is of the opinion that the cyanogen gas would impregnate the atmosphere and possibly snuff out all life on the planet.'[15] Call it a one-day lapse of judgement, but the reverberations would be felt worldwide.

The *Times* article was misleading in that Flammarion was the *only* astronomer at Yerkes to express grave concerns, though it clearly pointed out that his viewpoint was not in agreement with most scientists.[16] Flammarion was a credible figure, but with a penchant for the speculative. In 1893 he wrote a sensational novel, *La Fin du Monde*, on the dire consequences if a comet were to collide with Earth. Flammarion's scientific side soon got the better of him, leading to his recanting the suggestion of cyanogen extinction,

22

though this act received less fanfare in the press. In response to the public fears generated by the story, two days later the *Times* went into damage control, publishing another front-page comet story, proclaiming: 'No Danger From Comet'. It quoted astronomer W.J. Hussey of the University of Michigan, ridiculing the possibility of mass poisoning, labelling it as preposterous and joking that there wouldn't even be enough cyanogen gas to kill a single insect.[17] An editorial quickly followed the next morning, and while it was confidently stated that the Earth could pass through a dozen comet tails without any effect, the damage was done.[18] The *Times* editor was like a judge instructing a jury to 'disregard that last statement'. The final ingredient had been added to the cauldron. Meanwhile, Halley's Comet continued to grow in brilliance and, by mid-February, was visible to the naked eye as a bright star.

A flurry of stories quickly appeared in the press on cyanogen gas and its effects – though there was nothing to fear. It didn't matter that Halley's Comet had been recorded over thirty times since 240 BC without the slightest confirmed ill effect, or that the tail of the Great Comet of 1860 had also swept through Earth's atmosphere with no noticeable effect[19] Scores of astronomers became in demand overnight, some briefly attaining near celebrity status as journalists solicited their views on the possible harmful effects of the tail passing through the atmosphere. As is always the case in any discipline, a few scientists offered dissenting opinions. Possibly the most eminent was Flammarion, who was an accomplished science writer with a large following of admirers. Some astronomers, through their clumsiness in dealing with the press and with no malicious intent, inadvertently exacerbated the fears. For instance, the director of the French Meudon Observatory, expressed his view that the tail would harmlessly pass through the atmosphere, but also 'emphasized that the tail contained enormous quantities of cyanogen'.[20]

Astronomers are used to dealing with probabilities, and speaking in such terms often made the comet fears worse. Newspapers frequently did little to clarify the situation. The *Glens Falls Daily Times* in Upstate New York and the *Washington Post* were typical in their schizophrenic coverage. On 16 May the *Daily Times* quoted

23

Professor Andrew Cromelin of Greenwich University as stating emphatically: 'There is no probability that any effect will be produced.' Yet, in the same article, other astronomers' opinions were less convincing. Michael Giacohin of the Paris Observatory said that if the tail were to pass through the atmosphere, 'it is not at all probable that any injury to the earth or its inhabitants can be caused by such contact'. Giacohin's failure to give complete assurances must have been unsettling to some. An astronomy professor at the University of Michigan, J.M. Schaeberle, perhaps trying to dash rampant speculation, said: 'All predictions are purely speculative' which likely led to even greater speculation. Again, here was another prominent scientist who did not exactly instil confidence in the astronomical community – probably owing more to press ineptitude than any concerns he may have had regarding possible ill effects from the comet. Meanwhile, many reporters and editors did a poor job in separating fact from speculation and seemed to be conveying two different messages. And what did the journalist write in the same article that carried these quotes from the *Daily Times*? The reporter said that 'there is no probability that any sensible effect will be produced on the earth's atmosphere . . .'. Maybe so, but that is not what some of the experts said in this very article.

The respected *Washington Post* was also giving double messages. When Flammarion's doomsday scenario was telegraphed around the world beginning on 6 February, the *Post* cited several French astronomers, colleagues of Flammarion, who disagreed with his gloomy assessment. Yet just as one's faith is about to be restored in the noble profession of journalism, we are let down in the final paragraph. 'On the other hand, it is pointed out that the spectroscope has shown that there is a large quantity of cyanogen gas in the atmosphere surrounding Halley's Comet, and some chemists, such as M. Dastre, say that being practically without odor, the presence of the gas would not easily be perceived. A mixture of this gas with air would lead to certain poisoning.'[21] The article ended by citing the warning of M. Armand Gaut'er, cheerfully noting 'that in the presence of fire or a small electric spark, a mixture of cyanogen gas and air will explode'.[22]

By May, the *Post* was still raising eyebrows and blood pressure, with a report on the 11th about the comet's unpredictable nature and labelling the threat from cyanogen gas as not to be taken lightly. 'COMET QUITS ITS PATH. Wanders From Predicted Orbit; Surprises May Follow.' The sub-headlines were even more disconcerting: 'POISON IN ITS TAIL AGAIN. Cyanogen, Which Disappeared in March, Is Now Revealed by Spectroscope. Prof. Deslandres Says Hypothesis That Gas Is Liable to Affect the Earth's Atmosphere Is Not at All Absurd.' The article cites French astronomer Maurice Hamy of the Paris Observatory, reporting 'that the length of the tail has increased from five to ten degrees in three days'. Meanwhile, at the University of Dijon, Professor Deslandres said he could not assure the public that cyanogen would not impact life on Earth, while his colleague, B.M. Marchand, continued to warn 'that the comet shows important variations from its predicted orbit, which presage unexpected surprises'.[23]

The 12 May *Evening Telegram* of Elyria, Ohio, published the seemingly reassuring headline: 'People Don't Need to Worry – No Harm Will Come to Inhabitants When Earth Sideswipes Halley's Comet May 18.' Yet it's hard to imagine many readers being put at ease. The article reports on experiments conducted at Columbia University's large chemistry laboratories by astronomer S.A. Mitchell, intended to simulate the effects of cyanogen on humans. In trials that would never be approved by a modern ethics committee (and if they were, would likely result in monumental lawsuits), hoods of the deadly gas were placed in separate rooms at different densities. A student was placed inside each hood. 'It was found that the gas would have to be very dense to wipe out life, the tests merely causing temporary collapse or severe headaches.' This cheerful news was supposed to ease fears.

The popular *Harper's Weekly* published articles by two astronomers on the possible effects from the comet's tail on 14 May. In 'The Case for the Comet', astronomer D.J. McAdam of Washington and Jefferson College, discussed possible catastrophes resulting from Halley's close fly-by. In one scenario, McAdam speculated that various cometary gases could penetrate the atmosphere and cause widespread disease. 'When we pass through its tail in May we will be in a stream of hydrogen, probably mixed with marsh gas and other cometary gases. Disease and death have frequently been ascribed to the admixture of cometary gases with the air. Enough of such gases as are in the comet's tail would be deleterious.' While McAdam was right in his assertion that comets have often been associated with illness and death, such claims were folk theories, entirely without scientific foundation. For another apocalyptic scenario, he quotes the late British astronomer Richard Proctor (1837–88) who once suggested that a comet's tail sweeping over the Earth could trigger a massive explosion in the atmosphere if the hydrogen-laden tail were to mix with the Earth's oxygen. The prospect for human survival was not promising as the blast would create a deluge of Biblical proportions while 'leaving the burnt and drenched Earth no other atmosphere than the nitrogen now present in the air, together with a relatively small quantity of deleterious vapors'.[24] It didn't matter that Proctor's hypothesis was widely deemed as incredible by the scientific community and was based on outdated assumptions, or that Proctor had been dead for twenty-two years (points that McAdam failed to tell readers). It didn't matter how outlandish McAdam's speculations were, for he was a Professor of Astronomy at a recognizable college, and his far-fetched views were deemed credible enough to appear in a national magazine.

In the second *Harper's Weekly* article, 'The Case for the Earth', Columbia University astronomer Harold Jacoby argued that Earthlings had little to fear, though he was far from completely reassuring. 'Let us begin by considering the most unfavorable case that can be imagined – that a very massive comet approaching the earth near enough to be within the danger limit.' He said that such events could not be ruled out, though they were highly improbable.[25] While Jacoby was right, his case for the Earth being spared from any harmful effects was not nearly as forceful as it could have been. Most people were neither experts on comets, astronomy or physics, nor did they read *Scientific American* or *Nature*. The *Harper's* article epitomized the public's dilemma. The press was reporting mixed messages about the potential danger from the comet. The views of both astronomers – one radical, the other mainstream – were provided with equal space and respect, lending credence to the doomsday theorists. To the naive public, the comet catastrophe hypothesis received more legitimation than it would have in astronomical circles. What's more, the argument seemed so scientific.

Other wild theories abounded in the deluge of comet-related newspaper and magazine articles that appeared from April to mid-May. New York astronomer Edwin Fairfax Naulty expressed his expert opinion that the comet produces 'ethereal waves' capable of causing catastrophic events on Earth. 'The sweeping of this cometary cone of solar force does cause disturbances in the solar system. . . . The earth and all the planets are affected not only when they come within the actual cone, as the earth will tomorrow, but also by the ethereal waves set in motion by the comet's tail.' Naulty claimed that these waves were responsible for past disturbances on Earth including 'earth tremors, storms, and similar phenomena'.[26]

The most outlandish theory was by a scientist who postulated that the comet's tail, coming into contact with the atmosphere, might convert Earth's nitrogen into nitrous oxide or 'laughing gas'. According to this theory, the Earth's population would become delirious before succumbing to its fatal effects.[27] As mass extinctions go, this view is infinitely preferable to Proctor's hydrogen holocaust hypothesis. Still another theory held that the comet's tail might displace the Earth's magnetic pole, altering the planet's electrical potential and 'electrocuting every inhabitant of the globe'.[28]

In Europe, extremes of temperature combined with heavy rains drew associations with Halley's appearance, though nobody was panicking. When asked about any connection between the unusual weather and the comet, astronomer B.M. Marchand of the Paris Observatory stated that it was conceivable, due to the inexact state of science in 1910. He noted that variations in the comet's path could 'bring about unexpected results'.[29] Meanwhile, a US astronomer was forced to admit that it was impossible to predict the potential effects of a comet as erratic as Halley's 'when it doesn't know itself'.[30]

More scholarly and scientific publications rarely mentioned the poison gas concerns, reporting the comet's appearance in a strictly factual manner, choosing instead to discuss its brightness, speed, distance from Earth and projected path. *Scientific American* was typical. If one had read only this publication, with the exception of a couple of articles, they would have been oblivious to the debate.[31] A rare exception was Princeton University astronomer Morris Russell who, in a lengthy article, couldn't resist a passing barb to the doomsdayers. In the 16 April issue, he said: 'It would be about as reasonable to conclude that an arc-light was poisonous, after looking at it through a spectroscope from a distance, as to make the same deduction about a comet.'[32]

Beginning in late April, comet press coverage intensified, and, by May, many papers published comet stories almost daily. The *New York Times* was typical. With the exception of 2 and 4 May, Halley's Comet articles appeared in every issue for the month, and often there were several articles in the same paper. By mid-May unusual occurrences were being blamed on the comet, even though the tail was still millions of miles away. A freak late spring snowfall in Tennessee on 15 May was attributed to the celestial visitor, while a New York man, charged with wife beating, claimed the comet made him do it.[33] Meanwhile, in Wisconsin, some people were taking down their lightning rods, fearing that they would attract the 'electrical shock wave' that someone predicted. At the Bicêtre Hospital in Paris, an infirmary keeper was killed in an explosion after mishandling nitroglycerine. The blast sent many patients who were able, scurrying from the building, thinking the comet had struck.[34]

On Friday 8 May, the first major scare was reported in a telegraph dispatch from Bermuda. Coinciding with King Edward VII's death, people began looking to the skies and the comet as a portent. The comet appeared about 2 a.m. Early that same morning, towards the end of a lengthy 101-gun salute to the new King George V, as the final round was being fired at 3:52 a.m., many inhabitants swore that the comet's tail briefly turned red. Surely, the natives reasoned, this colour change was a sign, but of what? Many Jamaican dock workers, fearing that it was portending the Earth's demise, refused to load any more ships, got down on their knees and began praying. Some thought it was a sign that a war would mark the new King's reign.[35] 'They were speechless with fear and worked themselves up in their paroxysms of religious zeal to a perfect frenzy. It was not till the comet had faded from view and the daylight of Saturday had broken that they could be induced to go on again with their work.'[36]

THE AMERICAN REACTION

Across America there was an odd mixture of concern and delight. By early May the optimists held countless 'comet parties' and comet-watching excursions, while many pubs served 'Cyanogen Cocktails' (a concoction of crushed ice, French vermouth and apple jack). The New York correspondent for the London *Daily Mail* captured the mood in the Big Apple. 'America is reading, talking and joking about little else than Halley's Comet.' All-night comet parties were being held on the roofs of most major hotels, with the festivities lasting until dawn. 'Scores of men are giving breakfast parties at the leading hotels in overcoats, "on the tiles" with appropriate orchestral accompaniment.' At some of the more elaborate gatherings, guests were even given miniature silver telescopes as souvenirs.[37] On the 18th, the *Times* of Hammond, Indiana, printed the tongue-in-cheek front-page headline: 'If this is the last edition of THE TIMES we wish you a fond farewell.' Newspapers printed reams of comet-related poetry. Mr A. Grim summed up the comet hoopla with the following verse:

> It was the spring of nineteen hundred and ten,
> When Halley's Comet came again,
> And some of the people had a great fright,
> When a star with a tail on came in sight.
> On May eighteenth astronomers did say,
> That great big tail would flop this way,
> For two hours and a half in that Gas we would stay,
> How many would die they would not say.[38]

Entrepreneurs hawked a variety of comet-related products and souvenirs, expecting to spend their profits in this world. Some stores sold seats especially designed for comet-watching. In 1910, it was nearly impossible to escape the Halley's Comet media blitz. The comet theme was incorporated into hundreds of ads for an array of products: beds, light bulbs, soap, soda, and custard. Halley's Comet invaded all aspects of everyday life. Comet cartoons appeared in most newspapers, while comet-inspired poetry in the form of 'Letters to the Editor' were commonplace. Comet postcards were plentiful, as were comet jokes. The famous Ziegfeld Follies performed the song, 'The Comet and the Earth'.[39] The excitement and press coverage captivated the imagination of writer Samuel Clemens (Mark Twain), who was born in Florida, Missouri, in 1835, the year of the comet's most recent appearance. In 1909 he told a friend: 'I came in with Halley's Comet in 1835. It is coming again next year, and I expect to go out with it. It will be the greatest disappointment of my life if I don't go out with Halley's Comet.' He was not disappointed. Clemens died on 21 April 1910 in Redding, Connecticut, within hours of its closest passage to the Sun.[40]

The doomsdayers were also in evidence. In Pittsburgh, a minister proclaimed that the comet signalled the Second Coming of Christ, and spoke to packed audiences. Logging operations in eastern Texas were forced to temporarily close as so many lumberjacks abandoned their duties in order to attend revival gatherings.[41] Many suicides were reported in the 'final days' leading up to the tail's widely predicted rendezvous with Earth. The strain proved too much for several people who may have already been suffering from psychological disturbance. There has long been a link between both long- and short-term stress and an increase in the incidence of mental disorder. A man from Sommerville, New Jersey, convinced of the impending gaseous apocalypse, reportedly brooded for several days. Then, early one morning, police found the scantily clad man running down a street in a state of mental confusion, shouting something about being chased by both his mother-in-law and the comet's tail.[42] Near Walla Walla, Washington, a shepherd began to rant and rave about the comet and was given a new home – a padded cell. Meanwhile, another shepherd managed to nail himself to a homemade cross – at least two legs and one hand – before being 'rescued'.[43]

In Chicago, comet fears were blamed for several suicides and instances of 'disturbed' behaviour. Blanche Covington was reported to have been in a state of deep depression at the prospect of the city being wiped out by poison gas, and decided to end her life early by closing her doors and windows and turning on the gas oven. Alerted by a neighbour, police managed to save her. However, another Chicago woman succeeded in killing herself before the comet's tail arrived by inhaling illuminating gas.[44] In New York, a 25-year-old Bessie Bradley, a maid at Hastings-on-Hudson, reportedly killed herself, fearing impending doom when the comet did not appear as predicted in the press. 'The woman became greatly worried over the contradictory reports of what the comet would do and what it would not do. When no sign of it showed last night (May 18th) she grew so nervous that she could not sleep and this morning she went to her room to rest.'[45] She was found dead in her bed near lunchtime after turning on the gas. In Alabama, W.J. Lord was clinging to life after multiple suicide attempts. A deeply religious man, he was reportedly so distraught over the comet's passage, and believing he was a sinner, 'Lord is said to have made an attempt to shoot himself. Unsuccessful in this, he jumped off a roof and fell on his head, knocking out his teeth and sustaining other injuries. He then cut his throat and jumped into a well.'[46]

There were numerous reports of enterprising individuals selling 'comet pills' that were said to offer protection against the deadly cyanogen gas. In parts of Texas, two salesmen recruited agents to go door-to-door in many towns selling 'comet pills' and leather 'inhalers'. When the pair were arrested no one would testify against them, and the Sheriff soon decided to release them in order to appease an angry mob that had formed in front of the courthouse. They were intent on gaining the men's freedom so they could buy their 'life-saving' paraphernalia. An analysis of the pills revealed a mixture of sugar and quinine, the latter providing the desired bitter, medicine-like taste.[47] In parts of New York City, 'comet pills' were selling briskly at a dollar apiece. 'Comet protection pills' were also popular items in many other countries, with perhaps Haiti at the top of the list. According to the *Enquirer* of Cincinnati, Ohio, by mid-May much of the population of Port au Prince, Haiti, was frightened as officers of the passenger liner *Allegheny* reported that 'all the negro stevedores there, all the farmers roundabout, the servants, laborers, merchants, beggermen and thieves are rushing to the hut of a shrewd old voodoo doctor just outside the city, who is selling comet pills as fast as he can make them'. The native healer was quite the entrepreneur, recommending that people take 'one pill for every hour up to the time the comet begins to recede from the earth', though many were doubling the dose.[48]

Anxiety over possible harm from the comet was evident on the streets of New York City by the 16th. At the height of a busy afternoon on Columbus Circle, a mysterious object suddenly came hurtling to earth, slamming into the roof of an 8th Avenue trolley car, then shattering the woodwork. People went scattering in every direction fearing it was Halley's Comet. One poor man leaped from the trolley and onto the pavement for cover.[49] Women 'shrieked and fainted; the motorman was very shaky, and the conductor was on the ground almost as soon as the supposed aerolite'. Everyone breathed a sigh of relief upon realizing that a cooling fan had come loose from a fifth-floor window. Embarrassed pedestrians sheepishly went about their business.[50]

On 17 May, much of Chicago was in a state of great anxiety as most residents were preoccupied with the comet, fearing that 'the tail will wipe out all life'.[51] One report described the city. 'All else is forgotten. Comets and their ways and habits have been the principal topic discussed in the streets, cars, and elevated trains to-day. . . .'[52] In Lexington, Kentucky, it was reported that 'excited people are tonight holding all-night services, praying and singing to prepare . . . [to] meet their doom'.[53]

On the morning of Wednesday the 18th, employees at a real estate office in Topeka, Kansas, went to work and found a mysterious rock had smashed into the building. While there were fears it may have been part of the comet, it was later identified as a meteorite.[54] As the sun was setting in Boston, and droves of residents were awaiting the comet, a sudden clap of thunder immediately followed by darkening skies 'gave nervous folk who were anticipating strange happenings from the approach of the comet a mild shock'.[55] At about 10.50 that night, New York time, the Earth was projected to pass through the tail, though most scientists agreed that any poisonous substances would be so rarefied that the atmosphere would not be affected.[56] Some alarmed citizens went so far as to stuff rags in doorways, while opportunists sold gas masks and 'comet pills' to counter the effects of the gas. About 150 kilometres to the north-east in Providence, Rhode Island, anxious residents were out scanning the skies, though the city was shrouded in an eerie fog. At the time the tail was projected to envelope the atmosphere, some attributed the mist to the comet; others 'in the vicinity of the Great Bridge, catching a whiff of the familiar "Providence smell", were certain that they were able to trace the cyanogen gas of the comet's tail'.[57]

In New York City, many inhabitants partied through the night, though others were more apprehensive. Early in the evening, a group of Italian-Americans assembled near the corner of Broome and Mulberry Streets to view the comet. The mood was tense and as people crooked their necks and squinted skyward, a hush came over the crowd. Suddenly there was a fiery ball in the sky. 'La fina del mondo!' 'La fina del mondo!' Many collapsed to their knees, screaming in Italian that the world was ending. The commotion brought curiosity-seekers streaming from their homes to see what the fuss was about. Suddenly there was a burst in the sky and a shower of fiery sparks began raining down, panicking many in the crowd and prompting another round of fervent prayer. It was soon evident that the 'comet' was actually a rubber balloon, sent aloft by pranksters. Police soon arrived, dispersing the crowd.[58]

In parts of North Carolina and Kentucky, African-American farm labourers refused to work and instead were holding all-night prayer vigils, fearing the end of the world would occur as the comet's tail was due to sideswipe Earth.[59] In at least a dozen counties in western Georgia, there was a similar reaction.[60] To the north in Wilkes-Barrie, Pennsylvania, thousands of miners, most of them immigrants, threw down their picks and shovels and refused to go

33

underground, fearing 'the earth would be destroyed when enveloped in the tail of the comet'. They agreed that it was preferable to spend their last hours on Earth above ground. Many spent the day in prayer.[61] Workers at the Leadville and Cripple Creek mines near Denver, Colorado, had a different strategy. Workers there refused to remain above ground to reduce the risk of exposure to the comet's poisonous tail.[62]

The comet fever also produced some lighter moments. In the farming town of Towaco, New Jersey, two well-dressed young gentlemen told residents that they were scientists studying the comet. They said the comet would pass closest to the Earth at 3 a.m. on the morning of the 29th, and nearby Waukhaw Mountain would afford an exceptional view. The pair offered prizes in the form of gold coins worth $10, $5 and $2½ dollars for the three best descriptions. Much of the community trekked up nearby Waukhaw Mountain to get the best view but conditions were poor as the fog set in. When the dejected, groggy Towacoans returned to their homes, several large chicken coops had been emptied by the foxy hucksters. One man, Cyrus Doolittle, lost nearly 300 birds.[63]

In Alexandria, Virginia, on the night of the 18th, a Deputy US Marshal, Joseph F. Glover, got chills up and down his spine after straining to see the celestial wonder through a telescope – only to fall into the Potomac River after a wharf handrail gave way. After being rescued by friends, his spirits undampened, he went home to change into dry clothes and immediately return.[64]

Perhaps the most humorous report came from the tiny village of Gowanda in western New York. Several prominent, elderly villagers were peering through a large telescope purchased for public use in order to view the comet 'when the apparatus suddenly focused itself upon a hill. Immediately there appeared on the lens the figures of two people, said to be well known, in fond embrace.' After a brief conference, the group decided to abandon their search for the comet and focus instead on more 'terrestrial bodies'. A total of seven similar scenes were brought into focus. When the shenanigans of these amateur scientists were uncovered, it was reported that divorce suits were being contemplated.[65]

THE GLOBAL EXPERIENCE

Similar comet dramas were unfolding in other parts of the globe. While major panics were recorded in Russia and Japan, in Rome Pope Pius X denounced the hoarding of oxygen cylinders:[66] near the time of the comet's appearance, an urgent request was made to pharmacists for an oxygen tank to sustain a dying patient. Not one pharmacist had a single cylinder 'as it had all been taken by persons in splendid health who had been frightened lest the fumes of the gasses from the comet should choke them'.[67]

In France, cloudy skies dampened spirits. Paris was hit by an early morning deluge of rain. The rest of the city was calm as restaurants featured 'comet suppers' and 'comet balls', though in the countryside residents seemed more anxious. Many private individuals bought oxygen tanks and sealed off their cellars in order to survive any cyanogen contamination of the atmosphere. Their reasoning was that those who took such precautions could 'survive the brief period of contact of the two atmospheres, and they saw before them in this event a wonderful future of new experiences in a thinly populated world'.[68] In Madrid, Spain, there was little hint of concern and the mood was festive, though the spectacle was of great interest to those trying to foretell the future. One observer noted that a large number of astrologers dressed in 'long-pointed headgear and black tunics' were especially interested in glimpsing the celestial visitor. Most were carrying torches and 'long measures' in an attempt 'to take the scale of the mysterious astral body'. Unfortunately, clouds obscured the view from Madrid and much of the country.[69] Some Brazilian miners took their savings and, fearing imminent death from cyanogen gas, 'spent their money lavishly for things that could be enjoyed quickly'.[70] There were also several reported suicides in different countries due to the comet's appearance.[71]

In St Petersburg, Russia, many anxious residents spent the night in churches where some religious authorities had ordered 'continuous prayers'.[72] Poison gas fears from the comet prompted 'an extraordinary amount of nervousness' in parts of South Africa. One man placed a newspaper advertisement, stating: 'Gentleman having secured several cylinders of oxygen and having bricked up a capacious room wishes to meet others who would share the expense for Wednesday night. Numbers strictly limited.' Meantime, a prominent mine manager's wife was reportedly living in a special chamber deep in a mine, waiting for the tail to pass by before resurfacing.[73]

In the Caribbean on the night of 17 May, candlelit parades were held in San Juan and across the island of Puerto Rico as anxious residents sang religious songs and prayed fervently.[74] Confessionals were also busy. The next day 'large numbers of workmen failed to report . . . at the tobacco factories and plantations', forcing curtailment of pineapple shipments.[75]

The hilltops enclosing Mexico City were dotted with crucifixes surrounded by droves of anxious citizens. These prayer vigils had endured for ten days prior to the night of 'doom' as residents 'sought to avert the impending disaster with music, incantations, and weird ceremonies'. Many spent the preceding twenty-four hours in prayer; hundreds of others took refuge in mountain caves and canyons. When dawn broke over the horizon on the morning of the 19th and nothing seemed different, the once sombre masses began celebrating with dancing and feasts.[76]

The scene in England was relatively subdued following the recent death of King Edward VII on 8 May. Some Londoners remained at home, sealed up as best they could, with oxygen cylinders at the ready in case they were deemed necessary. But they were certainly the exception. According to the London *Daily Mail*, a great deal of tension was in evidence in 'the lower class foreign population and the poorer Dutch and coloured people' who were characterized as 'particularly anxious', as if anticipating a great calamity. In many British cities, people filled the streets, some jubilant, others nervous. By 4 a.m. when any danger seemed to have passed, there was a festive ambience across the countryside as cheers and sighs were heard and most people began drifting home.[77] In other parts of Europe people seemed less anxious, and there was more a feeling of celebration. In Germany, scores of 'comet picnics' were organized in the hills around Berlin and there were steamship excursions on the lake. According to one Berlin reporter, Germany was 'transformed into one large camp of comet seekers. Comet hats for women, with mother-of-pearl hatpins shaped like comets; comet walking sticks, umbrellas, textile goods, and brands of spirits are on sale.'[78] In Switzerland, many hotels and restaurants stayed open through the night, comet dances were popular, and there was a last-minute rush to reach some of the higher Alpine resorts before nightfall.[79]

In some parts of the world, opportunistic politicians used 'comet fever' to their advantage. For instance, in Constantinople, Turkey, authorities used comet fever as an ideal time to cleanse the city of its troublesome stray dog population. The idea sounded fine in theory – while much of the population would be up on rooftops at comet gatherings, police would sweep through the city streets, gathering up the nuisance pooches. As some city dwellers were fond of the creatures, the middle of the night on 18 May seemed like an opportune time to carry out 'the great dog roundup'.[80] In the meantime, residents of Constantinople spent a sleepless night. One dispatch from the city noted that most of the Islamic community spent the night on their rooftops and 'quaking with fear at the disaster they believed to be impending with the passing of the comet'.[81]

In reviewing the various press reports on reaction to the comet in both North America and Europe, a curious pattern emerges. In many instances when inhabitants were described as acting irrationally or panicking, this was commonly blamed on 'foreigners'. Immigrants made an easy target with their 'strange' customs and their failure to quickly assimilate. The press may have been reflecting the fear of foreigners that existed during this period.[82]

HEAVEN'S GATE AND COMET HYPE

In 1996, a similar wolf cry about a comet went up and resulted in the deaths of over three dozen people. In 1910, no one suggested that space aliens were flying behind Halley's Comet. The notion would have been absurd. Yet, after being bombarded with books, magazine articles, TV shows and documentaries discussing the likelihood of extraterrestrial visitations, the time was now right for another comet drama, on a much smaller but far more devastating scale.

Comet Hale-Bopp flew by Earth in 1997. There was no chance of Hale-Bopp crashing into or poisoning Earth. Yet, one night in November 1996, an amateur astronomer phoned the Art Bell radio show with a startling claim that a spaceship was behind the comet, hidden from view. At the time it was the most popular overnight radio show in America, being heard on over 330 stations, with a listening audience of over 10 million. The next night, political scientist Courtney Brown, of Emory University, known for his unconventional UFO beliefs, called in with confirming evidence: that a team of 'psychics' had determined that there was indeed an object trailing the comet and that it was an alien spacecraft. What's more, Brown said he had a photo of the ship taken by an astronomer at a top university. Brown asked Bell not to publish the picture until the astronomer had held a news conference. After two months of hype and speculation as to whether Hale-Bopp had a 'companion', no astronomer had come forward so Bell posted the photo on his website which had long been publicizing the spaceship claims. The photo was eventually revealed as a hoax and vehemently renounced by Bell himself, but it was too late. The claims fitted neatly into the pre-existing beliefs of a California cult, 'Heaven's Gate', members of which, believing the ship was coming for them, appear to have used the information on Bell's show to affirm their decision to commit suicide. On their website it read: 'Whether Hale-Bopp has a "companion" or not is irrelevant from our perspective.' It also had a link to Bell's homepage.[83]

On the afternoon of 26 March 1997 San Diego County sheriff's deputies found the bodies of thirty-nine members of Heaven's Gate. Cult members believed that their spirits would be taken aboard a spaceship that was hiding behind the Hale-Bopp comet. A note left behind read: 'Take the little package of pudding or applesauce and eat a couple of tablespoons. Pour the medicine in and stir it up. Eat it fairly quickly and then drink the vodka beverage. Then lay back and rest quietly.'[84] Ironically, one victim was 59-year-old Thomas Nichols, brother of Nichelle Nichols who played Lieutenant Uhura on the hit television show *Star Trek*.[85]

While it's easy to dismiss the episode as the work of a tiny lunatic fringe, Ronald Steel observes that Heaven's Gate members were not as radical as they may have first seemed. Their views on pacifism, celibacy and community are found in mainstream Christianity. Steel argues that religions are intended to 'offer solace, explain mysteries, provide standards of behavior and offer the promise of escape to a better world. The Heaven's Gate group would appear to be particularly benign, and even praiseworthy, in that its members were gentle, industrious, supportive and kind to one another. They did not try to coerce others into joining them. All they asked was to be left alone.'[86] The implication is clear. Under the right conditions, it could happen again.

The 1910 Halley's Comet poison tail scare was entirely unnecessary. The episode can be traced back to the publication of a single article in the 7 February edition of the *New York Times*, serving as a lightning rod for doomsdayers and quickly snowballing out of proportion to the actual infinitesimal danger that the comet's rarefied tail actually posed. At some future point, a large comet with a high concentration of cyanogen or other poisons could pass so close to Earth as to threaten human existence, or a comet could even crash into the Earth. But in astronomical terms, the odds are, well, astronomical. Astronomer Donald Yeomans calculates that the Earth will suffer a catastrophic cometary collision roughly once every 50 million years.[87] It *will* eventually happen. Being 'gassed' by a comet's poisonous tail in sufficient concentrations to harm people is even more remote. But by far the greatest danger to Earthlings is the more immediate threat posed by the mass media in crying wolf and generating needless worry before our number does come up.

THREE

The War of the Worlds Spooks a Nation: How It Happened

New York destroyed; it's the end of the world . . . I just heard it on the radio.

Anonymous woman in Indiana

The 1938 Martian invasion radio broadcast is one of the most memorable events of the twentieth century. The episode underscores the power of the media in several ways. The drama frightened hundreds of thousands of people across the United States and Canada, and demonstrates the remarkable influence of radio. It also highlights the power of the press which exaggerated claims of widespread panic and chaos. At the time, the newspaper industry had an axe to grind against Orson Welles and the increasingly competitive medium of radio which was depleting their advertising revenues, so they initially took great glee in not only reporting reaction to the broadcast, but exaggerating its effect. Regardless as to whether the motive was deliberate or subconscious, the press were looking for a reason to criticize radio, and the Martian broadcast handed it to them on a silver platter. Reports of panic were mostly limited to the New York–New Jersey region, where the fictitious radio play was set. Finally, adaptations of the *War of the Worlds* script have been broadcast by dozens of radio stations around the world. Most were uneventful. Several were boring flops. But a few which closely followed the Welles formula triggered varying degrees of fright and panic.

Shortly before 8 o'clock on the evening of 30 October, a 23-year-old theatrical prodigy named George Orson Welles (1915–85) stood before a small group of actors and musicians in a New York City studio of the Columbia Broadcasting System's Mercury Theatre of the Air. They were getting ready to present a re-creation of the 1898 science fiction classic, *The War of the Worlds*, by eminent British writer Herbert George (H.G.) Wells (1866–1946). Little did they know they were about to make history. Broadcast live over New York's WABC, the show would be carried live to 151 CBS radio affiliates across the country.

Shortly before airtime, Welles mounted a podium in the middle of the studio, sipped pineapple juice, donned headphones and signalled announcer Daniel Seymour to begin at precisely 8 p.m.[1] 'The Columbia Broadcasting System and its affiliated stations present Orson Welles and the Mercury Theatre on the Air in *War of the Worlds* by H.G. Wells.' After twenty seconds of live theme music from the in-studio orchestra, Welles was introduced: 'Ladies and gentlemen: the director of the Mercury Theatre and star of these broadcasts, Orson Welles.'

Welles began in a distinct professorial voice: 'We know now that in the early years of the twentieth century this world was being watched closely by intelligences greater than man's and yet as mortal as his own.'[2] After about a minute, Welles finished his opening lines and the drama then gave the appearance of being a typical radio programme of the era. A weather forecast was read, then an announcer said: 'We now take you to the Meridian Room in the Hotel Park Plaza in downtown New York, where you will be entertained by Ramon Raquello and his orchestra.'[3] Shortly thereafter, there was the first hint of trouble. 'Ladies and gentlemen, we interrupt our programme of dance music to bring you a special bulletin from the Intercontinental Radio News. At twenty minutes before eight, central time, Professor Farrell of the Mount Jennings Observatory, Chicago, Illinois, reports observing several explosions of incandescent gas, occurring at regular intervals on the planet Mars.'[4] It was then back to more of 'Ramon Raquello'.

The music continued to be interrupted at intervals with special bulletins of increasing length and gravity describing what were at first 'explosions' on Mars. As reporter 'Carl Phillips' filed a report from Princeton Observatory with a 'Professor Richard Pierson' who discussed the strange astronomical happenings, the Professor was handed a note from the New York Museum of Natural History which registered a major seismographic shock near Princeton. After more regular programming, the announcer came on: 'Ladies and gentlemen, here is the latest bulletin from the Intercontinental Radio News . . . a special announcement from Trenton, New Jersey. It is reported that at 8:50 p.m. a huge flaming object, believed to be a meteorite, fell on a farm in the neighborhood of Grovers Mill, New Jersey, twenty-two miles from Trenton. The flash in the sky was visible within a radius of several hundred miles and the noise of the impact was heard as far north as Elizabeth.'[5]

'Live' bulletins from the scene followed. The 'meteor' was later identified as a 'metal cylinder' that, before the announcer's eyes, sprouted legs and towered into the air. The cylinder contained hideous beings from Mars who opened fire with 'death rays', scorching anyone who opposed it.[6] The reporter announced: 'A humped shape is rising out of the pit. I can make out a small beam of light against a mirror. What's that? There's a jet of flame springing from that mirror, and it leaps right at the advancing men. It strikes them head on! Good Lord, they're turning into flame!' Shortly afterwards, dead silence from the on-the-spot reporter and a grave statement from the studio announcer: 'Ladies and gentlemen, I have just been handed a message. . . . At least forty people, including six State Troopers, lie dead in a field east of the village of Grovers Mill, their bodies burned and distorted beyond all possible recognition.'[7] From this point on, the drama gradually grew more and more unrealistic, yet many people were no longer listening, or if they were they were so frightened as to miss telltale signs that the broadcast was a drama. Later the announcer described a bleak and devastating scene as the Martian machines marched towards New York City: 'All communication with Jersey shore closed . . . army wiped out . . .'[8] Soon a voice was heard saying: 'I've just been handed a bulletin. Cylinders from Mars are falling all over the country. One outside Buffalo, one in Chicago, St Louis . . .'[9]

TIMING IS EVERYTHING

The drama appeared in newspaper schedules across the country on the day of the broadcast, clearly identified as a play, but many listeners did not make the association. For instance, on Halloween Eve, The *New York Times* printed the following radio listing: 'Today: 8:00–9:00 – Play: H.G. Wells's *War of the Worlds* – WABC.' The brief opening announcement also clearly stated its fictional nature, but it was common for listeners to miss the first couple of minutes as they shifted dials from other programmes. In 1938, there were also many live shows and they didn't always end exactly on time; some CBS affiliates would join the network late. Three other times during the play listeners were reminded of its theatrical nature, but these came much deeper into the programme, starting at the 42-minute mark, when it was too late as people were already frightened.

The most popular programme on the air at that time was the 'Edgar Bergen and Charlie McCarthy Show'. The show had phenomenal ratings as each week America's premier ventriloquist and comic, Edgar Bergman, would stage a variety show with his sidekick, wise-cracking wooden dummy Charlie McCarthy. They would open with twelve minutes of comedy, followed by a singer. A key point came at about eleven minutes and ten seconds into the drama. On this night it was Nelson Eddy performing 'Neapolitan Love Song'.[10] Listeners commonly tuned back and forth between radio programmes, especially near the beginning or during lulls. The practice was so common that it even had a name – 'airplaning' – the equivalent of modern-day 'surfing' with a TV channel changer. In 1937, Welles and actor John Houseman founded the Mercury Theatre, with their radio show by the same name beginning in mid-September 1938, in relative obscurity. Biographer Barbara Leaming remarks that each week Welles had a small window of opportunity in which to hook listeners. 'Each week their one big chance to attract listeners came when Edgar Bergen introduced a guest performer. At that moment, if the performer was not especially good, people across America would quickly turn the dial to hear what else was on before switching back. . . .'[11] Welles planned his script to include live dance music interrupted by special bulletins in order to grab the listeners' attention, especially those switching channels. Leaming suggests that Welles had intentionally used the technique to scare some listeners and that it worked beyond his wildest dreams.[12] Of those who began to 'surf' the dial for more interesting fare, about 12 per cent of Bergen's audience stopped at one of the over 150 stations that were broadcasting the Mercury Theatre. In fact, two separate surveys estimated that roughly 50 per cent of listeners to the Welles drama tuned in late, and missing the opening disclaimer, many believed it was a live news report.[13]

Immediately after the broadcast, Welles vehemently denied having any intention of deceiving listeners, noting that 'The Man From Mars' had often been the subject of radio fiction and part of the programme was in the form of a past-tense memoir.[14] Decades later he suggests otherwise, claiming that he had 'anticipated' the reaction.[15] Which Welles are we to believe? Based on the available facts, it seems plausible that Welles, intent on boosting his paltry audience share, calculated that some listeners would panic, but grossly underestimated reaction to the broadcast. This view is supported by an examination of earlier versions of the script which was significantly toned down compared to the broadcast version. Prior to its airing, CBS censors deemed the script too realistic and made no less than twenty-eight amendments. The working script used real-life names and places such as 'New Jersey National Guard', 'Princeton University Observatory', 'Langley Field', and 'Magill University', which were changed to 'state militia', 'Princeton Observatory', 'Langham Field', and 'Macmillian University'. 'The United States Weather Bureau in Washington D.C.' became 'The Government Weather Bureau' and 'St Patrick's Cathedral' was shortened to 'the cathedral'.[16]

The use of real names or real-sounding names and impersonations of government officials was clearly instrumental in convincing many listeners that the drama was really happening. In the Bronx, Louis Winkler of Clay Avenue said the broadcast was so realistic that it took his breath away, and describes the ensuing scene of pandemonium. 'I didn't tune in until the programme was half over, but when I heard the names and titles of Federal, State and municipal officials and when the "Secretary of the Interior" was introduced, I was convinced that it was the McCoy. I ran out into the street with scores of others, and found people running in all directions. The whole thing came over as a news broadcast and in my mind it was a pretty crummy thing to do.'[17] While the realism of the drama may seem implausible to contemporary radio listeners, for decades Mars had been the subject of frequent speculation about the existence of intelligent life, and news bulletins about the growing war in Europe were common. It is the modern-day equivalent of someone tuning in to CNN and being riveted to the TV by a catastrophic terrorist-related storyline, and assuming it was on all channels.

Near the end of the broadcast with the CBS switchboard flooded with calls, and policemen and reporters milling outside the studios, Welles stepped to the microphone to issue an apology, which sounded suspiciously as if it had been an intentional Halloween prank.

This is Orson Welles, ladies and gentlemen, out of character to assure you that the *War of the Worlds* has no further significance than as the holiday offering it was intended to be. The Mercury Theatre's own radio version of dressing up in a sheet and jumping out of a bush and saying Boo. Starting now, we couldn't soap all your windows and steal all your garden gates, by tomorrow night . . . so we did the next best thing. We annihilated the world before your very ears, and utterly destroyed the Columbia Broadcasting System. You will be relieved, I hope, to learn that we didn't mean it, and that both institutions are still open for business. So good-bye everybody, and remember, please, for the next day or so, the terrible lesson you learned tonight. That grinning, glowing globular invader of your living-room is an inhabitant of the pumpkin patch, and if your doorbell rings and nobody's there, that was no Martian . . . it's Halloween.[18]

Welles's apology did little to comfort or pacify those who had taken the broadcast as gospel. In Montclair, New Jersey, where hundreds

45

of community members were badly shaken, William Decker labelled the broadcast 'an outrage' and 'a disgrace', noting: 'It was the worst thing I ever heard over the air.'[19] In the aftermath of the broadcast, a Massachusetts man named George Bates sent a letter to the Mercury Theatre seeking damages of $3.25 for a new pair of black, size 9-B work shoes. He said he had bought a bus ticket to escape the invading Martians, but sixty miles into the trip realized it was only a drama. 'Now I don't have any money left for the shoes I was saving up for. Would you please have someone send me a pair of black shoes, size 9-B.' Theatre officials insisted on sending the money for the shoes despite objections from their lawyers, who no doubt feared that they may be setting a dangerous precedent.[20]

THE EFFECTS

The epicentre of fear was in central New Jersey in the vicinity of Grovers Mill and nearby Dutch Neck where there was near gridlock as thrill-seekers and rescuers were trying to reach the 'crash' site; others couldn't get away fast enough, speeding in the opposite direction.[21] At Grovers Mill, a suburb of Princeton in the town of West Windsor, New Jersey, hundreds of people arrived. Many searched without success for the imaginary Wilmuth farm, instead descending on the Wilson farm, assuming the reporter was mistaken.[22] Parts of New Jersey and New York City were most seriously affected, reflecting the content of the broadcast which described invading Martians attacking both states. Police in Trenton were kept busy with numerous requests for antidotes for the toxic Martian gas clouds and information on how to treat those already overcome. On North Clinton Avenue, two families told police that they had packed their cars with personal belongings, bundled family members inside, and were ready to head for the safety of the Rocky Mountains, and then head on to the west coast.[33] At a Princeton church a man ran in warning stunned congregants that the world was ending. A church in Kingston, New Jersey, closed early so parishioners could prepare for what was thought to be Judgement Day.[24]

An eerie fog which enveloped the region added to the fear. In one block in Newark, New Jersey, over twenty families fled their homes, covering their faces with wet handkerchiefs and draping towels over their heads to protect themselves from the 'poison gas'.[25] In Newark alone, fifteen people were treated for shock and anxiety at St Michael's Hospital.[26] Phone lines were jammed as police were swamped by frantic residents desperate for information on the 'gas raids from Mars'. At the *New York Times* offices, 875 phone enquiries were logged. At Manhattan Police Headquarters, the thirteen telephone switchboard operators could not keep up with calls.[27] Upon hearing the initial reports of a large meteor impact nearby, two Princeton University geologists even rushed to the 'impact site', only to find others, like themselves, searching in vain for the object.[28]

A New Jersey police officer wrote the following description of the panic in the daybook from the Port Norris Station: 'Between 8:30pm and 10pm received numerous phone calls as result of WABC broadcast this evening re: Mars attacking this country. Calls included papers, police departments including N.Y.C. and private persons. No record kept of some due to working teletype and all thru extensions ringing at same time. At least 50 calls were answered. Persons calling inquiring as to meteors, number of persons killed, gas attack, militia being called out, and fires. All were advised nothing unusual had occurred and that rumors were due to a radio dramatization of a play.'[29]

To a lesser extent, the effects of the broadcast were felt across the country. In Indiana a woman burst into a church shouting: 'New York destroyed; it's the end of the world . . . I just heard it on the radio.'[30] In Lincoln, Nebraska, hundreds of panicky residents jammed the police switchboard wanting to know if it was true and what they should do.[31] In St Louis, frightened residents huddled in the streets of some neighbourhoods to discuss a plan of action in the face of the impending war. In Pittsburgh, a man returned home during the broadcast only to find his wife clutching a bottle of poison, screaming: 'I'd rather die this way than like that.'[32] Across the border in Canada, Toronto radio station CFRB was flooded with enquiries from worried citizens.[33] In Washington State there was great anxiety as residents also jammed the phone lines of police, fire and newspaper offices in Seattle. Most terror-stricken were residents of Concrete, 100km to the north-east, when a power interruption caused pandemonium. Some loaded their families into cars and headed into the mountains; others fainted.[34] In Chicago, radio stations and newspaper offices were besieged with callers wanting to know the latest on the 'meteor' that had struck in New Jersey. On the campus of Brevard College in North Carolina, the scare reached such proportions that five students fainted and others were fighting to use the phones in order to call their parents to pick them up.[35]

THE POWER OF IMAGINATION

People's minds played tricks on them, illustrating the extreme variability of eyewitness testimony and suggestibility. One person became convinced that they could smell the poison gas and feel the heat rays as described on the radio; another became distraught and felt a choking sensation from the imaginary gas. In Hamilton, New Jersey, a frantic woman told police she had stuffed wet papers and rags into all of the cracks of her doors and windows but it was to no avail as the fumes were already seeping in.[36] During the broadcast, several residents reported to police observations 'of Martians on their giant machines poised on the Jersey Palisades'.[37] Upon hearing descriptions of Martians operating their towering metallic machines on three insect-like legs, several Grovers Mill residents opened fire at a huge outline barely visible through the fog – punching holes in the community's water tower.[38] A Boston woman said she could 'see the fire' as described on the radio; other persons told of hearing machine-gun fire or the 'swish' sound of the Martians.[39] One man climbed on a roof and told Bronx police: 'I can see the smoke from the bombs, drifting over toward New York. What shall I do?'[40] Of the people who claim to have actually seen the Martians, one emotionally distraught woman phoned Trenton Police from a vantage point near Grovers Mill, screaming: 'You can't imagine the horror of it. . . . It's hell!'[41]

In the excitement, some listeners created events that had never been described, underscoring the subjective nature of human memory reconstruction. For instance, Miss Jane Dean, a devoutly religious woman, who when recalling the broadcast said the most realistic portion was 'the sheet of flame that swept over the entire country. That is just the way I pictured the end'.[42] In reality, there was no mention of a sheet of flame anywhere in the broadcast. Some who had tuned in from the beginning, swore there was never a disclaimer. For instance, Sarah Jacob of Illinois said: 'They should have announced that it was a play. We listened to the whole thing and they never did.'[43]

Some terrified citizens tried to verify that what was being described on the radio was really happening, only to succeed in confirming the reality of an invasion. One person said that when they looked out and could see no cars coming down the street, they thought: 'Traffic is jammed on account of the roads being destroyed.' Another listener said that when they saw Wyoming Avenue busy with traffic, they assumed, 'people were rushing away'.[44] Despite staring contrary evidence in the face, some continued to interpret what they were seeing or hearing as supporting the Martian invasion. 'I stuck my head out of the window and thought I could smell the gas. And it felt as though it was getting hot, like fire was coming,' said one person.[45]

In London, H.G. Wells expressed agitation upon hearing news of the episode, remarking: 'I gave no permission whatever for alterations which might lead to the belief that it was real news.'[46] The Federal Communications Commission launched an immediate investigation of the broadcast. One FCC Commissioner, George Payne, advocated taking some type of action against CBS. 'People who have material broadcast into their homes without warnings have a right to protection. Too many broadcasters have insisted that they could broadcast anything they liked, contending that they were protected by the prohibition on censorship. Certainly when people are injured morally, physically, spiritually and psychically, they have just as much right to complain as if the laws against obscenity and decency were violated.'[47] Politicians also clamoured for action. Iowa

Senator Clyde Herring was clearly angry over such 'abuses', advocating legislation to prevent similar incidents in the future. 'Radio has no more right to present programmes like that than someone has in knocking on your door and screaming,' he said.[48] The City Manager of Trenton, New Jersey, was furious at the aftermath of the mass disruption and chaos to city life. Paul Morton sent an urgent message to the FCC Commissioners, urging them to take immediate action against the parties involved, warning that they were lucky no one was killed: 'If there had been a three alarm fire or other emergency during that interval, we would have been helpless.' Morton noted that the broadcast had 'completely crippled communication facilities' for the city's police department for three hours as concerned relatives from across the country were trying to get through to their loved ones. He was also critical of Welles, finding it difficult to believe that the broadcast was not a deliberate attempt to scare the public. 'I can conceive of no reason why the name of Trenton, and vicinity should have been used on this broadcast. The State Police were equally handicapped and it is indescribable the seriousness of the situation.'[49]

Despite protests from both politicians and the public, five weeks after its investigation began, on 5 December the FCC announced its ruling on the broadcast. Due to its limited mandate, the Commissioners' hands were tied. No laws had been broken. There was no way to formally restrict what went out over the airwaves as decreed in the FCC Radio Act of 1934.[50] As radio law historian Justin Levine notes: 'A basic obstacle that confronted the commissioners was the fact that no rule seemed to apply. The problem had nothing to do with their primary duties of preventing station interference or monopoly ownership within the broadcast industry. This was clearly not a case of obscene programming, nor could it even be termed indecent.'[51] Though concerned with censorship, the Commission decided not to impose new regulatory controls, noting that the actions taken by CBS since the episode 'were sufficient to protect the public interest'.[52] In its ruling, the Commission cited a letter from CBS stating that they would refrain from using the technique of live news interruptions and bulletins in any future dramas.[53] Angry Canadians were faced with a similar problem. Ontario Attorney-General Gordon Conant said: 'It is certainly not in the public interest that such broadcasts should be allowed.' Yet he expressed his powerlessness to take any action. 'I don't know of any action we could take,' he said.[54]

WAS THE IMPACT EXAGGERATED?

There is a growing consensus among sociologists that the extent of the panic, as described by Princeton University psychologist Hadley Cantril in his best-selling book *The Invasion from Mars*, was exaggerated. But regardless of the extent of the panic, there is little doubt that many Americans were genuinely frightened and some did try to flee the Martian 'gas raids' and 'heat rays', especially in the New Jersey–New York area. Based on various opinion polls and estimates, Cantril conservatively calculates that at least 6 million people heard the drama, 1.7 million of whom believed they were hearing a news bulletin, of whom 1.2 million became excited to varying degrees.[55] While there are some claims that hundreds of thousands panicked,[56] there is only scant anecdotal evidence to suggest that many listeners actually took some action after hearing the broadcast, such as packing belongings, grabbing guns or fleeing in motor vehicles. In fact, much of Cantril's study was based on interviews with just 135 people. Sociologist William Bainbridge is critical of Cantril for citing just a few colourful stories from a small number of people who panicked. Bainbridge reasons that, on any given night, out of a pool of over a million people, at least a thousand would have been driving excessively fast or engaging in rambunctious behaviour. From this perspective, the event was primarily a news media creation.[57]

Sociologist David Miller supports this view, noting that while the day after the panic many newspapers carried accounts of suicides and heart attacks by frightened citizens, these later proved to have been unfounded but have passed into American folklore.[58] Miller also takes Cantril to task for failing to show substantial evidence of mass flight from the perceived attack, citing just a few examples which did not warrant an estimate of over one million panic-stricken Americans. While Cantril cites American Telephone Company figures indicating that local media and law enforcement agencies were inundated with up to 40 per cent more telephone calls than normal in parts of New Jersey during the broadcast, he did not determine the specific nature of these calls. Miller contends that some callers probably wanted information such as which military units were being called up; where they could donate blood; or if casualty lists were obtainable. 'Some callers were simply angry that such a realistic show was allowed on the air, while others called CBS to congratulate the Mercury Theater for the exciting Halloween programme,' Miller writes. 'It seems . . . [likely] many callers just wanted to chat with their families and friends about the exciting show they had just listened to on the radio.'[59] Sociologist Erich Goode concurs with Miller's view but also notes that to have convinced a substantial number of listeners that a radio play about a Martian invasion was a real news broadcast must be viewed 'as a remarkable achievement'.[60]

THE POLITICS OF THE MEDIA IN 1938 AMERICA

In 1938, the print media and upstart radio were highly competitive arch-rivals, with radio viewed as an emerging threat to their advertising coffers. This antagonistic relationship may have prompted journalists to consciously or subconsciously exaggerate the extent of the panic in their initial press accounts.[61] The press commentaries and editorials were by and large condemning of Welles.[62] In an article entitled, 'Boo!' the 7 November issue of *Time* magazine conceded as much, noting that 'in the U.S. the press, no friend to radio, treated it as a public outrage'.[63] Justin Levine notes the conspicuous absence of 'independent historical accounts' detailing the severity of the reaction, with the exception of newspapers. He states: 'The anecdotal nature of the reporting makes it difficult to objectively assess the true extent and intensity of the panic.'[64] These suspicions are echoed by historian Timothy Crook: 'Somewhat suspiciously there were more newspaper offices than police stations swamped with frantic queries: "What is happening? Where's the nearest bomb shelter? What must we do?"' [65]

While the *Washington Post* published an editorial hinting at the need for radio censorship, on 15 November the paper printed a full-page ad questioning the effectiveness of radio advertising versus the press, noting that despite announcements as to the imaginary nature of *The War of the Worlds* drama, 'the public apparently failed to listen to them. "Who listened to him?" they asked rhetorically. "Who listens to what your announcer tells you about a product?"'

Welles was unhappy that in the wake of the broadcast, newspapers focused on the many lawsuits that were filed against CBS. Welles thought it was the press's way of striking back at radio's growing influence.[66] While $750,000 in damage claims were made by people asserting everything from broken bones to injuries suffered from tumbling down stairs – in reality, none of the suits succeeded in court. While most were widely viewed in the legal profession as 'pie in the sky', CBS settled a handful of suits without ever stepping inside a courtroom but never spent more than a few thousand dollars in total. For Welles, legal blame was a moot issue thanks to a clause in the contract, absolving the Mercury Theatre of 'all legal liability resulting from the content of our show'.[67] The fact is CBS was liable, but it was never really a major concern.

Science writer Keay Davidson suggests that the exaggerated nature of the panic, and failure to correct this oversight, reveals how scholars, novelists and intellectuals have conceived of ordinary working people as a blind, unthinking mob, easily led astray. Panic folklore about the 1938 broadcast reflects an elitist view of 'the masses' that has been used to justify unjust social policies and class oppression (i.e. 'You can't do that – the people will riot!'). 'The implicit message is blunt: most people are irrational and untrustworthy. The covert *political* message is: "Can the masses really be trusted to rule themselves?" "Don't they require a strong leader?" This question seemed urgent in Cantril's era, when the Hitler case suggested that the masses really could be manipulated easily by a charismatic leader equipped with the latest technologies of mass propaganda.'[68] Mass panic in reaction to the broadcast has been widely cited since 1938 to support government secrecy in the matter of UFO reports.[69] In 1999, US Senator Christopher Dodd cited the potential of a *War of the Worlds*-type panic in reaction to the Y2K computer scare. 'The worst thing the American public could do would be to withdraw funds in excessive amounts from their banks; to hoard medical supplies or . . . food or products like that in preparation for – something akin to The War of the Worlds. . . . That, in my view today, is the greatest threat that the Y2K problem poses – panic by the American public. . . .'[70]

It is undeniable that the 1938 panic occurred, but the extent remains debatable. The context of the broadcast was a key ingredient in triggering the scare. At the time, most Americans were heavily reliant on radio for news and entertainment. Political conditions were tense with Adolf Hitler continuing his incursion into Czechoslovakia, having recently annexed Austria. With each passing day, Europe was slipping closer to a second world war which would soon involve the United States. Listeners had grown accustomed to news bulletins interrupting regular programming with live reports from European war correspondents. Rapid progress in aviation technology was quickly 'shrinking' the world. The US would soon no longer be able to isolate itself, and it was well known that there was no coherent civil defence system against an aerial attack. With each passing day, Americans listened to bleak accounts of the widening war in Europe. Simon Callow describes this period in America as having a preoccupation with European affairs, a sense of pessimism and feelings of vulnerability, especially from the air, culminating in 'a mood of national jumpiness'.[71] It was within this context that the Welles drama, interspersed with a series of live field reports, would have appeared highly realistic. Cantril concluded that a contributing factor to the panic was the plausibility of the broadcast, as a substantial portion of listeners had assumed that the Martian 'gas raids' were actually a German gas attack on the United States and that the announcer had misinterpreted what he was seeing as a Martian invasion. Said one typical respondent: 'The announcer said a meteor had fallen from Mars and I was sure he thought that, but *in the back of my head I had the idea that the meteor was just a camouflage.* It was really an airplane like a Zeppelin that looked like a meteor and *the Germans were attacking us* with gas bombs.'[72]

Levine considers radio to be a particularly effective medium with which to perpetrate hoaxes as it can uniquely engage people while they are performing a variety of tasks, be it driving, typing or jogging. 'In terms of portability, radio remains second only to newspapers in its ability to follow the audience throughout their daily lives. Visual media – such as print, television, and the Internet, require the undivided attention of a static viewer in order to receive information.'[73] Levine points out that radio is the only medium at present that combines such elements as 'immediacy, portability, psychological impacts on the imagination, and the ability to reach listeners throughout their daily routines' and thus 'remains the most conducive for perpetrating hoaxes on unsuspecting audiences'.[74]

After the initial uproar, Welles's popularity soared. Overnight his name and face were instantly recognizable around the world, his radio ratings rose three-fold,[75] and Campbell's Soup quickly signed on as a sponsor.[76] Yet, Welles would never be entirely trusted again. In an ironic twist, he would become part of a cautionary tale on the dangers of 'crying wolf'. On 6 December 1941, during a live poetry reading on network radio, Welles was interrupted by a bulletin reporting the Japanese attack on Pearl Harbor. Many listeners refused to believe the report, suspicious of the coincidence.[77]

FOUR

How Could it Happen Again?
The Remarkable Legacy of the Martian Panic

Those who do not remember the past are condemned to repeat it.

George Santayana

There is widespread smugness today in America and other parts of the so-called civilized world that a similar reaction to that of the Welles drama, could not happen to them. There is a feeling that such episodes belong to the ignorant or primitive; that somehow, being more sophisticated, we are immune from such folly. Nothing could be further from the truth. If history teaches us anything, it is that those groups which grow complacent, arrogant and self-centred, are the very people who are most at risk. Could it happen again? The answer is 'Yes'. Since 1938, similar events have occurred several times.

Since Halloween Eve, 1938, the *War of the Worlds* production by Orson Welles and his colleagues has served as the inspiration for scores of radio adaptations. Many were pathetic productions suffering from various deficiencies ranging from poor acting to dull, unimaginative script-writing, leading to a general lack of believability. Deservedly and mercifully, most have been all but forgotten. Yet a few have caused significant short-term social upheaval or prompted the Federal Communications Commission to rewrite existing laws. Those that succeeded in causing fright and panic were those closely following the original Welles production format. In this chapter we will examine these episodes and the factors they share in common, beginning with two of the more notable incidents which occurred in South America during the 1940s.

CHILEAN *WAR OF THE WORLDS* SCARE (1944)

Shortly after 9.30 p.m. on 12 November 1944, panic erupted in several Chilean towns and cities after the broadcast of a version of the realistic 1938 radio drama loosely based on the H.G. Wells novel, *The War of the Worlds*. The play originated at a radio station in Santiago and was broadcast throughout the country on the Cooperative Vitalicia Network, causing thousands of terrified citizens to flee into the streets or barricade themselves in their homes.[1] Hundreds were affected in Santiago; in Valparaiso, electrician Jose Villarroel became panic-stricken and died of a heart attack. The script was the brainchild of American William Steele, former writer for the popular United States radio drama, 'The Shadow'. Ironically, and perhaps it is no coincidence, actor Orson Welles was the original voice of 'The Shadow', and Steele was undoubtedly familiar with Welles who was involved in the similar radio panic in North America six years earlier. Working with assistant Paul Zenteno, the duo set the invasion epicentre 15 miles south of Santiago in Puente Alto.[2] One provincial governor mobilized artillery units in preparation to repel the invading Martians. The broadcast was highly believable, including references to such organizations as the Red Cross and using an actor to impersonate the interior minister.[3] As in the previous drama, accounts of the invading Martians appeared as a series of 'news flashes'. The drama described in vivid, gloomy detail the defeat of the military, and destruction of the Santiago Civic Centre along with air bases and artillery barracks. The broadcast reported roads as jammed with desperate refugees fleeing the devastation.[4] Both the radio station and local press had announced the upcoming broadcast a week in advance, and once the play was under way, listeners were warned twice. After the broadcast, angry citizens pressured the government to close the station and suspend the play's creators but no official action was taken.[5]

ECUADOR MARTIAN INVASION PANIC (1949)

On Saturday night, 12 February 1949, a radio play based on *The War of the Worlds* by H.G. Wells, sparked pandemonium in

Ecuador. An Associated Press reporter on the scene said the broadcast 'drove most of the population of Quito into the streets' as panic-stricken residents sought to escape Martian 'gas raids'.[6] The drama described strange creatures heading toward Quito after landing and destroying the neighbouring community of Latacunga, twenty miles to the south. Broadcast in Spanish on Radio Quito, the realistic programme included impersonations of well-known local politicians and journalists, vivid eyewitness descriptions, and the name of the local town of Cotocallao. In Quito, rioting broke out and an enraged mob marched on the building housing the radio station and Ecuador's oldest and leading newspaper, *El Comercio*. Rampaging mob members blocked the entrance to the building, hurling stones and smashing windows. Some occupants escaped through a rear door; others ran to the third floor.[7] Groups poured gasoline onto the building and hurled flaming wads of paper, setting fires in several locations, trapping dozens inside and forcing them to the third storey. As the flames reached them, occupants began leaping from windows and forming human chains in a desperate bid to reach safety. Some of the 'chains' broke, plunging terrified occupants to their deaths.[8] Twenty people were killed and fifteen injured.[9] Army soldiers were mobilized to restore order, rolling through the streets in tanks and firing tear gas canisters to break up the demonstrators and allow fire engines through.[10] Damage to the newspaper building was estimated at $350,000.[11] Help was slow to arrive as most mobile police units had been dispatched to Cotocallao to repeal the 'Martians', leaving Quito with a skeleton police and military presence.

The tragic events began with the sudden interruption of a regular music programme with a special bulletin – 'Here is urgent news' – followed by reports of the invading Martians in the form of a cloud, wreaking havoc and destruction while closing in on the city.[12] 'The airbase of Marisal Sucre has been taken by the enemy and it is being destroyed. There are many dead and wounded. It is about to be wiped out', the announcer said.[13] A voice resembling that of a government minister appealed for calm so the city's defences could be organized and citizens evacuated in time. Next the 'mayor' arrived and made a dramatic announcement: 'People of Quito, let us defend our city. Our women and children must go out into the surrounding heights to leave the men free for action and combat.'[14] At this point, a priest's voice could be heard asking for divine forgiveness, followed by a recording of church bells sounding alarms throughout Quito. Positioned at the top of the city's tallest building, the *La Previsora* tower, an announcer said he could discern a monster engulfed in plumes of fire and smoke, advancing on Quito from the north.[15] It was at this point, according to a *New York Times* reporter, that citizens 'began fleeing from their homes and running through the streets. Many were clad only in night clothing.'[16] The panic was not limited to Quito. In some parts of the country hundreds of terrified Ecuadorians fled into the mountains to avoid capture, believing, according to the radio, that the Martians had already taken over much of the country.[17] The rioting, murder and public unrest was the most extreme reaction to a *War of the Worlds* radio re-creation, exceeding even the original 1938 episode.

The situation was so serious that the Defence Minister was appointed to head an investigation of the affair. In the following days, at least twenty-one people were arrested for their role in either rioting or being responsible for allowing the radio play to air, including the station's drama director Eduardo Alcaraz. Indictments were ordered against art director Leonardo Paez and station manager Alfredo Vergara, a script-writer, and his spouse, Maya Wong.[18] The station's operators claimed that Alcaraz and Paez were the broadcast's masterminds, having written and directed the play in secret.[19] Also arrested and charged with partial responsibility was *El Comercio*'s editor, Jose Alfredo Lierena.[20]

MARTIANS INVADE WESTERN NEW YORK (1968)

A local adaptation of the Welles drama, broadcast in western New York on Halloween night 1968, triggered widespread fear from southern Canada to the eastern seaboard. The remarkable saga began at about 11 o'clock on Thursday 31 October, and within several minutes stunned listeners were straining their ears to hear news of what was initially described as a catastrophic meteor strike. By the time the drama ended at a quarter past midnight, early Friday morning, many were shaking with anger to think that such a deception was perpetrated on the community. Airing on popular Buffalo radio station WKBW, with a powerful 50,000 watt signal, the drama incorporated the basic storyline of the 1938 play. Despite heavy advance publicity, once the programme began, it was difficult to distinguish from regular programming. Buffalo radio historian Robert Koshinski describes it as remarkably realistic: 'They played records, did commercials, played their jingles, and covered the story like they regularly covered stories.'[21] The broadcast was every bit as realistic and gripping as the Welles drama.

Programme Director Jefferson Kaye wrote the script which closely paralleled the 1938 version for the first few minutes, after which it became a local event set in Buffalo in the 1970s. Kaye and engineer Dan Kriegler intended to produce and direct the drama and had received permission to use the original Welles script, but abandoned the idea; practice readings with staff announcers were lacklustre and contrived, as the language was dated and sounded phoney.[22] Faced with the prospect of airing an incredible, boring broadcast bordering on the ridiculous, Kaye 'spiced it up' by having the Martians land on the Buffalo island suburb of Grand Isle, a few miles south of Niagara Falls. Adding to the realism, he let staff from WKBW radio and its television affiliate play themselves and report on the 'Martian attack' as if it was a live event. Reporters Jim Fagan, Don Lancer, Joe Downey, Sandy Beach and Irv Weinstein were given basic details around which to ad-lib. They were sent to mobile units in the parking lot, transmitting their reports back to the station to give them an authentic, live quality.[23] Kaye then spliced the different records together. A gifted announcer and writer, Kaye would later gain fame in the sports world as the voice of NFL films.

At 11 o'clock the pre-recorded production began when reporter Dan Neaverth signed off and aired a disclaimer. Joe Downey then read the news, ending 'with a seemingly innocent final story about mysterious explosions on Mars'[24] including an interview with an astronomer from local Niagara University. Near the start of the programme, disc jockey Sandy Beach did a typical show with occasional low-key news break-ins by Downey about reports of Martian explosions.[25] Suddenly in the middle of the song 'White Room' by Cream, a bulletin was aired describing a major traffic jam on Grand Isle. During the recording, Kriegler and Kaye were at the station adding live sound effects.[26]

More music and commercials, then the Beatles' 'Hey Jude' was interrupted by a bulletin from Joe Downey in the newsroom about an explosion on Grand Isle. 'It's been reported that a large meteor has struck the ground along East River Road on Grand Island setting off a series of fires and explosions. Several persons have been injured and as yet there is no confirmation regarding the number of people that may have been killed. KB total newsmen are already on their way to the scene. Repeating . . . it's reported a large meteor has struck grounds along East River Road on Grand Island. We'll have a special report in a few minutes.'[27] At this point, many listeners became engrossed in the story, failing to make the connection between the breaking news story and the scheduled Halloween drama. Many were completely fooled, not realizing the show had begun. Jefferson Kaye later said: 'All through that Halloween evening, people called WKBW radio. "When is the *War of the Worlds* going to start?" And we would tell them, "Eleven o'clock". Then promptly at 11 o'clock the show began. Then we started to get calls saying, "Well, where is it?" And we replied, "It's on. Listen."'

Excitement and fear continued to build in intensity. Soon Jefferson Kaye came on to inform listeners that the story was so serious that the station was going to present continuous, 'live' coverage of the events from KB newsmen in the field. As they recorded their takes, the ad-libbed format resulted in several reporters occasionally groping for their next lines or mispronouncing words. Kaye cleverly left many of these sequences in, adding to the spontaneous, 'live' quality of the broadcast. For those who may have been harbouring doubts as to the broadcast's authenticity, this technique erased many of their suspicions.

'This is Joe Downey in the WKBW newsroom. Right now there are ah . . . reported explosions and fires on Grand Island. Communications at this time are reported down. Telephone communications are down and other types of communication are very poor at this time on Grand Island. [There is much static and noise in the background as the broadcast signal seems to fade.] WKBW news is mobilizing its entire news department at this time . . . there is an unconfirmed report that a meteor exploded on Grand Island. Newsmen from KB are on their way right now to the disaster scene on Grand Island. WKBW newsman Henry Brock is now attempting to contact the Erie County Sheriff's Depar . . . ahh . . . Henry . . . Henry . . . Henry and the Sheriff . . .'

'Erie County Sheriff's Department . . . Deputy Macintyre here.'

Henry Brock: 'Hello, this is WKBW news . . . ah anything . . . ah . . . on that ah . . . goings on Grand Island tonight?'

Deputy: 'Well there's fires and there's damage . . . there's several lives that have been lost but ah we have no body count at this point. You know, I can't give you an actual report at this point. There's fire people here . . . there's military people . . . they're all over the place here . . . I can't really hardly give you actually any report . . .'

Then suddenly: 'This is Henry Brock in the KB newsroom. It has just been confirmed that Governor Rockefeller has mobilized the National Guard and contingents of the guard from the Western New York area are on their way to Grand Island.'

Shortly thereafter, a report from Jim Fagan who painted a very realistic on-the-scene report. 'I'm just off White Haven Road, Hank, not too far from the scene. . . . Right . . . several houses have been levelled to the ground and I can see ambulances . . . there are about three or four ambulances on scene that I can see. The attendants and the medics in these ambulances are now treating several of the people who have been injured here. My count is about twenty persons injured here at the scene.' KB reporter Henry Brock enquired: 'Whataya got, walking injuries or real bad ones?' To which Fagan responded: 'Hank, these people are badly crippled as a result of the injuries they've received.

Several people are unable to walk at all . . . and I see a number of people bleeding about the face.'

Later, Fagan describes a gruesome attack: 'My God, Don, there's something crawling out of the top of this thing. . . . The crowd's moving back . . . I'm moving back . . . I'm getting out of here . . . I tried to talk the Professor into moving out but he managed to talk some army lieutenant into approaching this thing. . . . He and the professor are now approaching. . . . Good God almighty Abraham, that was some sort of a red beam. They've burst into flames, the professor and the lieutenant. We're getting out of here. We've got to get out of here. The red beam, it's going off all over the place picking off people . . . one by one. There are bodies all over the place.'[28]

Shortly after midnight, WKBW-TV reporter Irv Weinstein was zapped by a Martian heat ray, leaving Kaye alone to close the drama 'by walking out onto Main Street and succumbing to the poison gas that had been wiping out the population of Buffalo all night. What followed was a somber close by Dan Neaverth that stuck to the original H.G. Wells novel explaining that the Martians themselves were wiped out by the common germ despite their victory over humanity.'[29]

Halfway into the programme, the phone began ringing continuously with worried callers. Realizing the anxiety he was generating, Kaye asked his engineer to open his microphone to interrupt the broadcast and remind listeners of its imaginary nature. Kaye says that he steadfastly refused as the drama had been sold and he was worried over the possible loss of advertising revenue.[30] Kaye threatened to pull the reel off the wall and was finally given control of the microphone to make a thirty-second disclaimer.[31] Between them, Buffalo police and the phone company logged over 4,000 calls from concerned listeners, the majority from outside the immediate Buffalo area. People called from as far east as Bangor, Maine, and as far west as San Francisco nearly 3,000 miles away. The station's signal can often be heard across much of the continental United States at night, when its transmission carries further.[32]

Once the drama ended, and after taking savage verbal abuse from scores of irate callers, Kaye says he became despondent thinking he would surely be fired in the morning. He hastily wrote out a resignation letter and slid it under the General Manager's door. By the following morning, the anger began to subside and he was surprised by the reaction from public and station officials who were generally supportive. Furthermore, it became evident that Kaye had tamed the powerful Federal Communications Commission who couldn't do a thing about the scare by carefully giving listeners ample notification of the event.[33]

Kaye recalls that after realizing they had been listening to a play, several people went to the station to complain. 'One man came to the back door with a baseball bat and was threatening to bash my brains out.' He thought the broadcast was real and headed toward Grand Isle to see the devastation, and in his haste, crashed his car into a utility pole.[34] Upon hearing reports of the 'attack' in Canada, Canadian National Guard units were deployed along the major border crossings including the Queenstown Bridge, Rainbow Bridge, and Peace Bridge.[35]

While professionally done, the play was not without flaws which went unnoticed by many: 'Several times reporters react to aircraft and explosions before the audience actually hears them because director Dan Kriegler had to add sound effects live to save tape generations. TV newsman John Irving describes the Grand Island Bridge explosion and has survivors being swept away by rapids some half-mile away just seconds later.'[36]

The episode is enlightening in that station personnel took extreme measures to ensure that listeners would *not* be frightened, although Kaye admits anticipating that some might be fooled.[37] Fearing a possible FCC backlash if the play backfired – which it did – for twenty-one days before the broadcast, WKBW undertook an unprecedented advertising campaign, airing frequent, daily promotions for the play, and mailing out hundreds of press releases to every police, fire and emergency service agency within their eight-county area of primary listenership in western New York and adjacent south-western Ontario, Canada.[38] On the day of the broadcast, the *Buffalo Evening News* even published a regular radio and TV news column by J. Don Schlaerth, telling readers of the airing of the programme at 11 p.m., complete with photos of WKBW's Dan Neaverth and DJ Don Wade.[39]

As a testament to the show's realism, Kaye says that a major Buffalo newspaper was even fooled, dispatching a team of journalists and photographers to the disaster scene, 'as confessed to us by an embarrassed photographer'. The same paper had been sent three separate notices warning of the upcoming broadcast. Meantime, a Canadian police department was temporarily unnerved by the broadcast. Kaye said: 'One unfortunate police chief from a small nearby city happened to be at his desk in the middle of the show when a man straggled into the police station with a wild tale of Martians invading the states.' The man had obviously been drinking and officers did not take his wild tale seriously. And where had he heard such an outlandish tale? When the man told them on WKBW, they incredulously tuned in, joining the programme in mid-stream. The police chief began handing out weapons in order to defend their community, only to hear a commercial and realize that the entire affair was fictional. 'Sheepishly they ordered pizza and sat down to listen to the rest of the show,' Kaye said. The embarrassed policeman himself had told the story to Kaye – but only on condition that he withhold his name.[40]

The failure of many listeners to discern the fictitious nature of the drama highlights the dangers of airing radio dramas that include live bulletins, and realistic, localized scenarios with familiar personalities. Kaye says that he learned a lesson from the event: 'You should never overestimate the sophistication of your audience.'[41] A modified version of the Kaye production was aired in 1971, and despite repeated promotions as to the time and date, a few concerned listeners called the station and emergency services.[42]

RHODE ISLAND'S *WAR OF THE WORLDS* SCARE (1974)

Several years later a similar broadcast would land another radio station in hot water, and prompt the FCC to seriously consider taking away its licence. Between 11 p.m. and midnight on Wednesday 30 October 1974, a local adaptation of the original 1938 *War of the Worlds* script was broadcast over another powerful radio station – WPRO in Providence, Rhode Island. The incident resulted in many frightened listeners in this tiny New England coastal state. The play had a similar opening storyline as the Welles drama. The script was vivid and localized with WPRO reporters covering a series of 'explosions' near Jamestown, the purported Martian landing site. Included was a description of a 'blue flame from Mars'. This was followed by reports of traffic jams and several fatalities, and a dramatic announcement that Governor Philip Noel was mobilizing the National Guard. WPRO reporters were sent to the scene, only to be vaporized by Martian ray guns. Prominent landmarks such as the two-mile-long Newport Bridge were 'blown up' in the alien attack.

The drama was aired during the Holland Cook show, a nightly feature between 7 p.m. and midnight. Cook, a local disc jockey who had only been working for about a month, at 11 o'clock began to play the taped invasion, which opened with a continuation of his regular music programme. Suddenly there was a bulletin about a meteor impact near Jamestown. The pre-recorded programme was produced by Jake Pacquin, but unlike the 1938 Welles broadcast, there was no opening disclaimer as to the fictional nature of the programme listeners were about to hear.[43] Further adding to the realism, WPRO did not begin to promote the Halloween show until 12.45 p.m. on the day of the broadcast, airing the adverts about one per hour.[44] Station management had notified various police agencies within the primary listening area prior to the broadcast and told listeners there would be 'a Halloween spoof' at 11 p.m. Area police departments logged over eighty telephone enquiries about the 'disaster', while the city fire stations and other radio and TV outlets reported being inundated with enquiries from anxious callers, as was WPRO which received over 100 calls.[45] Police switchboards statewide were jammed with calls from panic-stricken or angry listeners.[46] The impact of the broadcast was not nearly on the scale of the Orson Welles drama as, like the WKBW episode, the drama was not broadcast over a syndicated network of stations but on a single station. Another factor in reducing the panic was the late time at which it was aired.[47] By 11 o'clock, many listeners were already asleep and others were tuned in to their local TV news. The *Providence Journal-Bulletin* received about 500 calls in a one-hour period.[48]

The Federal Communications Commission was sent letters of complaint protesting at the broadcast, including accounts of frightened citizens speeding through the streets in an effort to reach home in order to protect their families. Some people altered their travel routes to try to bypass certain areas that the announcer had told people to avoid. One letter writer conveys the depth of the scare: 'We are not alarmists or gullible people but in the hour that we listened we were so afraid we called neighbors and our parents to warn them.'[49] One man left work after receiving a phone call from a friend telling him that his family, living near Jamestown, was in danger. A number of people were frightened and disorientated after being awakened by others and hearing disturbing details of the 'disaster'.[50] Even Providence Democratic Congressman William Babin heard the broadcast, noting that his nineteen-year-old daughter woke him after being 'really scared' by the show.[51] In East Providence some residents began 'crying and throwing up'.[52] Another caller told a reporter, their voice shaking, 'I was scared to death, running around the house with a gun. I can understand replaying the Orson Welles thing. But I listen to WPRO at morning and night [sic], and I never heard them advertise that programme.'[53] The station did not air a disclaimer until thirty-five minutes into the show.[54]

Following its investigation of the event, the FCC issued a reprimand to WPRO but did not suspend or revoke their licence. In doing so, it cautioned against using '"scare" announcements or headlines which either are untrue or are worded in such a way as to mislead and frighten the public . . .'.[55] An attempt to downplay the extent of the public reaction turned comical when station officials pointed out to the FCC that there was no public gathering at the 'landing site' as happened in the 1938 Orson Welles episode. The Commission replied that 'it would be reasonable to assume that the last place that those people misled by the broadcast would want to gather is at the Martian landing site'.[56] Despite the initial concern over the possibility of the station losing its licence, 'It was a powerful boost to our sales staff and boosted advertising revenues', Cooke said.[57] 'The programme showed just how easy it is to fool the public.'[58]

As is evidenced by the public reaction to earlier radio broadcasts of Martian invasion scares, disclaimers, even those played during the broadcast, are not always adequate to counteract the use of local announcers and live bulletins. The editors of the *Providence Journal-Bulletin* summarize this point well: 'There is no way in which any radio station or television can be sure that its early warnings about hoaxes will be heard by all those persons who may tune in on broadcasts at later hours of the day or evening. For that reason . . . full explanations ought to be offered as the show opens and at frequent intervals during productions.'[59]

MARTIANS INVADE PORTUGAL (1988, 1998)

During the final twelve years of the twentieth century, two more *War of the Worlds* scares would be recorded in Europe. On Sunday 30 October 1988, Radio Braga in northern Portugal caused hundreds of residents to become frightened after airing a drama about invading Martians. Intended as a tribute to the original 1938 broadcast on its fiftieth anniversary, hundreds began inundating police and fire agencies with telephone enquiries. While some got into their motor vehicles and sped away from the area, others actually headed toward the 'landing site' near the town of Braga.[60] After the broadcast, and upon learning of the deception, many residents became irate, holding protests outside the radio station's studios. Police were summoned to maintain order as up to 200 protesters turned out. Unlike the original Welles drama, the Portuguese counterpart was ninety minutes in length.[61]

Ten years later on Friday morning, 30 October 1998, Antena 3 (a subsidiary of Portuguese National Radio) in Lisbon, Portugal, aired a radio drama about invading Martians, triggering a regional panic. Broadcast in commemoration of the sixtieth anniversary of the infamous 1938 production this latest version of the Welles script (translated into Portuguese) was highly realistic. Hundreds of anxious residents deluged the radio station with phone calls; some left work while others felt sick in response to the news. While an announcer cautioned listeners at 7 a.m. that the drama would start in an hour, many did not hear the announcement. The play began with the report of a UFO landing in the town of Palmela, twenty-one miles south of Lisbon, which was followed by a series of news bulletins describing Martians heading toward Lisbon after destroying military units sent to stop them.[62]

THE POTENTIAL FOR MASS MANIPULATION

In 1964, WPEN in Portland, Oregon, aired a live broadcast of the *War of the Worlds* script. There was no panic in the streets or frantic phone calls to authorities. In fact, there have been at least two dozen adaptations of the *War of the Worlds* since 1938. In nearly every instance, nothing happened. So why were a handful of radio dramas able to frighten listeners where numerous others had not? Each of these 'successful' broadcasts shared several common features. They incorporated elements of Welles's original production, starting with a mysterious object coming to earth, usually initially described as a meteor, followed by 'live' bulletins of the event. The re-creations were very realistic using impersonators, local reporters who were trusted by their audience, and the names of real people and places. The quality of the productions was exceptional. Most of the 1938 script was authored by a young writer by the name of Howard Koch, relatively unknown at the time. Koch was gifted. He was to become famous after writing a masterpiece screenplay for one of the most acclaimed films of all time: *Casablanca*. The WKBW script was written by Jefferson Kaye, another gifted writer and radio mind who would go on to gain fame as 'the voice of NFL films'.

In every instance, disclaimers were broadcast prior to the event on the station and in the form of newspaper listings. In the WKBW case, disclaimers were broadcast weeks before, but were largely ignored, neutralized by the power of 'live' local reporters who were seemingly broadcasting from the scene of a seemingly real event. Audiences live with these radio personalities day after day, often for years. They become part of our families. We trust them.

It's interesting to note that contrary to popular belief, the Welles episode was not the first major radio scare. That distinction goes to the British. The parallels with the several *War of the Worlds* scares is striking. On Saturday evening, 16 January 1926, Father Ronald Knox began his regular radio show for the British Broadcasting Corporation. In the opening segment, Knox announced that he was presenting a comedy skit and that the upcoming stories were entirely fictional. However, many listeners across England and Ireland missed the opening disclaimer and took the show at face value.

The broadcast described a popular uprising, as an angry mob of unemployed workers was reportedly raging through London. A bloody massacre of the ruling class had purportedly taken place at St James Park; the National Gallery was said to be in ruins; trench mortars had taken down Big Ben. Meanwhile, the Traffic Minister was lynched from a tramway pole. 'The Clock Tower, 320 feet in height, has just fallen to the ground, together with the famous clock, Big Ben. . . . Fresh reports, which have just come to hand, announce that the crowd have secured the person of Mr Wotherspoon, the Minister of Traffic, who was attempting to make his escape in disguise. He has now been hanged from a lamp-post in Vauxhall Bridge Road.'[63] Perhaps appropriately, the programme ended with the destruction of the BBC office.

Once the show concluded, anxious listeners inundated newspaper offices with telephone calls asking for more details. Many were worried about the fate of friends and relatives in London or whether their properties were destroyed. According to one report, despite reassurances from journalists, 'rumours were still circulating in country towns and villages, and the fact that bad weather delayed the arrival of the morning papers was taken by many persons as confirmation that the worst had happened'.[64]

As with the original Welles drama that took place in the atmosphere of a looming war crisis in Europe, England was experiencing serious labour unrest and threats of major work stoppages. It was within this context that the Knox drama was set. It was plausible, exceptionally vivid, realistic in parts and well written. Knox was a brilliant writer, producing nearly one hundred scholarly books including his well-known *Enthusiasm: A Chapter in the History of Religion.*[65] Combined with the sound effects, the script came to life. The crumbling of buildings could be heard along with shrieks from the crowd and explosions in the distance.[66] From an examination of the script, it is clear that Knox never intended to deceive listeners. The drama was clearly satire to anyone who listened closely. Yet, the serious *tone* of the play, and the fact that it came from the BBC, fooled many listeners. Also like the Welles drama, it used a programme format of dance music, followed by 'live' news bulletins, then back to 'regular' programming again. It was a broadcast within a broadcast. 'That concludes the news bulletin for the moment; you will now be connected with the band at the Savoy Hotel [gramophone dance music can be heard] . . . London calling. You will now be given the weather report for tomorrow.'[67]

Shortly after that episode, an editorial in the *New York Times* entitled 'We Are Safe From Such Jesting', smugly suggested that Americans were practically immune from a similar occurrence. 'Such a thing as that could not happen in this country, or at any rate its harm would be confined to those who were listening to one of the 600 broadcasting stations. . . .' The editors failed to anticipate the proliferation of syndicated radio broadcasts transmitting a single programme to hundreds of stations simultaneously.[68] This situation was responsible in the two biggest reactions to adaptations of the H.G. Wells book – the 1938 Orson Welles production, and eleven years later when riots broke out in Ecuador. Today syndicated radio and television broadcasts are more common and popular than ever before. Whenever huge audiences are all tuned to the same programme, reading the same newspaper column or internet site, the potential for mass manipulation looms large.

FIVE

Media-made 'Monsters':
Four Tall Tales and Why People Believed Them

Things are seldom what they seem, skim milk masquerades as cream.
W.S. Gilbert, *HMS Pinafore*

Ignorance is the womb of monsters.
Henry Ward Beecher [1]

Over the years, members of the mass media have created an array of imaginary or exaggerated threats involving real or fictitious creatures. Sometimes these creations are deliberate fabrications; and sometimes the scares they produce are unintentional. These episodes, while infrequent, underscore the enormous influence and responsibility that the media has in our lives, and the ever-present potential for mass manipulation and social delusion. If we can be led to believe that ferocious animals are roaming the streets of New York City, devouring residents; that the carcass of a 300lb earthworm is lying across a Texas interstate; that 'kissing bugs' are attacking Americans in their sleep; or that a restless spirit is assaulting a BBC TV news crew, then we can be led to believe just about anything.

While some of these creature scares may seem so outlandish that they could involve only poorly educated, naive members of the public, it's important to realize the circumstances in which they occur. Each episode transpires within a unique context that renders it plausible to a segment of the population. In this regard, we are all potential victims, and those of us who are arrogant enough to think

72

ourselves too sophisticated to be fooled by such chicanery – we are especially vulnerable.

NEW YORK'S ZOO SCARE OF 1874

On Monday morning, 9 November 1874, thousands of people across the New York City region became panic-stricken after picking up their daily delivery of the *New York Herald* and reading that their fair city was under a state of emergency. 'AWFUL CALAMITY' proclaimed the headline. It was reported that several ferocious animals had escaped from the Central Park Zoo and were running loose throughout the city. From the descriptions, it was nothing short of a massacre. The National Guard was patrolling the streets and dead bodies were scattered everywhere. At the time of publication, the death toll had reached 49, with as many as 200 injured. Hospitals were overwhelmed. The situation was dire. In reality, the story was fictional, but stunned readers had no way of knowing that. Even the paper's editor, Gordon Bennett, was reportedly unaware of the hoax, and is said to have collapsed in his home after starting to read details of the catastrophe.[2] Many people chose not to venture out for the day.

The article came complete with vivid eyewitness accounts of the carnage. One man described the chaotic scene near the zoo, where several animals were purportedly fighting over the body of zookeeper Hyland Anderson, who was said to have triggered the breakout after poking a rhinoceros. 'But I could see nothing more than a mingling, gleaming mass, whence arose the most awful cries. Near to me, where Hyland lay, the lioness, the panther, the puma, and presently the Bengal tiger, were rolling over and over, striking at each other with their mighty paws . . . I could not help look at Lincoln, the lion . . . "By God, he's looking at me!" I said to myself. I saw him crouch. I turned and ran . . . I saw a young man fall from a blow of the awful paw, another crushed to earth beneath the beast's weight. . . .'[3]

The timing and context of the hoax were essential in selling it to the public. There were long-standing concerns over the safety of the zoo. Even the *New York Times* conceded that such an occurrence 'was not altogether unlikely to happen', noting that Central Park had 'the flimsiest cages ever seen'.[4] The accounts were extraordinarily vivid and detailed. One witness described a lion 'tugging and crunching at the arms and legs of a corpse, now letting go with his teeth to plant his paws upon the bleeding remains, and snap with his dripping jaws at another beast'. Another passage told of a panther gnawing on a man's head, while most gruesome of all was the description of a lion that had torn four tiny children to shreds, mangling 'the delicate little things past all signs of recognition'. In another incident, a panther was said to have leapt on an elderly woman, 'burying his fangs in her neck', while a young girl or boy was 'fearfully disfigured about the head and face'.

In the last paragraph, the story was unveiled as a hoax, but many readers never got that far. Under the subtitle 'The Moral of the Story', it was asserted that the reason for the deception was to shock New Yorkers into realizing how much of a danger the dilapidated zoo posed to the city's welfare. The *Herald*'s editors should have also considered the danger that their paper posed to the city's social tranquillity through irresponsible, alarmist reporting. Unofficially, the real reason for the exposé may have been to boost circulation. The rival *New York Times* was not amused, issuing a scathing editorial, labelling the incident 'intensely stupid and unfeeling'.[5] In adjacent New Jersey, the *Plainfield Times* reported that one of its prominent citizens, Henry Martin, was overcome by emotion while reading through the article and suffered a fatal heart attack.

Curiously, the hoax has had an unintended, far-reaching impact on the American political landscape. Shortly after the incident, political cartoonist Thomas Nast began to draw cartoons featuring the imaginary zoo breakout. As a result, as improbable as it sounds, the elephant – huge, clumsy, sloth-like – eventually came to represent the American Republican party, and the donkey – an ass – to symbolize the Democrats. As they say, 'Only in America!'

THE GREAT 'KISSING BUG' SCARE OF 1899

The 'kissing bug' is a generic term for numerous insect species that suck blood from mammals, so called for their tendency to pierce the exposed skin of sleeping victims, most often on the face and especially the lips. Other common names include the 'assassin bug', 'cone-nose' and 'big bed bug'. Its romantic nickname became popular during the summer of 1899, when scores of Americans claimed to have been bitten on the lips while sleeping.

After biting its victim, the kissing bug ungraciously defecates on the host, a practice which can transmit potentially fatal Chagas disease. In the faecal matter is a parasite which can severely damage the heart, nervous system, brain, colon and oesophagus. The dreaded bug is rampant in parts of Central and South America where 25 per cent of the population is at risk, an estimated 17 million are infected, and 50,000 deaths occur annually.[6] However, the species of kissing bug on the United States mainland rarely bite humans, and when they do – it's almost always in self-defence. In North America the chances of contracting Chagas disease is extremely low as the more polite northern 'kissing bugs' do not defecate while feeding, greatly reducing the transmission risk.[7] The bug's notorious reputation outside the US may have helped spark what became known as 'the great kissing bug scare' of 1899.

The scare can be traced to *Washington Post* police reporter James F. McElhone who, in the course of making his journalistic rounds in mid-June, began to note an influx of patients seeking treatment for 'bug bites' at the Washington City Emergency Hospital. Upon interviewing hospital physicians on 19 June, he learned that several people had indeed been treated for redness and swelling, typically on the lips, 'apparently the result of an insect bite'.[8] Curiously, no one ever saw their attackers in the act. On 20 June, McElhone published a speculative, sensational account of the flurry of 'bug bites' in Washington, describing victims as having been 'badly poisoned' and warning that it 'threatens to become something like a plague'.[9] It was quickly dubbed the 'kissing bug' and other Washington papers soon reported further 'attacks', followed by reports in papers along the east coast. News of these outbreaks was then spread nationwide.[10]

BITE OF A STRANGE BUG

– – – –

Several Patients Have Appeared at the Hospitals Very Badly Poisoned

Look out for the new bug. It is an insidious insect that bites without causing pain and escapes unnoticed. But afterward the place it has bitten swells to ten times its normal size. The Emergency Hospital has had several victims of this insect as patients lately and the number is increasing. Application for treatment by other victims are being made at other hospitals, and the matter threatens to become something like a plague. None of those who have been bitten saw the insect whose sting proves so disastrous. One old negro went to sleep and woke up to find both his eyes nearly closed by the swelling from his nose and cheeks, where the insect had alighted. The lips seems to be the favored point of attack.

. . . The matter is beginning to interest the physicians, and every patient who comes in with the now well-known marks is closely questioned as to the description of the insect. No one has yet been found who has seen it.

Across the country, people were on the lookout for any insect that vaguely resembled kissing bugs. In Exira, Iowa, Henry Bush captured one, 'his little life was squeezed out' and it was promptly exhibited in town.[11] New York City was especially hard hit. On 1 July, six patients were treated at Bellevue Hospital for what they said were kissing bug bites, though no one saw their attacker. Typical was the case of twenty-year-old Oscar Meltsner who said he was bitten 'on the face by a bug he thought was a mosquito, on Wednesday night. Thursday his face swelled up and Friday his left eye was closed'. He assumed it was the kissing bug.[12] On the evening of 2 July, kissing bug bites were reported by, among others,

Mrs Helen Veasy. Yet, as was typical of the bug's *modus operandi*, her attacker managed to escape without being positively identified. A *New York Times* reporter states: 'Mrs Veasy was sitting last night on the porch of the cottage when a large insect came sailing up to her in the semi-darkness and lighted for an instant on her lips. . . . As she raised her hand to brush it away, she felt a slight pain shoot through her upper lip. The bug then flew away before she could kill it. Within half an hour her lip had swollen to the size of a robin's egg.' The next day she consulted a doctor and the swelling was greatly reduced.[13] On the 11th, four new cases were treated at the Bellevue Hospital Dispensary, each with swollen lips.[14] During mid-July a series of 'kissing bug attacks' were reported along the coast at Newport in Rhode Island.[15]

Soon any insect bite or swelling or pain of any kind on or near the face was attributed to the sinister 'kissing bug'. Leland Howard, Chief of Entomology for the US Department of Agriculture in Washington, DC, describes the ensuing scare as a '*newspaper* epidemic, for every insect bite where the biter was not at once recognized was attributed to the popular and somewhat mysterious creature'.[16] His own Agriculture Department had initially identified the offender as *Melanolestes picipes*. Soon doctors and laymen were identifying *Melanolestes picipes* as the culprit. These allegations were surprising to entomologists as the accused had a previously good reputation. At the Philadelphia Academy of Natural Sciences, entomologists meticulously analysed the remains of numerous 'kissing bugs' collected by purported victims. Some of the specimens were provided by physicians. After considerable poking, prodding and eye strain, the bug experts soon announced that they had examined at least twenty-one different types of insects from among dozens of specimens. Remarkably, not a single 'kissing bug' or *Melanolestes picipes* was in the line-up of creepy-crawlies. Among those identified were houseflies, beetles, and bees. One person even sent in pieces of a butterfly![17] The problem was, *Melanolestes picipes* looked guilty. For instance, when a Chicago man managed to capture a so-called specimen, it simply looked the part. Despite the insect having made no attempt to bite anyone, a Mr F. Weinschenk described it in fierce terms: 'The bug is a strange looking insect and appears to deserve all the mean things that have been said of him. It . . . has a short, strong beak, with a point as sharp as that of a mosquito. Its color is nearly black. . . .'[18]

A separate investigation of reported 'kissing bug' bites in New York State by its top entomologist, Dr E.P. Felt, yielded similar conclusions. He notes that American species of kissing bugs were not aggressive and only attacked in self-defence. Of the many specimens of 'kissing bugs' sent to the State Entomologist in Albany for examination, 'All thus far received have proved to be harmless insects, lacking poisonous attachments.'[19] Most of these bugs were big and ferocious looking, and did not even remotely resemble the *Melanolestes picipes*, the kissing bug's so-called scientific name. Dr Felt said that reports of kissing bugs alighting on the lips were rare. 'This bug will not steal into a room and pounce upon a sleeping victim. To be stung, a person must go in its vicinity and cause it harm.'[20]

During July, newspaper accounts of kissing bug attacks grew increasingly sensational.[21] A report from a Chicago woman more closely resembled a vampire attack than a bug bite.[22] Not to be out done, in Brooklyn, a tailor named Paul Nichols described his encounter in terms so vivid as to resemble a 1950s-era drive-in monster movie. He said the bug 'had a head like a rat's and two long "fangs" and tackled his leg, instead of his cheek'. The insect put up quite a struggle flying about the room, but Nichols eventually managed to catch it and subdue it, being so disgusted by the vile creature that he promptly burned it. He said his leg was swollen for two days, and though he couldn't be certain it was a 'kissing bug', it was similar to press descriptions.[23] Near Fort Wayne, Indiana, a barefooted farmer named Jacob Meyer was relaxing on his property one July evening when he said a determined 'kissing bug' went into a steep dive, attacking the big toe of his left foot 'as if he was boring for oil'.[24] Like a fish story, the size of the abhorrent creature seemed to get bigger and bigger. In mid-July, when Lewis Winfield of Trenton, New Jersey, reported an attack, he claimed it was just under six inches long![25]

In mid-July at least two mysterious deaths were attributed to the 'kissing bug'. When a two-year-old Trenton, New Jersey, girl died on the night of the 9th, the attending physician blamed the bug after a 'red spot' had been found on the child's leg the previous week. In Chicago, about a week later, Mary Steger died six days after having been stung on the lip by something. Despite no clear proof, the death certificate read: 'Chief and determining cause of death, sting of kissing bug, consecutive and contributory tonsillitis', while the doctor later wrote that 'Mrs Steger had been suffering for a long time from tonsillitis and I think that the swelling may have spread to the tonsils and thus helped to cause the death . . . there is no doubt in my mind that the woman died primarily from the sting of a kissing bug.'[26]

At the height of the scare, kissing bug poetry began to appear. One read:

> Swift, with undiscerning glee,
> Through the land he goes,
> Kissing one upon the lips
> Or the chin or nose . . .
> Some of us well know thy worth,
> Gay philanthropist,
> Some of us who but for thee,
> Never would be kissed.[27]

Meantime, beggars in the city of Washington, DC, bandaged themselves and went about soliciting donations, claiming to have been out of work and requiring charity to subsist until their full recovery from kissing bug bites.[28] During the remainder of the summer, entomologists were in great demand, having difficulty just walking down the street or attending church services without being accosted on the subject. Dr Howard was of the opinion that many of the 'attacks' were simply mosquito bites that were exaggerated by frightened citizens. In some cases, Howard thinks the 'victims' were bitten by mundane bugs, but the patient, fearful of sickness and swelling, being certain they were victims of a 'kissing bug', may have developed psychogenic symptoms. But is this really possible? A stack of history books reveals numerous historical reports of people suffering hysterical reactions to insect bites in the form of tarantism.

TARANTISM

During the thirteenth century, in the region of southern Europe that is now Italy, there are numerous accounts of citizens claiming to have been bitten by the tarantula spider and experiencing an array of symptoms, the most conspicuous being an uncontrollable compulsion to dance. In fact, dancing was widely thought to be the only reliable cure so as to sweat out the 'poison'. Period physicians labelled the new illness tarantism, and episodes were common for centuries. Historian Harold Gloyne describes it as a 'mass hysterical reaction' to perceived tarantula spider bites.[29] Less common terms used to describe the behaviour includes tarantulism, *stellio, astaragazza*, and *tarantulismo*. Widespread, seasonal outbreaks persisted for 400 years, peaking in the seventeenth century; after which it rapidly declined to the point where only a handful of twentieth-century accounts are recorded. Tarantism is widely thought to be of psychogenic origin due to its many curious aspects, such as its almost exclusive occurrence during July and August. Historian Henry Sigerist states:

> People, asleep or awake, would suddenly jump up, feeling an acute pain like the sting of a bee. Some saw the spider, others did not, but they knew that it must be the tarantula. They ran out of the house into the street, to the market place dancing in great excitement. Soon they were joined by others who like them had just been bitten, or by people who had been stung in previous years, for the disease was never quite cured. The poison remained in the body and was reactivated every year by the heat of summer. . . .
>
> . . . Music and dancing were the only effective remedies, and people were known to have died within an hour or in a few days because music was not available.[30]

Tarantism symptoms included breathing difficulties, chest pain, headache, giddiness, fainting, trembling, vomiting, twitching, excessive thirst, appetite loss, and delusions. 'Victims' occasionally claimed that a sore or swelling was made by a tarantula bite, but such assertions were difficult to verify as the bite appeared similar to that caused by other insects. While the identical species of tarantula is common throughout southern Europe and is considered relatively harmless, frenzied reactions to perceived bites were almost exclusively found in the southern Italian state of Apulia. Curiously, during the Middle Ages some people tried shipping Apulian tarantulas to other regions but their bites failed to produce even a single case of tarantism. Modern tests on spiders have found nothing unusual with tarantulas from Apulia.[31] It's doubtful that another insect was responsible as most 'victims' never even claimed to have been bitten – by any insect – but would start dancing 'uncontrollably' in July and August.

Latrodectus tarantula is common in Apulia and can elicit psychoactive effects in those it bites, but it is not aggressive and moves slowly. In rare cases its bite causes symptoms that resemble some characteristic features of tarantism – twitching and shaking of limbs, weakness, nausea and muscle pain. Yet these symptoms are temporary and could not account for the range, scope or duration of tarantism episodes. *Latrodectus tarantula* is clearly innocent, being found in other regions of the world including the United States, all places where tarantism is not recorded.[32] The species most often associated with tarantism, *Lycosa tarantula*, the wolf spider, is a logical choice because it resides in southern Italy, is aggressive, ferocious in appearance and has a painful bite.[33] Yet its bite cannot produce symptoms even remotely resembling tarantism. It too is clearly innocent, as symptoms are minor and usually involve local pain and itching. Less common reactions include an increased pulse rate, nausea and light-headedness.[34]

Psychiatrists classify tarantism as a form of mass hysteria coloured by a person's unique set of beliefs about the world. Other psychogenic symptoms include the reported necessity of dancing to certain musical scores as the only reliable cure. The most common curative tunes were variations of the tarantella, a dance taking its name in the eighteenth century from the Italian port city of Taranto. The tarantella is a whirling, fast-paced dance featuring brief, repetitive phrases that build in intensity. While dancing typically endured intermittently for days and occasionally weeks, those affected eventually declared themselves 'cured', only to relapse in subsequent summers. At other times, 'victims' reported being 'infected' by simply being near someone who had been bitten or by simply touching or brushing against a spider. Still others were afflicted summer after summer upon hearing musicians playing tunes that were intended to 'cure' those who had supposedly been bitten.[35]

How did psychogenic reactions to imaginary tarantula bites originate? They may have begun as ancient Greek religious rituals that were intended to produce a catharsis.[36] Over the centuries they may have evolved into tarantism. Clearly, most North American 'kissing bug' bites reported in the summer of 1899 were social delusions by jittery citizens misidentifying mundane insect bites. Some, however, may have been psychogenic in origin. Correspondingly, most tarantism 'victims' seem to have been play-acting in order to achieve ecstatic states similar to many modern-day charismatic religious groups. A few may have been experiencing psychogenic reactions, truly believing they had been bitten by the tarantula.

GHOSTWATCH

Our next example of media manipulation produced neither psychogenic reactions nor mass hysteria, but did frighten the wits out of many British people – especially children. Some of those who were terrified required psychiatric treatment for post-traumatic stress disorder. At 9.25 p.m. on Halloween evening of 1992, the television arm of the BBC aired what appeared to be a serious ninety-minute documentary on the supernatural. Promoted as an investigation of the paranormal, *Ghostwatch* was billed as a live broadcast from 'the most haunted house in Britain'. The house was located in Northolt, Middlesex, where a divorcee named Pam Early and her two daughters had reported a series of ghostly happenings over the years:

strange voices, noises, and harassment by a poltergeist that reportedly moved objects about the modest three-bedroom home. The programme ended up scaring the bejesus out of England, prompting widespread public outcry, and was never shown again until its release on video a full ten years later. This is despite the show's remarkable success, with an estimated viewership of over 11 million. Response to the programme was overwhelming. BBC phone lines were flooded with an estimated 20,000 calls from mostly irate listeners and a deluge of letters quickly inundated BBC offices.

Ghostwatch featured four distinguished, well-known British TV personalities: Michael Parkinson and Mike Smith who were depicted in the studio; and Sarah Greene and Craig Charles were on location in the house. The show began by introducing a taped segment in which we are introduced to the haunted family, including a spooky scene from the girls' bedroom where a video camera purportedly captures eerie flashing lights, shouting and banging. The most dramatic scene involves a lamp which rises from a table, then smashes into pieces.

From the very start, the show was gripping as respected, charismatic British talk show host Michael Parkinson walked across the set to address the audience. His facial expression serious; his tone, no nonsense. 'The programme you are about to watch is a unique investigation of the supernatural. It contains materials which some viewers may find disturbing.' The tension and drama gradually built throughout the show, as occasionally 'live' calls were taken in the studio for the public to call with comments. Next the capabilities of the infra-red cameras were discussed. About thirteen minutes in, Parkinson took the first viewer 'phone call' – Mrs Staplefield of Slough thought she saw a ghostly figure dressed in black, standing in the bedroom. Soon Pam Early began describing the haunting which had begun in 1991 involving an entity that she called 'Pipes', a disfigured old man in black robes – so named when his initial ghostly clamouring was blamed on poor plumbing. An array of spooky noises were heard in the house, and after about an hour, a sudden breakthrough. They appeared to catch Suzanne, her daughter, making the noises. Ah! A big sigh of relief. Apparently the whole affair was a hoax. Parkinson beamed: 'We set out to catch a ghost . . . and we mark out an exposure of a hoax.' But the plot quickly thickened and soon there were more twists and turns. Before long, all Hell broke loose as events quickly spiralled out of control. Suzanne's face was suddenly, spontaneously, covered with scratches. Before the show ended, the girls began speaking in tongues; Sarah Greene was dragged under the stairs to her doom; Parkinson himself was possessed by an evil force.

The show's writer, Stephen Volk, said the programme was crafted as a 'scripted drama' in order to grab the audience's attention and fool them into thinking it was real, but only at the very beginning. The decision to present the 'investigation' as live (it really wasn't) with familiar announcers, greatly enhanced its credibility. 'We thought that people might be puzzled for two, perhaps five minutes, but then they would surely "get" it, and enjoy it for what it was – a drama. The curious thing about *Ghostwatch* is that while one part of the audience didn't buy it for a second, another part believed it was real from beginning to end.' [37]

The show was actually filmed during the summer of 1992, though the house was decorated with Halloween trappings for effect on the assumption it would be shown on or near 31 October. On that night the cast and crew got together for a few drinks and to watch it 'live'. Volk says, 'When Ruth arrived from TV centre to report that the BBC phone lines were jammed, we knew we had created an effect far beyond anything we had anticipated.' According to Volk, 'If we were guilty of anything, we were guilty of underestimating the power of the language of "live TV" to convince people that what they are watching is real. On the Monday morning after transmission, school teachers cancelled lessons to discuss the programme. Kids across the country were arguing about whether "Pipes" the ghost actually appeared, and if so, how many times.'

PUBLIC IMPACT

The *British Medical Journal* reported on two separate cases of post-traumatic stress disorder that were diagnosed in ten-year-old British boys and attributed to watching the show. Described by their parents as 'worriers', the boys had trouble sleeping, frequent nightmares, were afraid of the dark or to sleep alone. They suffered panic attacks, depression, irritability, separation anxiety, memory and concentration problems, as well as intrusive thoughts and images about the show. In one case, the boy became so frightened that he couldn't bear to keep watching, and soon sought constant reassurance that ghosts and witches could not harm him. He could not even sleep alone with the light on, had flashbacks and would hit his head in a vain attempt to rid himself of thoughts of the show. The boy clung to his mother more and more, and she had a difficult time even getting him to attend school by himself. Unable to cope any longer, she finally sought professional help. Her son recovered, but only after being hospitalized for eight weeks.

The case of the second boy was similar to the first, though not as severe. Once the show was over, he felt ill, weepy, and became convinced that his room was being watched. He refused to enter it. When his parents let him sleep with them, he would talk excessively about his fear of ghosts, to the point where he needed repeated assurances during the night. It soon became too much to handle so they sought help. This boy also eventually recovered and they were both able to get over their excessive fears with behavioural therapy which included not discussing *Ghostwatch* or topics related to ghosts.[38]

Just how much of a lasting effect do frightening shows like *Ghostwatch* have on people? While most research focuses on the short-term effects of watching frightening TV programmes, Kristen Harrison of the University of Michigan has found a worrying long-term impact. Surveys were taken at two large American universities where students were asked if they had ever been frightened over a long period of time after watching a TV show or film. The results were alarming. About 9 per cent said they had been frightened for up to a year or longer, but that the fear had dissipated. Just over 26 per cent reported that the fear endured for at least a year *and was still continuing*. Half of the subjects reported eating or sleep disturbances as a result of being scared by the media, while about

35 per cent said they either dreaded the frightening behaviour or avoided it altogether. Over 18 per cent dreaded or avoided 'situations related to the depicted situation' such as swimming after watching the film *Jaws*.[39] Yet, some people didn't even realize the impact of the media until finding themselves in a similar situation. One student said that while she 'had fun' watching *Jaws*, 'I was surprised at the effect it had on me when I went swimming in Wisconsin lakes. . . . If someone yelled "Jaws!" and I was in the water my heart would start racing and I would fly out of the water. It lasted a good year.'[40]

One viewer's death was tied directly to *Ghostwatch*. Five days after watching, and obsessing with fears of ghosts, eighteen-year-old Martin Denham hanged himself from a tree near his family's home in Nottingham, known by locals as the 'Witch Tree'. Denham had learning difficulties and was highly impressionable. His suicide note read: 'Mother do not be upset. If there is [sic] ghosts I will now be one and I will always be with you as one. Love Martin.'[41] Denham's mental age was equivalent to a thirteen-year-old. There is little doubt that if the show had not been broadcast Denham would still be alive today.

WHY IT WORKED

Why was *Ghostwatch* so believable? Perhaps the biggest factor was the 'Parkinson Effect'. Presenter Michael Parkinson oozed credibility and he was in a familiar role – that of discussing important news events. In fact, he played the part so well, that Volk said it even fooled people who expected to see a drama, not a documentary. 'One friend of mine, whom I'd told the week before that I had a drama on TV at 9.30 the following Saturday, phoned to tell me that she totally believed it was happening for real. I said, "But I told you I'd written it!" "Yes, I know," she said, "but as soon as I saw Michael Parkinson I thought you must have got it wrong!"'[42] Sarah Greene was also a readily recognizable face, known and loved as one of the stars of the hit children's TV show *Going Live*. Her husband Mike Smith was also a respected TV personality on family-orientated shows. This husband and wife team would certainly have had an impact in making the show seem believable to both children and parents. These presenters were 'part of the family' and when they seemed to fall into trouble, many viewers already had an emotional investment in their well-being. In this way, there was built-in character development. Many in the audience deeply cared about what was happening to these presenters whom they had grown up with, as if a family member had been in trouble. Another realistic touch was the use of popular TV comedian Craig Charles who was shown interviewing neighbours during the episode, playing himself and providing comic relief.

Ghostwatch was framed in such a way as to affect many viewers on a personal level. For those believing the 1938 Welles drama, it was feared that a Martian or German gas attack was under way – an event that was likely to seriously disrupt their lives. Very few events are perceived by a large number of people as directly affecting their lives. The assassination of John F. Kennedy and the death of Princess Diana were remarkable events in that they had a deep personal effect on large numbers of people who in their own minds had made a personal connection with Kennedy or Diana. The attacks of 11 September 2001 also struck a chord with people around the world as almost anybody could have had the misfortune to have been on one of the doomed flights or touring the World Trade Center on that fateful morning. *Ghostwatch* was presented as a 'live broadcast', capturing listeners with the sense that they were watching something extraordinary unfolding before their very eyes; a collective seance that could potentially affect their lives. Many viewers took it personally, thinking that they were potentially vulnerable. The format was similar to other popular, dramatic, real-life programmes of the period such as *Hospitalwatch, Crimewatch, Watchdog,* and the nature production, *Badgerwatch.* Many of these shows relied on viewers phoning in with their own insights and tips.[43]

Adding to the realism, members of the Society for Psychical Research were pictured sitting at phone banks answering questions and writing down 'psychic' experiences from viewers. Those answering the phones were actually from the Society, and they were hoping to get reports of 'psychic' experiences, but they also quickly explained to callers that the show was a drama and not real. It certainly appeared real as millions of viewers would have recognized the phone number – 081 811 8181 – which was the same number that was used for several real-life call-in shows including *Crimewatch*. Another strategy to add realism was the use of a 'live' satellite link in order to interview experts such as a 'Dr Sylvester' in New York, who was offering the sceptical view. Representing the believers was 'Dr Lyn Pascoe' from the Society for Psychical Research. Satellite link-ups were a familiar element in many British news programmes, as was the format of soliciting opinions from opposing experts on the topic at hand.

Ghostwatch used the familiar faces of prominent TV personalities, each playing themselves. The use of 'live' bulletins interrupting programmes had been done before, such as in the 1994 American TV movie *Without Warning*, which, ironically, was first aired on Halloween night. It describes a series of asteroid fragments striking Earth. The impacts turn out to be part of an invasion of Earth, complete with convincing news bulletins. The movie prompted a number of complaints from angry viewers who had been briefly fooled into thinking the event was really happening. For instance, a CBS affiliate in Fort Smith, Arkansas, received dozens of phone calls from anxious residents wanting to know more about the 'news' of the 'disaster', while others were upset that Fox, NBC and ABC had not yet broken into regular programming to cover the story live.[44] While *Without Warning*'s use of news bulletins was mildly convincing to a relatively tiny number of inattentive viewers, *Ghostwatch* had a much greater impact on audiences because, in the days prior to its showing, it was being promoted as a 'live' documentary. A variety of devices were used to heighten its realism, such as a series of technical miscues that one might expect from doing a live show, and, about an hour into the programme, the announcement: 'Those joining us for the next scheduled programme should be aware we are staying with these events.'[45]

Was *Ghostwatch* part of a deliberate attempt to give its viewers a Halloween fright? It would seem so, though, like the Welles drama, its impact was greater than anyone's expectations. In fact, writer Stephen Volk states that on several occasions he thought the plug might be pulled on the show, and wasn't certain as to whether it would go on air, even up to the last minute, because of nervous corporate sponsors, 'but we made it by the skin of our teeth', Volk said.[46] A similar recognition of the potential to deceive listeners was realized in the 1938 Welles drama as CBS censors made numerous alterations to the script in the week prior to its airing, changing real names and places to similar sounding but imaginary ones. A statement issued by the BBC soon after *Ghostwatch* was broadcast, notes that most callers were seeking reassurance that it was not real, and once relieved they became angry and felt duped.[47] Despite the public outcry, some of those involved were unrepentant. Michael Parkinson angered many by pointing the finger of blame at viewer ignorance, shrugging off the BBC's responsibility in the affair. He accused those who took the drama as real, of 'living under a stone for the previous two weeks. I have no concerns whatsoever about the show. You always get a certain percentage who believe everything on TV is real. If people were scared, we did our jobs well.'[48]

THE TEXAS EARTHWORM HOAX

The story was only 200 words in length, and was buried on page three, but it created a brief sensation near the Mexican border town of Laredo, Texas (population 130,000). While it may sound hard to believe, it really happened. In early March 1993, the *Morning Times of Laredo* published a bogus account of a giant 300lb earthworm measuring 79ft in length. The creature was reportedly found dead, draped across Interstate 35, jamming up traffic. One motorist described the creature as 'a grey, fat, rubbery thing'. The incident highlights the influence of the mass media in the information age, and how susceptible society is to journalistic hoaxes.

According to the story, entomologist Luis Leacky from Laredo State University had located a mucus trail along the interstate, speculating that the creature had mutated from the nearby Rio

Grande. Laredo police and US Border Patrol officers reportedly converged on the scene in rubber gloves, removing the mammoth worm with the help of two cranes and a large truck.[49]

Local police were deluged with hundreds of calls from inquisitive residents as scores of excited people drove to the scene to glimpse the fictitious worm after the journalist who created the story, Carol Huang, wrote: 'Because federal environmental guidelines do not outline the proper disposal method for large, earthworm carcasses . . . authorities have left the creature in the Target store parking lot until Monday, when zoologists and Environmental Protection Agency (EPA) officials are expected to arrive from Washington.'[50] Even before the store opened, a Target worker said that curiosity seekers kept asking if the worm carcass was inside the building.[51]

Huang, who was dismissed from her job the same day, says she wrote the account on her computer as a joke but several days later said she was flabbergasted to see it in print. The news editor who allowed the story to appear, Thomas Sanchez, left his job shortly after the incident, saying the account ran 'by accident'.[52]

The story had elements of credibility and even fooled a scientist from Texas A&M University who phoned the paper and offered to rush to the scene and examine the worm with a vanload of equipment. For instance, the Rio Grande was notorious for pollution, and even though the notion that an earthworm could mutate in the chemical soup to reach such incredible dimensions was scientifically impossible, to the average person it had an air of plausibility. The purported interview with a professor at Laredo State University, the Luis Leacky who supposedly confirmed the incident, would have further eroded lingering doubts.

Some details were so vivid as to lend further credibility, such as the idea that police would use rubber gloves to handle the carcass. The idea that the federal officials would delay taking any action until hearing from the EPA on proper disposal of the carcass, fits neatly into the environmentally conscious 1990s. The federal government is well known for its bureaucracy and foot-dragging, especially when the EPA is involved. There is much dissatisfaction with the agency as it's widely thought to have too much power. For example, when any new business construction is proposed, the builders must get an environmental impact statement before they can even break ground.

At first glance, the Texas earthworm hoax seems too implausible. Could many people actually take such a story seriously! A newspaper account of a giant worm of such incredible proportions seems not only to stretch the limits of plausibility, but to exceed them. But that is exactly what was reported to have occurred in southern Texas. Yet all someone needs to do is look at that part of the world and it makes sense. It was the local culture which rendered the story plausible. Laredo is located along the Mexican border. Strange tales of giant earthworm-like creatures 3ft thick and reaching lengths of 75ft have long circulated through parts of South and Central America. The creatures reportedly live in lakes and ponds. They are referred to as the *Minhocão* in Brazil, from the Portuguese *minhoca* or earthworm; as the *sierpe* in Nicaragua; and are also known by other names including *Surubin-Rei*.[53] These exaggerated tales of giant worms may have been the inspiration for the popular 1990 movie *Tremors* starring Kevin Bacon, where a colony of carnivorous earthworms burrowed under the ground in the south-western United States.

THE MORAL OF THE STORY

In this chapter we have examined four episodes of media manipulation. In three cases the stories were outright bogus, while as for the 'kissing bug', its exploits were greatly exaggerated. Yet, for those who were taken in and believed these reports, for a brief time, they *were* real. There *were* lions and tigers roaming through New York; there *was* a nefarious spirit attacking a BBC film crew. And therein lies the real danger – there *were* real consequences besides the anger and chuckles by the public when it was over. In 1874 some people *did* stay home from work for fear of being eaten on the way. *Ghostwatch* unduly alarmed thousands of British children, causing fear and nightmares. In 1899, how many Americans spent sleepless nights worrying about being the next victim of the 'kissing bug?' How many people feared going out or sweated through the summer by sleeping under a bed sheet to avoid being bitten? As for the Texas earthworm report, well, if the press is capable of convincing readers of the existence of something as implausible as a giant worm, can another zoo deception or kissing bug scare be far off?

In our post-11 September world, where many people are already feeling on edge, members of the media need to tread carefully in terms of what they produce, and think through the potential effects on their audience. For instance, if another 'kissing bug' scare were to be created, some may suspect it is a superbug created by terrorists; or that animals escaped from a zoo were actually let out by terrorists. During each age, a handful of major themes are reflected in the form of popular fears – fears which may result in public reactions that we cannot anticipate. If similar broadcasts were to occur today, they might trigger widespread fear that a biological or chemical terrorism attack was actually under way.

Plausibility and timing are also important. To successfully deceive the public, there has to be a plausible story occurring at the right time and place. *Ghostwatch* would not likely have been viewed as plausible and hence real in an atheistic society where the existence of poltergeists was not accepted as part of the natural world. The Texas earthworm hoax would not likely have succeeded in New York or London. While growing up, many people living in the border region between the US and Mexico have heard stories of giant earthworms living in bodies of water. As implausible as it may seem to the rest of us, the earthworm article was probably meant as a spoof on people who believe in such tales – and believe they did.

SIX

Europe's Mad Cows and Bad Coke: Terror at the Dinner Table

No passion so effectually robs the mind of all its powers
of acting and reasoning as fear.

Edmund Burke[1]

Coke has long been promoted with the advertising slogan, 'The Real Thing'. Yet, when it comes to triggering mass hysteria, reality usually counts for little. Perception is everything. Executives of the Coca-Cola company learned this lesson the hard way in 1999. During that summer, nearly a thousand people in Belgium and France became sick after drinking 'tainted' Coke and other soft drinks made by the Atlanta-based cola conglomerate. Soon, all products made by the world's most recognizable brand name were ordered off the shelves by worried governments in many European countries including Spain, Germany, Holland, Luxembourg and France, costing the giant soft drink company tens of millions of dollars. An investigation at Coca-Cola quickly uncovered two problems. Coca-Cola's CEO, M. Douglas Ivester, followed a time-tested public relations strategy. He bravely fessed up by facing the crisis head-on. Ivester accepted blame, issuing a public apology for the mistake and hinting that hygiene at the bottling plant in Antwerp may have been sub-standard. 'Quite honestly, we let the people of Belgium down,' he said.[2] There was only one problem. Independent tests would later exonerate the company. Coke was innocent. There was nothing harmful in the various Coca-Cola products that had supposedly sickened so many Europeans. The sickness was all in their heads, triggered by an odd smell and taste,

93

the cause of which was harmless. The frenzy that followed the first 'outbreak' was so intense and convincing that even Coca-Cola officials believed that they were to blame.

The poison Coke scare began on 8 June 1999, when thirty-three pupils at a Catholic secondary school in the small, prosperous town of Bornem, near Antwerp in Belgium, were rushed to a nearby hospital after they felt ill shortly after drinking containers of Coca-Cola. After the first ten students reported feeling sick, the school nurse made frantic enquiries, in an attempt to trace the cause. She soon had her answer: the only factor the students shared was their having drunk Coke. At this point, staff members reportedly went from room to room, asking students if they had consumed Coke and if they felt sick. In the annals of mass hysteria, it was the equivalent of someone shouting 'Fire!' in a crowded theatre. It is not surprising, then, that shortly afterwards, another twenty-three students reported feeling ill and were admitted to hospital. The symptoms were varied. Some began to complain of stomach pain; others had difficulty breathing. Nausea, dizziness and light-headedness were also common. Examining physicians were initially puzzled and could find no indication of any abnormality as urine and blood samples all tested within normal limits. Following the time-tested strategy of 'Do no harm', and seeing that the pupils were in no immediate danger, they prudently held off from administering medication. As a precaution, some were given oxygen, which is relatively harmless. Fifteen were kept in hospital overnight for observation. The following day, four more students were examined at the hospital complaining of similar symptoms. Like the earlier group, their symptoms were also unremarkable. In all, thirty-seven students ranging in age from ten to seventeen were admitted – twenty-eight girls and nine boys.[3] In an ironic twist of fate, one of the pupils, fourteen-year-old Ann DeMan was leading a field of other students in a contest sponsored by Coca-Cola in which she stood to win a portable CD player.[4]

The Bornem incident made headlines across Europe that evening and in the next day's newspapers. In the following days, seventy-five Belgian schoolchildren claimed similar ill-effects from drinking Coke at four other schools. Eleven students in the tourist community of Bruges on 10 June were reportedly stricken after drinking Coke or Coca-Cola soft drinks. The next day at Harelbeke, seventeen more were afflicted. The tainted Coke crisis was quickly spiralling out of control, threatening to become a national emergency. On 14 June, thirty-five more students were added to the growing list of affected students. On the same day, at a school in Kortrijk, twelve reports of Coke-related illness were recorded.[5] The main symptoms in these subsequent cases were abdominal pain, nausea, headache, trembling, light-headedness, palpitations, and malaise. Curiously, seventy-two of the seventy-five students affected in these schools were girls.[6] Coca-Cola announced a recall of certain Coke and Fanta containers on 11 June, and by 14 June, all Coca-Cola products were barred from sale in Belgium. For Coke, it was the biggest crisis in its 113-year history. For Belgium, the 'Coke crisis' dominated news and people were talking of little else.

At this point it seemed that the situation couldn't get much worse. It did. In the wake of media saturation of the 'poisonings', symptoms quickly spread from being a series of isolated school incidents to every region of Belgium. From the time of the first reported illness outbreak on 8 June through 20 June, the Belgian Poison Control Centre was flooded with phone calls from jittery citizens fearful of being the next victims. During this span, 1,418 phone calls were recorded. Of these, 943 callers said they began to feel unwell after drinking Coke, and to a far lesser extent, other drinks – some of which were not even manufactured by the Coca-Cola Corporation. Fanta, Sprite, Minute Maid, Lipton Iced Tea, Nestea, Aquarius – even Pepsi Cola were said to have caused illness reactions. There was no rhyme or reason to the reports. There was no obvious geographical pattern and calls were scattered from across the entire country.[7]

On 15 June, Coca-Cola officials issued a remorseful statement claiming that they had at last pinpointed two causes of the outbreak. First, it was stated that transport pallets treated with fungicide were responsible for contaminating 'the outside of some cans'. It was assumed that those who became ill had ingested some of the toxins after drinking directly from the cans. Second, it was said that some bottles had been dispensed with 'bad carbon dioxide'.[8] These findings were then sent to prominent Belgian toxicologist Dominique Lison at the Catholic University de Louvain in Brussels. After studying the results, Dr Lison made a stunning announcement. In his expert opinion, the chemical traces were not sufficient to have caused illness. He believed the most probable explanation for the symptoms was mass hysteria.[9] 'The analyses revealed the presence in some bottles of very low, but odorous amounts of hydrogen sulphide (about 5–15 ppb), possibly originating from the hydrolysis of carbonyl sulphide. In other words, the carbonation process hadn't worked properly, causing an odd smell. Small amounts of 4-chloro-3-methylphenol were found on the outside of some cans (about 0·4 µg/can). In both cases, it is unlikely that such concentrations caused any toxicity beyond an abnormal odour. No other notable chemicals had been found.'[10] A similar conclusion was also reached by an *ad hoc* working group advising the Belgian Health Ministry.[11] While the reports supporting the mass hysteria theory caused considerable controversy and debate among the Belgian public and the medical community, science had spoken.

By the end of June, the episode had subsided. The recall is estimated to have cost Coca-Cola between US$103 and $250 million dollars. The ban on Coke products in Belgium was lifted on 23 June.[12] It wasn't until 31 March 2000 that a Belgian government report officially issued its exoneration of Coke products, concluding that mass hysteria was the real culprit.[13] Reports of similar illness symptoms were reported in at least eighty-eight people in France during June, and it is thought that mass hysteria in the wake of the Belgian media publicity was also to blame in those cases.[14]

Belgium's veteran Deputy Prime Minister, Luc Van den Bossche, who was assigned to deal with the crisis, was reportedly furious at Coca-Cola for not revealing its formula, telling aides that the Corporation deserved the recall and bad press for not being more forthcoming.[15] Toxicologists have suggested that company officials had 'shot themselves in the foot' by underestimating the seriousness of the illness reports and its potential impact on sales of Coke products.

In spite of the magnitude of the crisis facing Coke officials and its future, and pulling its products off store shelves, some scientists noted that Coca-Cola representatives were inexplicably 'casual in providing data from the chemical analyses of their products. The documents that we received were often no more than faxed messages and loose notes, with insufficient details. . . .'[16] But in hindsight it may not have been arrogance, incompetence or even aloofness that sealed Coke's fate in prolonging the scare. It may have been understandable shyness on the part of company officials to reveal information about its secret formula. For in order to more accurately assess what exactly happened, scientists naturally wanted to know as much as they could about the formula. For Coca-Cola it was the equivalent of someone asking Colonel Sanders to hand over his secret recipe of eleven herbs and spices for Kentucky Fried Chicken.

THE SEEDS OF THE SCARE

What became widely known as 'the tainted Coke scare' was the culmination of a series of food scares that had frayed the nerves of Europeans throughout the 1990s. Preoccupation with food safety began to weigh on the minds of Europeans with the 1995 'Mad Cow' scare which would dominate headlines until early 1999. From the late '80s to the early '90s, over 160,000 cattle across Europe were diagnosed with bovine spongiform encephalopathy (BSE) or 'mad cow' disease. Then, in the mid-1990s, British Health Secretary Stephen Dorrell announced that ten young British citizens had recently died from a rare human form of 'mad cow' disease known as Creuzfeldt-Jakob disease (CJD). He also said there was a possibility that they contracted the disease from eating infected beef. Like its bovine-attacking relation BSE, CJD affects nerve cells in the brain, causing a loss of coordination, Alzheimer's-like symptoms and eventually certain death. In the final pathetic, agonizing days, the patient's brain wastes to such an extent that it resembles a sponge – hence the term 'spongiform'. By 27 March 1996, the European Commission voted to ban the import of British beef and beef products including semen and embryos. This occurred even though the odds of getting CJD are about one in a million. But as each new CJD case was diagnosed, there were fears that it may have come from having eaten tainted beef. By 1999 the scare was starting to subside when a new fear arose – dioxin.

In early 1999, the 'dioxin crisis' captured the headlines across Belgium, when a tank filled with recycled fats used in the production of animal feed was inadvertently contaminated with PCBs (polychlorinated biphenyls), dioxins and other pollutants. Hundreds of Belgian farms received the contaminated feed, though the actual levels of contamination were minute. The incident led to a massive concern among chicken farmers when the feed was dispensed to the fowl. The delay in announcing the contamination to the public (the incident was leaked to the Belgian media months later in May) fomented a political confidence crisis which led to the resignations of the Ministers for Agriculture and Health.[17] In May, it was widely reported in the media that animal feed in the country had been contaminated with toxic agents. The reports triggered widespread anxiety across Belgium, starting with a massive recall of chicken and eggs and, soon, of most dairy and meat products. By early June, at the time of the first Coke incident, the 'dioxin crisis' was dominating Belgian news and all aspects of Belgian life.[18] 'The issue of the safety of modern foods had become pervasive, with one of the main messages aired by scientists being that even minimal amounts of chemicals could seriously affect health.'[19] The tainted Coke scare had come at a time when many Europeans, especially Belgians, would become anxious at the sight of a cheeseburger or fried chicken. The time was ripe for the new scare.

MAD COWS

The 'mad cow' saga started on 22 December 1984 when a farmer in Sussex, southern England, noticed one of his cows acting strangely. Its head would shake uncontrollably. It had difficulty walking. It became aggressive. When cow number 133 died on 11 February of the following year, scientists were startled when they began testing the carcass. Its brain was full of tiny holes. The diagnosis:

spongiform encephalopathy. Scientists had seen this disease before in sheep, but never cows. Even more alarming, soon more of farmer Stent's cows were showing identical symptoms. A new term was coined: bovine spongiform encephalopathy or 'mad cow' disease. Bovine relates to cattle; spongiform denotes the sponge-like appearance of the ravaged brain; *enkephalos* and *pathos* are Greek for brain and disease.[20] Shortened to BSE, at first scientists were puzzled as to how this horrific disease could have 'jumped' from sheep to cattle. They soon had their answer. Cattle feed made from the ground-up remains of sheep suffering from scrapie, the ovine form of the disease, had got into the cows' food supply. It was a human-made disaster. While the use of such feed was soon banned, there were fears that BSE could jump to humans.

With strict new feeding measures in place, the incidence of BSE peaked between 1992 and 1993, affecting just 0.3 per cent of British herds and has declined ever since.[21] No one was too worried until 1995, when the fear of contracting BSE began to cause worldwide alarm after a nineteen-year-old Englishman named Stephen Churchill died of a mysterious disease. While it resembled the rare, dreaded, brain-wasting Creutzfeldt-Jakob disease, it clearly wasn't plain CJD. His brain was remarkably similar to that of cow 133 that had died a decade earlier of 'mad cow' disease, which then spread through British cattle herds. A frightening scenario was taking shape – the possibility that Stephen had contracted BSE from eating meat from a sick cow.[22] Millions of Britons and other Europeans had eaten British beef over the past few years. Would some or all eventually develop the BSE, slowly, agonizingly losing control of their bodies as their brains were eaten away? The illness was soon identified as a new variant of CJD. Many scientists are convinced that BSE has crossed into humans in the form of CJD. It seems that somehow the prions or aberrant proteins accumulate in the brain and eventually turn it to mush. The other piece of bad news is that prions are virtually indestructible and remain active even at temperatures as high as 2,000° Celsius.

In 1996, scientists at London's Imperial College predicted that millions of people could develop new variant CJD. The following year they estimated that upwards of 10 million people could die from this strange new disease. By 1998, this estimate was lowered to half a million. In 2002, scientists estimated that there would be thirty-two deaths from the new disease during the year. The actual figure was seventeen.[23] The scientists were wrong. There was not and has not been a spike in the number of new variant CJD cases, and the incidence of plain CJD remains the same – about one per one million. It seems that beef lovers aren't all going to die from mad cow disease after all. CJD is extremely rare. More people die of lightning strikes each year. The only way one can contract forms of CJD from eating beef is if one eats either part of the spinal column or brain. Dr Jean Weese, an expert on BSE, says that based on research into the BSE–human connection, the results are reassuring. 'We've simply not seen any evidence of this prion in red muscle mass. From everything researchers have been able to determine, it only turns up in brain and spinal tissue.'[24] In fact, if one wants to worry about illnesses, there are many more ailments that are far more common than CJD. You are much more likely to die from flu, walking across the street, or of a heart attack during sex. While there are more preferable ways to die (with expiring of a heart attack during sex being fairly high on the list), the fact remains that a mass outbreak of CJD is not on the cards. If it were to happen, it would have occurred by now. As physician Scott Ratzan remarks, the link between mad cow disease and CJD 'turned out to be wrong. We still don't know how humans contract CJD. But what is clear is that people don't get it by eating meat from cows or lamb. The mad cow prion has only been found in the brains of cattle afflicted with the disease, not in muscle tissue.'[25]

MAD COW AND CANNIBALISM – AN UNLIKELY LINK

While the BSE scare seems frightening and unprecedented, it is not. A remarkably similar disease to BSE and CJD, which is also caused by prions, has occurred for centuries in the jungles of Papua New Guinea but never spread outside the region. Since the early 1900s, scientists have been aware of a strange illness among the Fore people. It was a medical mystery. It usually took about two years for the disease to run its course and kill its victim. Between 1957 and 1968, over a thousand natives died from this terrible sickness. It was always fatal. Known among the Fore as *kuru*, meaning 'to shiver or tremble', scientists were baffled as to the cause. At first, victims would act as if they were intoxicated, staggering about and having difficulty speaking. Their bodies would shiver as if they were freezing despite living in the steamy tropics. Soon they grew unable to walk and gradually lost the use of their muscles which would twitch and jerk uncontrollably. These poor souls were also plagued by sudden, dramatic mood swings. Sometimes they would begin to laugh uncontrollably, accounting for why this disease was also known as 'the laughing death'. Near the end, victims would lose almost all control of their bodies. Curiously, Fore women were eight times more likely to get the ailment than men. The breakthrough came when American physician Carleton Gadjusek cracked the code. The natives were cannibals who ate their dead relatives. When a Fore died, people would come to feast on the body. Males favoured eating the muscles, hoping that it would make them stronger; women focused on the brains, hoping it would increase their intelligence. For the women, it turned out to be a deadly choice as the brains, Dr Gadjusek found, occasionally contained prions. For his role in eradicating *kuru*, Dr Gadjusek was awarded the Nobel Prize for Medicine in 1976.[26]

The national crises over mad cow disease and tainted Coke were unfounded. These scares were fuelled by the mass media which exaggerated the threat based on speculation and fear, not science and reason. The reality was hyped far beyond the real threat. The moral is clear – if you are so inclined, do not hesitate to dig into a juicy hamburger and wash it down with a tall, cold glass of Coke – but avoid the brains and spinal column. By stopping the practice of Fore cannibalism, *kuru* has been eliminated from New Guinea. Similarly, the ban on using ground-up animals for feed should stop any potential epidemic of BSE among humans. While people will, in extremely rare cases, continue to contract CJD, and while the exact mechanism of transmission is not yet fully understood, it is clear that the incidence of such cases – about one per one million people, poses absolutely no health threat to the general public. No, we're not all going to die of mad cow disease or CJD. The only epidemic that we need to quell is the unnecessary epidemic of fear and misinformation.

SEVEN

The New American Witch-hunts: Creating the Sex Abuse Epidemic

Talk of the devil, and he is bound to appear.

Proverb

Throughout history, especially during times of crisis and fear, groups of people have engaged in horrific crimes in the name of truth, justice, and self-preservation: even if the events that provoked those crimes were imaginary. Among the most notorious were the medieval European witch-hunts which began about 1350 and endured for nearly four centuries. This bloody era is characterized by unspeakable butchery and barbarity to an array of social misfits whose only crime was not fitting the arbitrary period definition of 'normal'. As a result, anyone unlucky enough to have been mentally unstable, disabled, or born with deformities, made easy targets. Other marked people included eccentrics and assertive women, and anyone who was unpopular or looked and acted differently to the norm. The accused were charged with conspiring with the Devil to cause an array of misfortunes – sudden mysterious deaths, floods, drought, plagues, fires and crop failures. These unfortunate souls were ready-made scapegoats for the various problems facing community and church authorities at the time. Hundreds of thousands of innocent men, women and children were forced to endure unimaginable horrors: slow, agonizing torture, live dismemberment, drowning, hanging, and more often, being burned at the stake – alive. What's more incredible and tragic is that these horrors were carried out on the flimsiest of evidence. Even animals were brutally tortured and burned. Witchcraft historian Rossell

Hope Robbins estimates that 200,000 perished in what is now Great Britain and continental Europe, more than half in Germany. Sociologist Erich Goode, using more contemporary studies, places the figure closer to half a million.[1]

The witch-hunts are a tragic part of human history that many would like to forget. When discussing these events, many people do so with a sense of alienation – that somehow the perpetrators were not part of the human family, that somehow our ancestors, as ignorant and misguided as they were, were an entirely different species belonging to our distant past. Surely, they reason, such events could never happen again, or if they do, certainly not on a broad scale. Surely, the medieval European witch-hunts and the Salem witch trials of 1692, are gross, shameful examples of human folly that could never recur in a modern, well-educated society. Yet, starting in the late 1970s, a new therapeutic fad swept through many American psychotherapy offices – the search for so-called 'hidden memories'. This approach was and is based on the dubious notion that a variety of common psychological problems, ranging from eating disorders to drug addictions, stem from repressed memories of childhood molestation. In other words, patients would walk into psychotherapy offices having absolutely no conscious memory of sexual abuse during childhood, only to be convinced otherwise by overzealous therapists who inadvertently invented imaginary abuses using such dubious techniques as hypnosis and vague touchy-feely methods like visual imaging and journalizing. This is not to suggest that none of these patients had been sexually abused – a horrific crime if there ever was one – but that a great many people were falsely accused based on fictitious evidence.

The first part of this chapter describes how the medieval European witch-hunts were fuelled by the development of the printing press and publication of books such as the *Malleus Maleficarum*. These publications greatly contributed to the epidemic of false accusations by confirming and legitimizing popular notions of witchcraft, and detailing signs to look for: 'odd' behaviour, witch marks, spectral evidence. Parallels are then drawn with the sudden modern-day upsurge in reports of sex abuse, the presence of satanic kidnapping cults and the existence of 'multiple personality disorder'. Each of these 'epidemics' was predicated on similar ambiguous, subjective criteria, resulting in scores of people being erroneously diagnosed or falsely accused, leaving many lives in shambles.

THE *MALLEUS MALEFICARUM* CREATES AN 'EPIDEMIC' OF WITCH ACCUSATIONS

In 1486, the book to read was the *Malleus Maleficarum* (generally translated as 'The Hammer of Witches') by Dominican monks Jakob Sprenger (1436–95) and Heinrich Kramer (*c.* 1430–1505).[2] Unfortunately, relatively few could read it. Most of the population of western Europe were illiterate: literacy was the privilege of churchmen and scholars – and most of the scholars were churchmen. If this wasn't limiting enough, the book was written in Latin, further narrowing the field of potential readers. While Latin – like English today – was the tongue in which international affairs were conducted, many were familiar only with their own vernacular.[3]

Nevertheless the book was a best-seller, as books went at the time. Its popularity and influence were both immediate and lasting: it was reprinted some twenty times in the following two centuries, apart from more than thirty translations. The reason is not hard to find. This was a book about the Devil writ large, a subject of universal interest and fear; and it was a book about witchcraft, a subject of particular interest now that the Catholic Church had determined the practice was heresy but that to disbelieve in witchcraft was equally so. This was a matter which concerned not only every churchman but every administrator. For though administrators and churchmen did not always see eye to eye, the secular authorities knew that to defy the Church could make life difficult. So what the *Malleus* had to say was of urgent interest to all. Indeed, the authors made it clear that their book was aimed at both secular and ecclesiastical readers: it was intended as a practical handbook for everyone whose duties included purging society of witchcraft. Its major impact was to prompt judges who were without religious affiliation or under the control of the Church, 'to investigate and prosecute, and to teach them to employ the inquisitorial processes which assure confession and conviction'.[4] This was confirmed on 6 November 1486, when at Brussels, the Holy Roman Emperor Maximilian I signified his wish to protect the Papal Bull, and specifically the inquisitors Sprenger and Kramer: all his subjects were commanded to render them aid and favour.[5]

The *Malleus* was by no means the first publication to deal with these topics. A considerable literature on demonology and witchcraft was already circulating when Sprenger and Kramer set to work.[6] Their book was far from original. It drew heavily on such works as Johannes Nider's widely respected *Formicarius*, published in 1475, which had been written some time before, during the Council of Basel, 1435–7. But Nider, and other authors of the day, were considerably less rigorous than the two Dominicans. Their writings were academic treatises, penned by scholars for scholars, by theologians for theologians. In other words, they were written by the elite, for the elite. Any relevance to the man in the street would be asserted by intermediaries – the priests and magistrates to whom the man in the street looked for guidance. In an age without popular media, the average person had no means of knowing what was going on in the rest of the world; his only sources of information were official pronouncements and word of mouth.

What the *Malleus* had going for it was the blessing of the highest possible authority, the Pope himself. Consequently it was seen as virtually the official pronouncement of the Church: which was tantamount to the word of God. Even with this backing, however, its acceptance was neither instant nor universal. As a matter of course, Sprenger submitted his book to the theological faculty of the University of Cologne. The university had wielded great power ever since 18 March 1479, when Pope Sixtus IV issued a brief, approving the institution's role in suppressing heresy by giving it the authority to censor books. Surprisingly, though Sprenger was a member of the faculty, his book was not well received. Only four faculty members approved of the book, and even these had reservations.

None the less, the shrewd and determined authors went ahead and published an 'Approbation' by the four professors, giving the misleading impression that this was an official approval emanating from the university: a further approbation was added later, which seemed to indicate that all eight members of the faculty approved the book, but this was an outright forgery. This latest approbation was not included in editions which might be seen in Cologne, and so had no immediate consequences: but it is significant that when Sprenger died in 1495, he was not granted the customary requiem mass by his university. The very fact that this sleight of hand was necessary shows that the inquisitors by no means held the high ground: tragically for the world, however, their devious methods prevailed and even those questioning the book's presumptions found it safest to keep their doubts to themselves.[7]

It is generally thought that Kramer was the major author, and that part of his motivation was to regain the approval of Church authorities after his high-handed methods in Austria had led to disgrace. In Tyrol, he was despised by the community after justifying his witch-hunt by encouraging a woman of ill-repute to crawl into an oven with the Devil, after which she began naming names of local Satanic allies. These unfortunate residents then underwent excruciating torture at the hands of Kramer. The atrocities stopped only after Kramer was expelled by the Bishop of Brixen.[8] To have Sprenger as a co-author was a judicious move, for Sprenger had a lofty reputation and a university position. Neither was a polished author; the book is rambling, discursive, and lacks elegance.[9] Furthermore, it is sloppily written and suffused with bad scholarship: for example, they derive the etymology of the word 'femina' (woman) from 'fe' (faith) and 'mina' (less), reflecting their negative attitude to women.

The intellectual level of the book is appalling. Here is an example of the kind of evidence which the authors saw fit to present to their readers:

In the town of Waldshut there was a certain witch who was so detested by the townsfolk that she was not invited to the celebration of a wedding at which nearly all the other townsfolk were present. Being indignant because of this, and wishing to be revenged, she summoned a devil and, telling him the cause of her vexation, asked him to raise up a hailstorm and drive all the wedding guests from their dancing; and the devil agreed, and raising her up, carried her through the air to a hill near the town, in the sight of some shepherds. And since she had no water to pour into the trench (for this is the method they use to raise hailstorms) she filled it with her urine. Then the devil suddenly raised that liquid up and sent a violent storm of hailstones which fell only on the dancers and townsfolk. And when they had dispersed and were discussing among themselves the cause of that storm, the witch shortly afterwards entered the town; and this greatly aroused their suspicions. But when the shepherds had told what they had seen, their suspicions became almost a certainty. So she was arrested, and confessed; and for this, and for many other witchcrafts which she had perpetrated, she was burned.[10]

We may marvel that a fairy tale such as this – and the book is crammed with similar absurdities – could be presented by two reputable theologians as credible evidence for the evil of witchcraft, and no doubt it was the inclusion of such tales that caused so many scholars, even among those who recognized witchcraft as an authentic danger, to reject the *Malleus*. But they were in a minority; the majority either swallowed it whole or pretended to do so for the greater truths they supposed the book to contain.

THE CREATION OF EVIL

The importance of the *Malleus* was that it epitomized a remarkable change of Church policy – perhaps the most fatal decision it made throughout its history. Until the fourteenth century, sorcery had been practised widely, at the level of popular magic: it was folklore, popular wisdom, commonplace in everyday life. It was punishable only if harm was done; no one was executed simply for practising it, and indeed in the tenth century Charlemagne prohibited the burning of witches as a pagan custom. From the Church's point of view, guidance was provided by the *Canon Episcopi*, a ninth-century document which was embodied in the Canon Law. In essence, it denied the whole idea of witchcraft: the supposed arts of witches, the Sabbat and flight included, were illusions or fantasies originating in dreams. Far from witchcraft being considered a heresy, it was the belief in witchcraft which was heretical.

The *Malleus* set out to transform this loose hotch-potch of popular sorcery into a perceived evil menace, threatening the Church and indeed all society. As a result, witchcraft was considered not simply to be a fact, but a heretical fact; a witch was a heretic who by definition was perpetrating treason against God by allying him or herself to the Devil. Now it was disbelief in witchcraft which was judged to be heretical and therefore punishable. The world had been turned upside down.

How did this extraordinary turnaround occur? Social factors no doubt played a part. Europe had been devastated by plagues and wars, but these were nothing new; they had afflicted the populace often before without bringing about a witch mania. Without the Church's reformulation of the image of witchcraft, there may have been local disturbances, but it is highly doubtful that there would have been carnage on the epidemic scale which rolled across the map of Europe, steamrolling everything in its path. For that to occur, a wide and powerful authority was needed, and at that time there was only one effective authority transcending geographical or political boundaries: the Church.

In December 1484, Pope Innocent VIII promulgated the Bull *Summis Desiderantes Affectibus*, deploring the spread of witchcraft in Germany. But it went further than simply lamenting the situation: it vested authority to end this fictitious evil in his beloved 'sons' Jakob Sprenger, dean of Köln University, and fellow monk Heinrich Kramer. With that mandate, the witch mania can be said to have become official.

Two years later the two Dominicans issued the *Malleus Maleficarum*.[11] Their opening sentence proclaims the authors' position: 'The belief that there are such beings as witches is so essential a part of the Catholic faith that obstinately to maintain the opposite opinion manifestly savours of heresy.' Since disbelief in witches was heresy; since the ways to recognize a witch were so many and varied; and since the means of extracting a confession – every conceivable torture – was a legitimate procedure, the book constituted, in effect, a licence to kill, torture and maim.

It is this universal applicability of the witch myth which explains why the Protestants, though they jettisoned much of Rome's traditional teaching, accepted the teachings of the *Malleus*. Had the Protestants rejected it as a contemptible production of the Church of Rome, the witch mania might have been half as devastating. But belief in the Devil was part of the primitive Church teaching to which the Protestants claimed to be returning, so they accepted the *Malleus* as a laudable return to fundamental Christian principles. The consequences were far-reaching as the authorities in Protestant countries such as Scotland and Switzerland were just as ruthless as those in France and Germany.

The man in the street, even if he could read, was unlikely to read the *Malleus*, but its teachings became the model for the witch-hunters, and thus became imposed on the populace at large. The model was not entirely an artificial construct: indeed, one of the reasons it was able to captivate the popular imagination was that it built on existing beliefs. Though the 'wise woman' living on the edge of the village was a valued member of the community, she was also the object of fear and suspicion; so it was not difficult for the inquisitors to persuade the community to see her as an agent of the Devil. Village sorcerers had always been suspected of practising magic on their neighbours by bringing about cattle sickness and harvest failure, impotence, miscarriages, and fatal accidents of every kind. They were widely believed to be capable of magical flight, and the nocturnal activities of 'ladies of the night' under various names were a staple of popular dread – the modern-day equivalent of the bogey man.[12] But now these activities were seen as part of a larger plan, executed as part of a collective effort perpetrated by evil-doers in cahoots with the Devil.

Many of the elements were already present in people's minds: the churchmen simply wove them into a coherent system, restructuring traditional beliefs into an explicit, logical myth.

Because so much of it was what people had always believed, they did not question the new rationale. Now, when they were arrested and questioned, it was not the old crimes of sorcery but the new witchcraft heresy to which they confessed. What the churchmen now had to do was to convince the world that these collective practices were a reality.

The other achievement of the *Malleus* was to persuade the authorities that the evil of witchcraft was so destructive, the menace so imminent, that any means were justified in combating it. Consequently the normal rules of law could be set aside. Any witness was acceptable, however dubious, and an accuser could even retain his anonymity. Consequently anyone might accuse others of well-nigh any crime, without bearing the usual consequences of false accusation.

Few books have done as much harm as the *Malleus*, despite the fact that only a tiny minority of those affected by it could actually read it. Perhaps this very exclusiveness helped to protect its message from criticism; perhaps if more had been able to read it, more voices would have been raised against it. So great was its impact on humanity that Rossell Robbins states that the book and its notorious authors 'set back the orderly development of civilization several hundred years' [13]

THE AMERICAN SATANIC RITUAL ABUSE EPIDEMIC 1970s–1990s

Following such blatant, appalling examples as that of the European witch mania, and the injustices in Salem, Massachusetts, in the late seventeenth century, it might be thought that such mass delusions could never recur. But they could, and did. At the close of the twentieth century, in one of the most highly educated and developed cultures the world has ever known – that of the United States of America – there broke out an epidemic which has many parallels to the medieval witch-hunts. Though none of the accused was actually burned at the stake, many were accused and imprisoned on false or non-existent evidence, others were driven to commit suicide, and tens of thousands of lives were ruined, families broken apart, careers destroyed, relationships left in tatters. Yet the evidence on which this was done was no less flimsy than that which had taken so many innocent lives to the stake five hundred years before.

What had changed was the level of communication. The twentieth-century epidemic was fuelled by radio, the press, television. Yet here, too, it is possible to identify a single influential book as central to the inflaming of popular opinion: *The Courage to Heal: A Guide for Women Survivors of Child Sexual Abuse*.[14] Like many of the books of guidance written to help possible victims come to terms with their situation, it reads more like a feminist tract than a reasoned, balanced guide. *The Courage to Heal* is better written, subtler and more sophisticated, more user-friendly; but it is equally destructive, inviting comparison with the *Malleus*. *The Courage to Heal* was a best-seller and was enthusiastically received by the popular press.[15]

The authors are nothing if not practical. The person who thinks she or he has been sexually abused is counselled to adopt a different strategy towards those who are likely to be supportive and those who will be hostile. 'Confrontations [with abusers or their kin] can be incredibly empowering because you learn that you are strong and powerful.'[16] Though fundamentally its aims are not so very different from those of the authors of the *Malleus*, the approach is utterly different. Here everything is affirmative, seen as if from the victim's point of view, thus reaffirming over and over that the reader is a victim. But like the *Malleus*, it assumes the worst is true.

During the repressed memory controversy, thousands of people, particularly women, came or were brought to believe that they possessed 'hidden memories' concealed within. These memories were generally of being abused, particularly sexually, during their childhoods. Often, the abuse was thought to have occurred in the context of 'satanic' rituals, during which they were forced to undergo and participate in such anti-social practices as incest, rape, murder and cannibalism. The psychological conflict created by unconscious awareness of these childhood adventures led, it was claimed, to the creation of alternate personalities ('alters') who knew about them even though the individual's conscious primary personality had suppressed the memory.

A VIEW OF

THE INHABITANTS OF THE MOON,

AS SEEN THROUGH THE TELESCOPE OF SIR JOHN HERSCHEL.

The Great Moon Hoax. In the pre-photographic period artists' impressions, such as this contemporary engraving of Bat-men and Beaver-People on the Moon, were accepted as authentic representations. Many of the *Sun*'s readers believed that this fanciful scene was what Herschel saw through his telescope. (*Mary Evans Picture Library*)

PUNCH, OR THE LONDON CHARIVARI.—February 5, 1887.

THE " CATCH-PENNY."

Policeman. "NOW THEN, YOU MISCHIEVOUS YOUNG RASCAL,—STOP THAT!"

The Catch-Penny. Long after the birth of the sensational 'penny paper' in the 1830s, editors were seeking to attract readers with sensationalized stories. Sir John Tenniel's cartoon from the satirical journal *Punch* dates from 1897, but a hundred years later circulation-hungry journalists are still up to the same catch-penny tricks. (*Mary Evans Picture Library*)

Himmellegemet

Tegning af Axel Nygaard

Nu har vi Kometen i Sigte,
alt vejrer vi Blaasyrens Duft —
dog turde det være en Fabel,
at Halen er bare Luft.

Nej, skulde vi støde paa Bæstet,
saa ser man af Billedet her
de Folk har vist slet ikke Uret,
som siger, at Enden er nær. *sm.*

In the eye of the beholder. As the tail of Halley's Comet passed through the Earth atmosphere in May 1910 it triggered a variety of responses. In some countries it was haile with enthusiasm, as depicted in this charming cartoon from the Danish weekly *Klods-Han* but elsewhere it created alarm and fear of widespread poisoning. Optimists and pessimis alike had access to the same facts: the difference was made by the way the press chose t interpret those facts. (*Mary Evans Picture Library*)

The young prodigy, US film actor, producer and director Orson Welles was responsible for arguably the greatest hoax of the twentieth century, the 1938 Martian invasion scare. (*Mary Evans Picture Library*)

Welles the actor? An apparently contrite Orson Welles is surrounded by reporters the day after the Martian broadcast. Welles said he had no intention of scaring anyone. Decades after the controversy had died down, Welles said that he had expected all along that a public panic would occur. (*Mary Evans Picture Library*)

The War of the Worlds, 1898. The first Martian emerges from the cylinder as the deadly inva
commences. The illustrations by Alvin Correa to a French edition – arguably the finest depict
of Wells's novel – vividly express the confrontation between extraterrestrial beings and the citi
of Victorian England and invite readers to imagine themselves in such a situation. (*Mary E.
Picture Library*)

THE MODERN EDITOR AND HIS BOSS.

From *Puck*.

The modern editor and his 'boss'; the pressure to publish 'sensational' news, as depicted by the US satirical magazine *Puck* in the 1890s. A century later, little had changed as the European 'Mad Cow' and 'poison Coke' scares were fuelled by knee-jerk media reports that were based on fear, not science, and emphasizing sensational scenarios. (*Mary Evans Picture Library*)

The Tarantula. Was the Great American Kissing Bug Scare of 1899 a form of mass hysteria created by newspaper reporters? A similar type of hysteria involving fear of the tarantula reportedly swept through southern Europe during the Middle Ages. Its cure was said to be dancing the tarantella. (*Mary Evans Picture Library*)

American anthropologist Dorothy Billings with Walla Gukguk, president of the Tutukuval Isukal Association (TIA), successor to the (President) Johnson Cult. (*Mary Evans Picture Library*)

MALLEVS

MALEFICARVM,

MALEFICAS ET EARVM

haeresim frameâ conterens,

EX VARIIS AVCTORIBVS COMPILATVS,

& in quatuor Tomos iustè distributus,

QVORVM DVO PRIORES VANAS DÆMONVM versutias, praestigiosas eorum delusiones, superstitiosas Strigimagarum caeremonias, horrendos etiam cum illis congressus; exactam denique tam pestiferae sectae disquisitionem, & punitionem complectuntur. Tertius praxim Exorcistarum ad Dæmonum, & Strigimagarum maleficia de Christi fidelibus pellenda; Quartus verò Artem Doctrinalem, Benedictionalem, & Exorcismalem continent.

TOMVS PRIMVS.

Indices Auctorum, capitum, rerúmque non desunt.

Editio nouissima, infinitis penè mendis expurgata ; cuique accessit Fuga Dæmonum & Complementum artis exorcisticæ.

Vir siue mulier, in quibus Pythonicus, vel diuinationis fuerit spiritus, morte moriatur Leuitici cap. 10.

LVGDVNI,

Sumptibus CLAVDII BOVRGEAT, sub signo Mercurij Galli.

M. DC. LXIX.

CVM PRIVILEGIO REGIS.

Malleus Maleficarum title page, Lyon, 1669. The 'Hammer of Witches', authored by Dominicans Jakob Sprenger and Heinrich Kramer and authorized by Pope Innocent VIII, is the most influential book promoting the existence of the witchcraft heresy. Though the text ludicrous to the point of absurdity, its lofty credentials ensured that it exerted widespread influence: probably no book has been responsible for so much misery and so many deaths. (Mary Evans Picture Library)

Opposing the Martians. William Dock stands ready to hold off the Martians in his farm near Grovers Mill, location of the attack in the Mercury Theatre broadcast. Did Mr Dock really have time to make this neat stack of sandbags on hearing of the invasion? Photographs such as this add an extra dimension to the hoax: it could not have been made at the time, obviously, so it can only be a reconstruction set up a day or two later by the media, to lend credence to what had now become a media event. (*Mary Evans Picture Library*)

FALSE MEMORY SYNDROME

The key to the modern American epidemic of child sexual abuse centres on the concept of False Memory Syndrome or FMS. This loosely defined term refers to the so-called recovery of false memories, typically during psychotherapy sessions, involving adults who claim that parents or relatives sexually abused them as children, and that these memories were repressed due to the traumatic nature of the offence. It is known by various synonyms: 'repressed memories', false memories', 'hidden memories', 'recovered memories' and 'pseudo-memories'. FMS is the historical equivalent of 'spectral evidence' on which many witchcraft accusations were based. For instance, during the 1692 Salem witch scare, the twenty poor souls who were executed were all convicted on 'spectral evidence' whereby accusers claimed that spirits of the accused had left their bodies and visited them, especially at night, causing torment or misfortune. It was nearly impossible to refute such claims. In 1692, it was widely believed that witches could take any shape or form, adding to the anxious atmosphere as potential witches were everywhere. Two dogs were even accused and executed.

Psychologist John Kihlstrom defines FMS as occurring when someone comes to believe in the reality of a traumatic experience that never occurred. He remarks: 'We all have memories that are inaccurate. Rather, the syndrome may be diagnosed when the memory is so deeply ingrained that it orients the individual's entire personality and lifestyle, in turn disrupting all sorts of other adaptive behaviors.' Kihlstrom further notes the presence of avoidance and obsession. 'False Memory Syndrome is especially destructive because the person assiduously avoids confrontation with any evidence that might challenge the memory. Thus it takes on a life of its own, encapsulated, and resistant to correction. The person may become so focused on the memory that he or she may be effectively distracted from coping with the real problems in his or her life.'[17]

False Memory Syndrome was devised in the early 1980s by the False Memory Syndrome Foundation. The organization was formed in response to the dramatic escalation of child sex abuse claims that began to sweep across the United States during the early 1980s. Mark Pendergrast chronicles the genesis of the repressed memory movement, noting that prior to about 1970, incest and sexual abuse were relatively rare occurrences, and even through the mid-'70s, most abuse claims involved conscious recall.[18] The organized search for repressed child abuse memories can be traced back to psychiatrist Judith Herman, affiliated with Harvard University. In her 1981 book, *Father–Daughter Incest*, Herman made reference to the existence of an informal network of private practice psychotherapists in the vicinity of Boston, Massachusetts, who were searching for patients with repressed memories of child sexual abuse. Herman's psychotherapy reportedly involved such techniques as dream analysis and the use of hypnosis to induce age regression.[19] By the mid-'80s, the issue was being widely reported as an epidemic.

THE MODERN AMERICAN SEX ABUSE SCARE

In 1988, the repressed memory movement crystallized with the publication of *The Courage to Heal* by California creative writing instructor Ellen Bass and her pupil, Laura Davis.[20] The book, which sold nearly 800,000 copies, is based on a self-fulfilling prophecy, targeting females with vague suspicions that they may have been abused, but who have absolutely no initial recall. With a sense of authority, urgency and vagueness reminiscent of the *Malleus*, Bass and Davis were able to foster a full-scale, nationwide witch-hunt. And how does anyone determine that they have been abused? Bass and Davis explain: 'Often the knowledge that you were abused starts with a tiny feeling, an intuition. It's important to trust that inner voice and work from there. Assume your feelings are valid. . . . So far, no one we've talked to thought she might have been abused, and then later discovered that she hadn't been. The progression always goes the other way, from suspicion to confirmation. If you think you were abused and your life shows the symptoms, then you were.'[21] The foggy, ambiguous nature of abuse signs and symptoms discussed by Bass and Davis are chillingly reminiscent of Salem.

THE McMARTIN NIGHTMARE

Startling claims of a hidden epidemic of child sexual abuse are the stuff of which headlines are made, and Bass, with her Harvard affiliation, gave these claims instant credibility. Fuelled by *The Courage to Heal*, the 'hidden epidemic' of sexual abuse allegations reached dizzying heights with the spotlighting of the crisis on high-profile television chat shows, creating an emotionally charged climate in which many, especially women, came to believe that they too had suffered hidden abuse. The reality of the danger seemed confirmed by court cases such as the McMartin trial – said to be the longest and costliest trial in American legal history, and certainly one of the most publicized – in which the managers of a pre-school were accused of sexually abusing their pupils.[22] The accused were school founder Virginia McMartin, her 62-year-old daughter Peggy McMartin Buckey, her 28-year-old grandson Ray Buckey, 29-year-old grand-daughter Peggy Ann, and three other childcare workers. They were indicted in March 1984 on no less than 115 counts of child abuse inflicted on 360 children. Later the number of counts was raised to 354, based on statements from 34 infants. How could so many children be wrong? The public reasoned that they must have been guilty. The authorities, convinced that there must be a reality behind the nationwide concern, went to work with enthusiasm.

The McMartin case occurred in Manhattan Beach, California, and epitomizes how easily people were accused and convicted in the court of public opinion. In August 1983, one of the parents at the school noticed her child had a red bottom. Suspecting sexual abuse, she told the police who soon circulated a letter to all 200 parents with children at the school, warning of possible criminal acts: oral sex, fondling of genitals, sodomy, and asking if they thought their children might be the victims of similar practices. For the next seven years, the court heard a stream of incredible stories from the therapists who interrogated 349 children, mostly three- or four-year-olds. Many children denied any abuse; others went into lurid detail. They had been raped and sodomised by Ray Buckey. Female teachers had inserted pencils into their orifices. They had played

115

games involving weird sexual practices. They had watched animals being slaughtered at sacrifice rituals. They were forced to drink rabbits' blood. Some of their abusers were strangers in black robes: others were identified from photographs. One child even fingered the Los Angeles District Attorney! Many claimed to have been photographed in sexual situations, yet not a single photo was found despite a $10,000 reward offer. They told of flights in aircraft, voyages in submarines, and being abused in hot-air balloons. The longer the case dragged on, the more incredible it became. Many of the descriptions were impossible, such as children describing, at the prompting of interviewers, how they and the teachers ran naked round the playground alongside a well-travelled road. One child told of having sex with Ray while going through a public car wash, though no vehicle is allowed through the tunnel with occupants, and in any case the time factor made it impossible.

How had so many false stories been created? The prosecution's case eventually fell apart after shoddy interviewing methods were revealed. The tape recordings show that the 'interviews' with the children were packed with leading questions such as 'Did you ever see anything come out of Mr Ray's penis?' to which the children were cajoled into acquiescence. According to one research team who reviewed the evidence: 'There was not one spontaneous "disclosure" on any of these tapes. . . . On all of the videotapes shown, the children repeatedly denied witnessing any act of sexual abuse of children. The interviewer ignored these exonerating statements and continued to coax and pressure the child for accusations.'[23] While the accused were eventually set free, each had a stigma attached to their names that would never be entirely erased, for millions continued to believe that justice had not been done, that the Buckeys were guilty and that the children were indeed the victims of a conspiracy. By now the school's reputation was destroyed, and all associated with it were ruined. The price tag for the McMartin witch-hunt was $15 million.

In Salem, it had been Massachusetts Governor Sir William Phips who put an end to the injustices after speaking out when his own wife was under suspicion of witchcraft, issuing a moratorium on further witch trials. In modern America, a tireless advocate for the falsely accused has been University of Washington psychologist Elizabeth Loftus. The former President of the American Psychological Association, Loftus and colleague Katherine Ketcham, identify four tenets which fuelled the sexual abuse incest scare.

The first factor was the view that *incest was occurring in epidemic proportions*. In the late 1970s and early '80s, slowly gathering storm clouds were forming with allegations that sex abuse occurred on a far greater scale than most people had ever imagined, with several books detailing case histories of female abuse. By the mid-'80s, several so-called experts claimed statistical backing for the assertions of Dr Herman and others. A 1985 survey by the *Los Angeles Times* stated that about 38 million Americans were sexually molested during childhood.[24] The next year, Diana Russell published her startling book, *The Secret Trauma: Incest in the Life of Girls and Women*, claiming that of 930 California women randomly contacted and interviewed, over half reported sexual abuse before age eighteen (including claims of non-physical genital exposure).[25] Despite numerous flaws, Russell's study helped to ignite the sex abuse 'epidemic', such as interviewers being exposed to 'ten hours of pre-interview indoctrination on the horrors of rape and incest'.[26] One reason for the epidemic numbers of persons being labelled as having abused childhoods was the new definition of incest and abuse. For instance, in *The Courage to Heal*, Bass and Davis offer examples that can be interpreted as either 'violations of trust' or 'non-physical incestuous' behaviour, including a father 'leering when you entered to use the toilet' or if as a child you felt that 'your stepfather was aware of your physical presence every minute of the day, no matter how quiet or unobtrusive you were. Your neighbour watched your changing body with an intrusive interest.'[27]

A second factor in triggering the American sex abuse epidemic centres on the assumption that *repression is commonplace*. As a result, many people who suspect they were a child sex abuse victim – but have no conscious recall – have allowed their therapists to hypnotically regress them so they can find out what happened. The experience is thought to serve a positive function for the victim as a cathartic release for memories that have been 'bottled-up' for years. Yet most child sex abuse victims *can* vividly recall their molestation. For them, psychologist Dennis Coon notes, the problem is, 'they can't forget what happened to them, not that they don't remember it'.[28] Just as science could not confirm the suspected existence of witches, the evidence for repressed memories is not supported by any known theories of memory, which involves a rather straightforward process of encoding, storing and retrieving. The belief in repressed memories is a form of Voodoo psychology that remains unproven. The lack of evidence prompts forensic psychologist Terence Campbell to ask: 'Do traumatic experiences interfere with the encoding state of memory, and if so, how does this interference occur?' The same questions can be asked for the storage and retrieval stages of memory. Campbell states: 'Current theories of trauma and memory loss neglect to answer these important questions. These theories suggest *why* people might engage in repression, but they fail to specify *how* repression supposedly occurs.'[29]

Another factor in the sex abuse upsurge is predicated on the belief that recovery is possible once repressed memories are unveiled. The final pieces in the epidemic are the specific techniques used to reveal 'hidden memories'. Loftus and Ketcham state that when many patients first seek help from psychotherapists for various problems – from eating disorders to sexual difficulties and addictions – there is an assumption that the underlying cause is childhood sexual abuse. The so-called diagnostic criteria are so ambiguous as to be present in almost anyone at some time. Psychotherapist E. Susan Blume offers thirty-four signs suggestive of incest including such ridiculously broad indicators as '[w]earing a lot of clothing, even in summer; baggy clothes; failure to remove clothing even when appropriate to do so (while swimming, bathing, sleeping); extreme requirement for privacy when using bathroom'.[30] While some abuse victims no doubt have these feelings, far too often those with perfectly normal childhoods have identical feelings and were never abused. Renee Fredrickson lists such vague indicators of having been sexually abused to include being terrified of basements and sexual promiscuity.[31] Could we get much more vague?

There are several different subjective methods used by psychotherapists to uncover 'hidden memories'. Imagistic work involves focusing on an image believed to be from childhood, then 'describing in great detail every sight and sensation relating to the image and adding, whenever appropriate, subjective interpretations'.[32] Dream work involves interpreting dreams related to possible sexual abuse while body work entails body massage and manipulation techniques that can supposedly uncover hidden memories of abuse. Journal writing is just like it sounds, writing down thoughts and impressions of possible abuse on a frequent basis. Some therapists believe that such memories can be accessed by stimulating any one of the five senses.[33] These fuzzy techniques are far from scientific and can easily lead patients astray.

Another important consideration in the False Memory Syndrome debate are the numerous studies suggesting that the recall of traumatic events is typically altered. A dramatic example of this process occurred when Loftus and her colleague Jacquie Pickrell were able to get many people to believe they had met and shaken hands with Bugs Bunny at Disneyland when they couldn't have. About one in three subjects exposed to a bogus print ad picturing the famous cartoon character at Disneyland, said they had met him there. This scenario was impossible because the Bugs Bunny trade mark is the property of Warner Brothers. Pickrell found the study 'frightening' because of the ease with which people can create false memories. 'It's not only people who go to a therapist who might implant a false memory or those who witness an accident and whose memory can be distorted who can have a false memory. Memory is very vulnerable and malleable. People are not always aware of the choices they make.'[34]

SATANIC CULT AND RITUAL ABUSE SCARE

From about 1983 to the mid-'90s, stories began to circulate that a network of Satanic cults were ritually abusing or killing America's youth. There were reports that tens of thousands of children were being kidnapped or murdered each year for sacrificial purposes, or forced to take part in orgies, or exploited in child prostitution and pornography, supposedly favourite activities of Satanists. These cunning Satanists were reportedly able to repress their victims' memories of the events, the result being that most people were supposedly unaware of what they had done, or had done to them, as children. Supported by such books as *The Courage to Heal*,[35] and reinforced by television appearances, lectures and meetings, police forces were alerted to the danger, and seminars and conferences asserted the existence of a nationwide, perhaps even international network of abusers. It turned out to be a huge waste of valuable police time and resources that could have been put to use fighting real crime.

At least sixty rumour-panics were triggered in various sections of the United States during this period. After 1993, claims have continued, but in a more sporadic fashion. Many sociologists classify these episodes as moral panics which coincide with the breakdown of the traditional family and a desire to find scapegoats. They are viewed as cautionary tales for guilt-ridden, absentee parents – a metaphor for prevailing concerns over the weakened family and its diminished capacity to protect children.[36] The Satanic ritual abuse scare can be traced back to 1980 with the publication of *Michelle Remembers*.[37] Set in Canada, the book purports to be a true account of Michelle Smith's childhood nightmare of anguish and abuse at the hands of a Satanic coven. Written with her psychiatrist Lawrence Pazder, *Michelle Remembers* is the first known story of a 'repressed memory' involving Satanic ritual abuse. As such, and like the *Malleus* and *The Courage to Heal*, it provided a blueprint for others to follow, who were later to claim that they too were sexually traumatized by a Satanic coven. Michelle describes a horrific childhood with two alcoholic parents. Her mother died when she was just fourteen; her father then left the family and she was raised by her grandparents. During the late 1970s, Smith began attending therapy sessions with Dr Pazder, whom she was later to marry. Pazder placed her under hypnosis in order to release 'repressed' memories of her abuse. Smith told an intriguing story of having been mistreated by a group of Satan worshippers including her own mother.

Over the course of several months, Michelle's 'repressed' memories flooded back in vivid detail. Among her chilling disclosures was being stripped naked and placed in a cage filled with snakes. Other supposed eyewitness accounts include the butchering and burning of foetuses, killing kittens and being forced into revolting sex acts. If these weren't bizarre enough, she even claims to have had horns surgically attached to her head and a devil-like tail affixed to her lower spine! Even more implausible, following this horrific ordeal, Michelle was allowed to leave with her mother, after which she supposedly repressed all memory of these abuses.[38] Smith's claims are as unbelievable as they are dubious. For example, neither of her two sisters could recollect the 'abuse'.[39] David Alexander concurs: 'As for bringing Smith's tormentors to justice, it should be relatively easy to identify them, even years later, since the members of this "cult" reportedly cut off the middle fingers of their left hands as a sign of obedience to the Prince of Darkness. Unfortunately, no independent evidence has surfaced to corroborate any of the claims made by Smith.'[40]

THE MORAL PANIC ABOUT SATANIC RITUAL ABUSE

Sociologist Jeffrey Victor identifies several factors responsible for nurturing the Satanic cult scare. First is the widespread appearance of beliefs within segments of American society, of the existence of a new type of deviant – dangerous Satanic cultists – and the serious, growing threat that they supposedly posed to American children. The 'panic' began with sporadic rumours and warnings by authorities such as clergy, law enforcement, cult experts and psychotherapists. While the mass media did not start the scare, it did help to spread the claims.[41] The ritual abuse scare grew separately out of the child sex abuse panic and the expanding perception that the sexual abuse of children is a hidden epidemic. As a result, Victor states, 'the general public was more receptive to the self-appointed authorities who lent credibility to SRA stories'.[42]

Another factor in the Satanic abuse epidemic was the expanding role of authorities who are important in not only defining what constitutes deviant behaviour, but also in evaluating and legitimating emerging claims about supposedly new societal threats. If these new claims are not deemed credible by authorities, they fail to gain a foothold in society. However, new authorities, especially from the medical community, are being increasingly relied upon by law officers, justices, legislators and court juries due to their specialist knowledge, and present their interpretations of information and evidence that are often viewed as indisputable scientific fact.[43] Victor argues that at the time of the SRA epidemic in the early 1980s, psychotherapists and social workers were not fully accepted within the medical profession and were keen to gain greater respect and recognition. He believes that the 'discovery' of this hidden epidemic focused the media spotlight onto their 'noble' profession, giving them the credibility that they so much desired. Victor states: 'If this important discovery could be confirmed in the courts of law and science, these specialists could obtain well-deserved recognition and respect for their work.'[44] These same psychotherapists and social workers spread the SRA message initially through conferences and seminars, and later gaining the media spotlight as part of the broader child molestation scare.[45]

The sudden proliferation of Satanic ritual abuse reports during the 1980s also occurred as the result of flawed investigation methods for evaluating reports of deviant acts and helped trigger the epidemic of False Memory Syndrome. Techniques such as hypnosis, dream interpretation and guided imagery have all been linked to the production of false memories.[46] Victor believes that three main groups are responsible for the Satanic ritual abuse scare. Traditionalist Christians have a moral world-view attributing the cause of evil acts to Satan. This perspective views Satanists as literal agents of the Devil, whose intentions are 'to spread immorality of all kinds in order to destroy the moral order of American society and hasten Satan's takeover of the world'.[47] A second major group who helped to fuel the SRA cause, were social conservatives such as certain 'feminist' and 'Christian' psychotherapists, concerned with the decline in American morality.[48] A third group – radical feminists – have a demonological view of patriarchy and its many sexual aggressions against women and children, including incest and rape.

Victor says: 'Skepticism about accusations of SRA is regarded as being one more attempt by men to discredit women and children's testimony about their sexual victimization. The anomaly that many of the people accused of SRA are mothers or female child care workers is ignored or is attributed to male manipulators.'[49]

WHY THE SATANIC RITUAL ABUSE SCARE?

Accounts of organized Satanic ritual sexual abuse function in modern society as a form of scapegoating. All cultures have a concept of evil. As strange as it sounds, we need evil. Evil functions to bring societies closer together and fosters unity. Evil gives us a common, clear-cut enemy to rally against. In today's Western society we are heavily influenced by Christianity, and correspondingly, evil is typified by Satan. For most of the second half of the twentieth century, communists conveniently filled this niche. The rise of the Satanic cult threat is an 'invented' evil that conspicuously coincides with the break-up of the Soviet Union and the communist bloc as a new evil quickly filling the void.[50] Victor believes that creating moral scapegoats promotes social stability by 'providing a target for displaced aggression and unifying the conflicting elements within a society – by defining some category of people as being traitors to, or deviant from, the overarching moral values of that society'.[51] On a different level, Victor thinks that the creation of Devil cultists violating America's youth reflects widespread anxieties about internal conflicts among parents. 'There is a great deal of parental guilt today; many parents feel guilty about leaving their children at day-care centers or about having little time to spend with them or about being reluctant to use their authority to guide their children's choice of entertainments and friends or about feeling unable to guide the moral values of their children.'[52]

THE SUDDEN 'EPIDEMIC' OF MULTIPLE PERSONALITY DISORDER

The belief in repressed memories also played an influential role in another 'epidemic' during this period – Multiple Personality

Disorder. The sudden appearance of tens of thousands of cases in America over just two decades, and its virtual absence around the globe, can only be explained by psychiatric politics and the American penchant for psychotherapy.[53] It may not be coincidental that American psychotherapy rakes in over a billion dollars annually, yet quality control and oversight are sorely lacking.[54]

The sudden appearance of MPD is remarkable. Before 1973, a mere 75 cases had ever been recorded. By the 1980s there were an estimated 40,000 cases. So what happened to create the sudden upsurge in reports? Two influential media events. In 1973, the sensational, best-selling book, *Sybil* was published by psychotherapist Cornelia Wilbur. *Sybil* is the story of Shirley Ardell Mason of Lexington, Kentucky, who purportedly had over a dozen separate personalities – all struggling for control of her body. Three years later, actor Sally Fields starred as Sybil in a television movie. Soon people across the country were reporting that they too were suffering from MPD, and psychotherapists obliged.[55]

Faced with patients presenting psychological problems for which they could not account, many therapists suspected an inner conflict caused by hidden memories of childhood abuse. They asked: 'Do you feel different from other people?' or 'Do you often feel taken advantage of?'[56] and sometimes such simple questioning was sufficient to bring out hidden memories: others had to be coaxed out with hypnosis. It was at this stage that MPD became a fashionable diagnosis. Most of these patients had approached their therapists with standard psychiatric problems like depression and relationship troubles, only to be diagnosed with some deeper underlying cause – alternate personalities.[57] *Most of these patients had no conscious recall of having been molested, prior to visiting their therapist and having the idea suggested.* Supposedly, as a survival strategy, their 'memories' were 'hidden' by entrusting them to an alter ego who became their guardian. By encouraging the alter egos to come out and reveal the childhood ordeal, a therapist could guide the afflicted adult to come to terms with his or her past and then rebuild their life.

Psychologist Nicholas Spanos believes that the sudden influx of MPD tells us more about the fuzzy profession of psychotherapy than

124

it does about the existence of MPD. The diagnosis of having multiple personalities fits neatly into the already fermenting sexual molestation scare. 'During this period, MPD therapists also became incest-resolution therapists, and by the 1980s, the alter personalities of MPD patients began increasingly to be conceptualized as the repositories of memories of sexual abuse that were hidden from the main or host personality. In short, the enactment of MPD came increasingly to involve the recovery of more and increasingly horrendous abuse memories that were "held" by more and more alter personalities.'[58]

It had already been noted that childhood abuse – though not of the Satanic kind – featured in many MPD cases. Eugene Bliss went so far as to assert that the 'evidence suggests that most personalities . . . are produced by abuse and mistreatment, usually in childhood'. Though he describes the world of his MPD patients as a 'land of fairy tales', he insists that the tales were built on a substratum of fact; in cases in which he had been involved, 'all traumas were verified as actual occurrences, with two exceptions'.[59] Few therapists, however, went to so much trouble to verify their patients' claims, insisting that it was sufficient to 'believe the patient'. By the mid-1980s, one in four MPD patients traced her problems to ritual Satanic abuse; by 1992 the figure had doubled.[60]

The therapy sessions were intense and traumatic. The patient would be questioned for hours on end to persuade her – most sufferers were female – to disclose her life-history. Any hint she gave would be seized upon as evidence: it didn't have to be verbal – a body movement could be a 'body memory', so that a patient experiencing chronic arm pain might recall that she was hung up by the wrists in a Satanic ritual.[61] This procedure was uncomfortably reminiscent of the exorcisms of allegedly possessed persons in the seventeenth century. The patient, already weakened or disorientated by whatever was afflicting her and often numbed by years of treatment, found herself confronted by a professional who was already convinced that the MPD was there, latent and waiting to be extracted. The therapist became an authority figure commanding emotional dependence. Generally more educated than the patient, professionally versed and experienced, supportive and encouraging, it is not surprising that a patient would be keen to retain this favour by stifling her doubts and giving the therapist what she or he wanted. Alan Siegel remarks: 'Patients in psychological crisis welcome an explanation of their turmoil and inner disarray. Often they long for a reason for their pain, and are vulnerable to the therapist's convictions and beliefs about the causes.'[62] Therapists justified themselves by citing Freud who once said: 'We must not believe what they say, we must always assume, and tell them, too, that they have kept something back because they thought it unimportant or found it depressing. . . .'[63]

These therapy sessions were usually long-drawn-out affairs: the therapists themselves admitting that it took an average of 6.8 years between the time a patient was first assessed and the 'accurate' diagnosis of MPD.[64] One of the earliest and most influential books on MPD, the case of Sybil, describes therapy sessions enduring eleven years, and requiring more than two thousand visits to her therapist! Frequently, treatment ceased only when the patient could no longer afford to pay, or the insurance ran dry. Even if a fusion of the personalities was triumphantly achieved, post-fusion therapy was required to maintain stability in over 90 per cent of cases, and even then relapse was frequent. Richard Kluft, one of MPD's strongest advocates, asserted that a patient's cure frequently left her with 'single personality disorder' and that retraumatisation led to relapse in virtually every case.[65]

The one-to-one sessions were only part of the process, moreover. Once the alters had been coaxed out of their hiding places, they were welcomed to self-help and support groups, workshops and reinforcement events of all kinds, given books and newsletters to read. Patients who may have been self-conscious about their histories now felt welcomed and encouraged. They were made to feel privileged rather than persecuted: they were on the high road to self-fulfilment. 'Patients often re-create themselves in the mold of the survivor, their beliefs forming the basis of a new identity and world view.'[66]

The process of creating an alter ego was explained to Bliss by one of his patients, speaking as one of her personalities, who said of her:

'She creates personalities by blocking everything from her head, mentally relaxes, concentrates very hard, and wishes.' Bliss perceptively points out: 'The crux of the problem is whether patients are consciously playing a role or are someone else.'[67]

For the therapist, it was an enticing challenge. Jack Leggett sums it up: 'If someone comes into my office and it's kind of a depression and I'm kind of working through their life, it's not as exciting as if I'm in a life-and-death struggle with devil personalities and hooker personalities and little-crying-child personalities.'[68] A revealing incident occurred when therapist Cornelia Wilbur, while treating Sybil, temporarily entrusted her to a colleague. When Sybil came to therapy with Dr Spiegel, she asked 'Do you want me to be Peggy, or can I just tell you. . . . When I'm with Dr Wilbur, she wants me to be Peggy.' Spiegel replied that it was her decision whether to be Peggy or not. Sybil was relieved, choosing not to exhibit different personalities while he was conducting the sessions.[69]

What brought the epidemic to an end was the stark absence of any convincing supporting facts. Official investigations, while not denying that some child abuse did indeed take place, showed that it was almost always a family matter, and not a scrap of evidence for the wilder claims was ever produced.[70] Joan Acocella notes that victims had been advised: 'To say "I was abused", you don't need the kind of recall that would stand up in a court of law.'[71] It was bad advice: ultimately they did need such evidence. In the early stages of the epidemic, supposed victims not only accused their parents but sued them, and were awarded large sums by the courts: but later in the epidemic, the strategy backfired as accusations were directed against the therapists. For instance, 35-year-old Elizabeth Carlson had been led by her therapist to 'remember' that she had been molested as a child by some fifty relatives – her parents, grandparents, and even her great-grandparents. When she came to realize the absurdity of the charges, she sued her therapist and was awarded $2.4 million in damages.[72] Which was just as well, for the cost of those weekly sessions, year after year, was very high: one innocent family incurred medical costs of over $3 million for therapy which included the hospitalization of two sons aged four and five for three years, where they provided details of the murder and cannibalism they had performed as members of a Satanic cult. Another patient spent two years in a private psychiatric hospital at a cost to her insurers of $1,200 a day. When her insurance money finally dried up and she was no longer able to receive treatment, her MPD conveniently went away.[73]

An important role in the return to reason was played by the False Memory Foundation, created in 1992, and supported by several leading psychologists as well as families who said they were falsely accused of abusing their relatives. In a notable experiment to demonstrate how easily false memories can be implanted in a suitably suggestive subject, social psychologist Richard Ofshe 'fed' a false incest event to an accused father, and the following day the father recalled it as fact, narrating it in florid detail entirely supplied by his own imagination.[74] Gradually the more extreme claims were withdrawn; more and more therapists were successfully sued for implanting false memories in their patients. The MPD epidemic had risen and was sustained on the basis of ritual abuse. When it became evident that there was little or no evidence for ritual abuse, the epidemic collapsed.

The effect was to cast doubt on the whole concept of multiple personality. Clearly, MPD had been extravagantly over-diagnosed: if multiple personality fantasies could so easily be created, perhaps the very concept was itself a delusion. In the 1994 edition of the *Diagnostic and Statistical Manual of Mental Disorders*, the Bible of the mental health community, MPD was discreetly replaced by DID – Dissociative Identity Disorder. Referring to the MPD movement, Paul McHugh aptly observes: 'In but a few years we will all look back and be dumbfounded by the gullibility of the public in the late twentieth century and by the power of psychiatric assertions to dissolve common sense.'[75]

What happened in the 1980s was that therapists came to believe that MPD provided the explanation for the 'hidden memories' which they believed their patients to possess, and which would reveal their involvement in ritual abuse. They set to work in the belief that they were revealing these personalities, unaware that instead they were creating them. This was facilitated by two aspects of mental activity for which insufficient allowance is generally made: on the one hand, the capability for fantasy-creation, vividly illustrated by the Ofshe experiment mentioned above; on the other, the tendency to role-playing which all share.

FROM WITCHES TO SEX ABUSERS: COMING FULL CIRCLE

There is little doubt that many patients invented 'hidden memories' of childhood sexual abuse, Satanic ritual abuse, and Multiple Personality Disorder – all with the unwitting aid of their psychotherapists. How prevalent is the creation of these fantasies? What percentage of patients, having absolutely no recall of child sexual abuse prior to seeing their therapist for an unrelated issue, invented such memories with the encouragement of their therapists after using such subjective techniques as hypnosis and dream analysis? Childhood sexual abuse is a heinous crime that is often perpetrated on the very young – society's most innocent and vulnerable. Therefore, many older patients may recall only fleeting images of such abuse. Yet there is a terrible danger here. False Memory Syndrome and the creation of fantasies that are 'teased out' by well-meaning therapists, have created a tragedy that is every bit as devastating as real sexual abuse. Child molestation is a sinister crime perpetrated on innocent victims and often leads to an array of psychological problems that the victim must endure throughout a lifetime. However, there is a double tragedy here. In their zeal to stop these terrible crimes, some psychotherapists have created a flurry of false accusations that are equally as catastrophic and far-reaching as the crimes they are intended to thwart. Even more remarkable are the parallels between the witch-hunts and False Memory Syndrome. To understand the present, we must understand the past. We have come full circle.

EIGHT

Terrorism Scares – the Phantom Menace

Dangers bring fears, and fears more dangers bring.
Richard Baxter[1]

When it comes to reporting, all forms of mass media are a far cry from the fair and balanced image that they typically project. This is especially true in times of crisis – most notably on the sensitive subject of terrorists and terrorism. The definition of just who is a terrorist, and what is an act of terrorism, is highly subjective and depends on which side of the political fence you are standing. One person's freedom fighter is another's terrorist. The English language *New Collins Dictionary* defines terrorism as 'the systematic use of violence and intimidation to achieve some goal'.[2] By this definition, George Washington and many rebellious British colonists in the New World could easily be labelled as terrorists. Washington and his fellow revolutionaries advocated the violent overthrow of a sovereign government. In the years leading up to the Revolutionary War, disgruntled colonists used violence and intimidation against many of their fellow British subjects, especially tax collectors. They stole and dumped British tea and set fire to the homes of suspected Crown loyalists. Once the war was under way, it was a similar story on the battlefield. American soldiers were notorious for breaking with time-honoured conventions of warfare. It was a pragmatic strategy if David was to defeat Goliath. An undisciplined, ragtag army of former British colonists were fighting the greatest army on earth. The only chance the Americans had to succeed was to fight 'dirty' with tactics of the

130

weak. There are accounts of American soldiers marching in formation with their musket butts turned upside down – a sign of surrender – only to fire on shocked, approaching Redcoats. Although some historians contend that they were unaware of this convention, their use of other tactics suggests otherwise. On numerous occasions Americans intentionally did not wear their uniforms, making it difficult to readily identify a soldier's loyalties. American ships sailed under the safety of the Union Jack – only to suddenly hoist a rebel flag and attack British vessels as they pulled alongside. Sniping from behind trees and deliberately targeting British officers was considered uncivilized and barbaric conduct. To the British, they were terrorist acts. To the Americans, they were acts of practicality and survival. Many of the concerns over present Western terrorism fears centre on the plight of the Palestinians and their quest to reclaim their homeland. There are many parallels with the rebellious American colonists and the feelings of Palestinian powerlessness and displacement. While no one is advocating suicide attacks, such incidents are the weapons of a weak, desperate people, trying to even the score against a superpower and fight for what they view as their legitimate homeland.

There is little media balance when it comes to reporting on this emotional subject. The media on both sides project a relatively black and white, good versus evil struggle. The same is true of embedded reporters during the 2002 Iraq war. The term is an oxymoron. Once a journalist is embedded, they cannot possibly remain objective. 'Embedded reporter' is a synonym for 'in bed with reporters' – literally. For instance, US and British journalists could not report certain information such as their unit's specific geographical position. Others took up weapons and fired on the Iraqis. Western journalists and US military commanders were quick to protest when the bodies of American soldiers were shown on Middle Eastern TV. Yet shortly after the death of Saddam Hussein's sons Uday and Kusay, the US military showed little hesitation in deciding to publicly display their bodies. Most Western news agencies quickly obliged. The plain truth is that there is a flagrant double standard bordering on the absurd when it comes to wartime reporting, where the home side views every soldier as a hero and offers few pictures of wounded civilians or their own dead. The enemy is stereotyped as evil and not playing fair. This is understandable. Reporters are human, and during crises they rally around their own flags and any semblance of fairness and balance goes out of the window. So it is with the terrorism scare.

There is no question that the world faces a genuine threat from the use of nuclear, chemical and biological weapons. What *is* questionable is the tendency for the media, especially in America and Britain, to exaggerate the threat. Public fear over the potential damage from weapons of mass destruction may prove more harmful than most real scenarios. The greater threat is from overzealous reporting which engenders needless fear, disrupts everyday routines, siphons off money and personnel for homeland security, and fosters witch-hunts against innocent people such as Muslims and Arab-Americans. How much needless anxiety was generated when Homeland Defense Secretary Tom Ridge urged his fellow Americans to have plenty of duct tape and plastic wrapping on hand to protect their homes in case of a chemical or biological attack in their neighbourhood? While it may be prudent to take some precautions such as having an ample supply of food and water on hand, it may be better to simply keep a well-stocked liquor cabinet in the unlikely event that your particular neighbourhood is targeted.

Extreme public reaction to perceived terror threats is nothing new and can be traced back centuries. The mere threat of such attacks has triggered many episodes of mass hysteria and social delusion. Every terror scare is framed within a unique set of social and cultural circumstances which render it plausible. Media-generated terror scares are nothing new: the media is influential in both spreading and legitimizing the false or exaggerated belief which engenders the fear. This chapter examines several outbreaks of psychological illness and fear in such geographically diverse places as southern Europe, the Middle East and the United States. In each case, media coverage played a significant role in triggering chemical or biological terror fears where little or no real threat existed.

THE MILAN POISONING SCARE OF 1630

Johannes Gutenberg invented the printing press in 1455, forever revolutionizing mass communications. By the early 1600s, one-page sheets known as the *coranto* were irregularly appearing across Europe, briefly summarizing news from across the continent though they were often preoccupied with the commercial sector, not always timely, or able to be read by citizens of ordinary literacy. During the early 1600s, dispatches and government proclamations were routinely printed and posted for the public to read. These tended to be much more 'of the moment' as they were often printed by local governments and distributed relatively quickly across a city or region. For all intents and purposes, due to their more prompt nature, they were the historical equivalent of the mass media.

It is against this backdrop that in 1630, the 'Great Poisoning Scare' swept across Milan, Italy. The episode coincided with pestilence, plague, and a prediction that the Devil and evil-doers would poison the city's water supply.[3] The Italian writer Count Alessandro Manzoni describes the episode in his novel, *I Promessi Sposi* (The Betrothed). Across Europe at the time there were widespread fears that certain people were intent on spreading plague throughout the continent either by witchcraft or 'contagious poisons'. The seeds of the scare were sown in 1629, when King Philip IV signed a dispatch that was sent to the Milan governor, warning him to be on the lookout for several Frenchmen who, having escaped from a Spanish prison, were thought to be on their way to the city, possibly to spread plague by use of 'poisonous and pestilential ointments'. The King's ominous message was passed on to the city's senators and health commissioners, and soon circulated across Milan. The threat was not widely deemed to be credible and any fears quickly faded.

The King's dispatch was nearly forgotten when the plague broke out in Milan in May 1630. Some residents began to suspect a plot involving poison as vague fears and suspicions began to crystallize into a city-wide panic.[4] On the night of 17 May, a number of residents claimed to have witnessed several people placing what seemed to be poison on a partition in the city cathedral. The head of the city's health board and four of his fellow committee members went to the cathedral to investigate. In a subsequent letter to the governor, members of the health board said that they had gone so far as to conduct experiments with the mysterious substance on dogs, without any harmful effect. They said the investigation was undertaken 'to exceed in caution, than from any conviction of necessity'. To sooth the frayed nerves of jittery residents, they had the furniture removed and cleaned.[5] Much to their surprise, these actions had the opposite effect. Instead of dissipating fears, removing the items backfired and lent credence to rumours that the cathedral had been poisoned. Manzoni states: 'This mass of piled-up furniture produced a strong impression of consternation among the multitude, to whom any object so readily became an argument. It was said, and generally believed, that all the benches, walls, and even the bell-ropes in the cathedral, had been rubbed over with unctuous matter.'[6]

When city-dwellers awoke the next morning, they grew even more fearful after noticing mysterious stains on many doors and walls around the city. 'In every part of the city they saw the doors and walls of the houses stained and daubed with long streaks of I know not what filthiness, something yellowish and whitish, spread over them as if with a sponge.'[7] Disregarding the possibility of some mischievous prank, there was alarm that the sign of the awaited poisoning was at hand and that the city was doomed.[8]

Despite verbal reassurances from the health board, which then circulated through the city in order to maintain calm, fear was growing by the hour as their actions had created the impression that poisoners were intent on terrorizing the city. Board members held an urgent meeting and wrote a letter on the 19th, that was printed up and distributed on the 21st, calling on *anyone* with *any* information as to the identity of the perpetrators of the enigmatic marks, to be rewarded for their revelations and receive a full pardon if they were in some way involved. The proclamation read in part, 'that this crime should by any means remain unpunished, speciallie in times so perilous and suspicious, we have, for the consolation and peace of

134

the people, this daie published an edicte'. On the one hand, commission members were vehemently denying that there was any threat posed by the marks; on the other hand, their actions in posting the edict only served to further fuel fears. Citizens reasoned: 'If there is nothing to worry about, why issue such an urgent proclamation?'

Homeowners lit straw and began burning the spots. Meanwhile, the hunt was on to identify the evil ones who would perpetrate such a bold and dastardly act. Suddenly, dozens of people were on the list of possible suspects and became the subject of great scrutiny. Manzoni remarks: 'Among those who believed this to be a poisonous ointment, some were sure it was an act of revenge of Don Gonzalo Fernandez de Cordova, for the insults received at his departure; some, that it was an idea of Cardinal Richelieu's to desolate Milan, and make himself master of it without trouble; others, again – it is not known with what motives – would have it that the Count Collalto was the author of the plot, or Wallenstein, or this or that Milanese nobleman.'[9]

Soon, strange stains – either real or imagined – were again spotted across Milan: on walls, doors, public entrances. Some stains had probably long been there, only to be 'found' during the intense hunt for marks, with residents scrutinizing every nook and cranny of the city. Armed with the conviction that poisoners were about, it was almost inevitable that poisoners would be found. Fears intensified as 'all eyes were on the look-out' for the 'poisoners'. In the scare that ensued, many people were killed, badly beaten or imprisoned. Italian writer Giuseppe Ripamonti describes two eyewitness accounts. In the first, a man was spotted in church wiping a bench before sitting down, when he was accused of smearing poison on the seat.

> . . . an old man, more than eighty years of age, was observed, after kneeling in prayer, to sit down, first, however, dusting the bench with his cloak. 'That old man is anointing the benches!' exclaimed with one voice some women, who witnessed the act. The people who happened to be in church . . . fell upon the old man; they tore his grey locks, heaped upon him blows and kicks, and dragged him out half dead, to convey him to prison, to the

135

judges, to torture. 'I beheld him dragged along in this way,' says Ripamonti, 'nor could I learn anything further about his end; but, indeed, I think he could not have survived many moments.'[10]

In another incident, Ripamonti recounts that three young visiting Frenchmen were studying various antiquities in the city including Milan Cathedral. They were standing outside the building, apparently admiring the architecture. 'One, two, or more passers-by, stopped, and formed a little group, to contemplate and keep their eye on these visitors, whom their costume, their headdress, and their wallets, proclaimed to be strangers, and, what was worse, Frenchmen. As if to assure themselves that it was marble, they stretched out their hands to touch it. This was enough. They were surrounded, seized, tormented, and urged by blows to prison.'[11] Fortune smiled upon the trio as the hall of justice was nearby. The judges found the men innocent and set them free. One could not blame them if they had decided to hightail it out of the city, for paranoia and suspicion were on every street corner.

In another instance a Signore Mora, a pharmacist and barber by profession, was found with several preparations containing unknown potions and was accused of being in cahoots with the Devil to poison the city. Protesting his innocence, his resistance was broken after prolonged torture on the rack, admitting to cooperating with the Devil and foreigners to poisoning the city and anointing the doors. His spirit broken, he named several accomplices who were eventually arrested and tortured. They were all pronounced guilty and executed. British journalist Charles Mackay writes that 'The number of persons who confessed that they were employed by the Devil to distribute poison is almost incredible', noting that 'day after day persons came voluntarily forward to accuse themselves'.[12]

CREATING THE 'MAD GASSER' OF MATTOON

Another terrorism scare, this one involving an imaginary chemical weapons attack, took place in a small American midwestern city whose residents were facing a crisis of a different nature as the media warned of the possible use of such weapons by the Axis powers. Two and a half months after the D-Day invasion of Normandy in September 1944, the Allies were entering the German fatherland in an offensive that would eventually doom the Nazi regime. Amid such reports, a series of mysterious gas attacks were recorded in the American heartland in sleepy Mattoon, Illinois. The 'gassings' made international news as people read accounts of the 'phantom anaesthetist' or 'mad gasser' – a nefarious, shadowy character who was said to be sneaking up to houses at night and spraying the occupants with a noxious gas through open windows. After two weeks and dozens of 'gassings', a joint investigation by local, state and federal authorities concluded that the entire affair was a figment of the imagination.[13] The episode can be traced to the publication of a single newspaper article that triggered the scare. Events quickly spiralled out of control as other newspapers followed suit and citizens began redefining shadowy figures and unfamiliar odours as the work of the gasser.

The 'mad gasser' episode cannot be understood without examining the context of the times. During the early 1940s, dozens of popular and scientific periodicals discussed the emerging 'poison gas peril' facing the world, in publications such as *Newsweek, Popular Science*, and the *American Journal of Public Health*.[14] As the tide of the Second World War turned increasingly in favour of the Allies, so did concern that German commanders, desperate to defend the fatherland at all costs, might resort to gas warfare.[15] Such a scorched-earth policy would have been futile, but could have inflicted massive, horrific civilian and military casualties on both sides. In fact the Allies were so concerned that the Germans might use poison gas during their 6 June 1944 D-Day invasion of Normandy, that they had a plan to retaliate within forty-eight hours with two bombing raids of 400 planes each, all loaded with chemical weapons designed to hit selected targets. Gas warfare expert Frederic Brown states that D-Day was the 'most dangerous period for German [gas] initiation' – a credible threat that was widely discussed in the press during the latter months of 1944.[16]

Terrifying images of gas warfare from the First World War were still fresh in people's minds as the topic remained in the public eye through the interwar period. From the time a deadly chlorine cloud was unleashed by German soldiers at Ypres, Belgium on the afternoon of 22 April 1915, gas warfare had struck fear into the hearts of people around the world. Poison gas claimed about 90,000 lives during the First World War, and injured over a million more.[17] The spectre of gas warfare would haunt Americans for the next two decades. During the 1920s, the thorny issue of stopping the rapidly emerging arms race involving chemical and biological weapons was widely discussed in the American press. While US representatives signed the Geneva Gas Protocol in 1925, it triggered a firestorm of controversy and debate that would endure to the end of the decade as the Senate steadfastly refused to ratify the Protocol. The issue was emotional and divisive and many veterans groups, most prominently the American Legion, made media spectacles out of denouncing the treaty during their annual meetings. Other opposition groups were the Veterans of Foreign Wars, Reserve Officers Association, Spanish-American War Veterans, and Military Order of the World War, but there were splinter groups favouring ratification.[18]

In the 1930s, several influential books appeared on what was commonly known as 'the poison gas scare'. These include Elvira Fradkin's *The Air Menace and the Answer*, J.M. Kenworthy's *New Wars; New Weapons*, and *The British Way of Warfare* by Liddell Hart.[19] Fradkin worried that rapid aeronautical progress combined with advancements in chemistry could lead to a human catastrophe.[20] The League of Nations also kept the issue alive with a series of conferences and publications addressing the issue.[21] By the late '30s, amid fears of Europe slipping into another world war, the issue of chemical and biological warfare was weighing heavy on Americans. The fact that Americans were so preoccupied with the subject resulted in the 1938 *War of the Worlds* broadcast being widely interpreted to have been a surprise German gas raid, by listeners who assumed that the announcer had mistaken the Germans for Martians.[22]

During the Second World War, military analysts on both sides were gravely concerned with the possible use of poison gas.

Historians Robert Harris and Jeremy Paxman note that 'years later it is difficult to appreciate just how great the fear of gas was' for both the military and civilians.[23] By mid-1944, the poison gas scare reached new heights. As the tide had clearly shifted in favour of the Allies, it was widely feared in both civilian and military circles that the Germans might resort to chemical weapons. While this never occurred, in the study of social delusions perception is everything. There is a common legal saying that 'possession is nine-tenths of the law'. In the study of mass hysteria, the motto should read, 'Perception is nine-tenths of belief'. In 1944, the *New York Times* published 112 articles under the subject heading of 'chemical warfare' – that's roughly an article every three days.[24] About this time, many respected and widely read publications discussed the possible use of poison gases,[25] and whether the Allies should use them first.[26] Commentators in such newspapers as the *Washington Times-Herald*, the *Chicago Tribune*, and the *New York Daily News* were in favour of a first strike; others thought this was an incredibly dangerous idea, fearing that the Germans would get wind of the notion and launch a pre-emptive strike.[27]

THE GASSER STRIKES

It is within this context of social paranoia over the imminent use of gas warfare that the 'mad gasser' saga unfolded. The residents of Mattoon didn't simply conjure up visions of the gasser out of thin air. But why Mattoon? For one thing, residents were especially edgy following news that an escaped Nazi was loose in the area (he was later found and never made it near the city).[28] On the very day of the 'attack', an Associated Press story on the possibility of a poison gas attack on American soil circulated widely throughout the state. It warned: 'If Nazi extremists bent on ruling or ruining should employ gas against civilian populations in a bitter end resistance, the allies would be in a position through air strength to drench German cities. . . . Recurrent rumors that the Germans are preparing to initiate gas warfare bring no official reaction here.' As if anxiety levels weren't high enough, a series of burglaries were reported in the days prior to 1 September.[29] The woman involved in the first reported attack was Mrs Aline Kearney. What were *her* personal circumstances? She was especially jittery, having cashed her government allotment check of $75 dollars earlier that day. What was the last thing she'd done before retiring to bed? Counted her money. The 'mad gasser' did not simply occur, it grew out of a unique set of circumstances.

At about 11 o'clock on Friday night, 1 September, an anxious Aline Kearney went to bed with her three-year-old daughter Dorothy. Her husband, Bert, was away driving his taxi. Her sister Martha was awake in a front room while Aline's other daughter and Martha's son slept in a back room. Suddenly Aline noticed a sickening, sweet smell that she attributed to a gardenia flower patch near an open window, inches from the bed. She summoned Martha to ask if she could smell it too, but she couldn't and soon left. As the scent intensified, Aline noticed that her throat and lips felt dry and burning, and there was a paralysing sensation in her legs. She screamed for Martha, who again rushed in but this time said she *could* detect a strange odour. After being told of the 'paralysis', Martha alerted a next-door neighbour, Mrs Earl Robertson, who phoned police about the 'gassing'. Police found no trace of an intruder.[30] After hearing of the 'attack', Mr Kearney reached home about 12.30 a.m. and claimed to glimpse a figure near the bedroom window. Police again searched fruitlessly. He said the man was tall, wore dark clothes and a skullcap.[31]

ALARMIST PRESS COVERAGE

The next day the *Daily-Journal Gazette*, Mattoon's only large circulation newspaper, published a sensational front-page account of the 'gassing', proclaiming: 'Anesthetic Prowler on Loose. Mrs Kearney and Daughter First Victims . . . Robber Fails to get into Home.' The paper treated the gasser as a fact, noting that the paralysing sensation in Mrs Kearney's legs abated after thirty minutes. Her daughter said she felt ill for a little while but quickly felt better again. Curiously, no one else in the house felt any ill effects whatsoever.[32] Aline Kearney's 'attack' couldn't have been too serious – she never even saw a doctor.

The *Gazette* was read by 97 per cent of families in the city.[33] The article suggested that there may be more 'victims'. After reading the *Gazette* story, four other residents soon came forward to report similar 'gassings', that they said occurred at their homes before or near the time of the Kearney incident. Mrs George Rider said she was alone with her two sleeping children, awaiting her husband's return from work. Having an upset stomach she began drinking excessive amounts of coffee. She later admitted to drinking 'several pots' and then took stomach medication before vomiting. Until this point, there was no sign of the gasser. She next lay in bed near her children with the window shut and then heard a peculiar noise – like a 'plop' – followed by an odd smell and a feeling of lightheadedness. This was accompanied by finger and leg numbness. Just then her baby began coughing. She assumed that the gasser had forced the fumes through a bedroom window.[34] Mr and Mrs Orban Raef claimed the gasser struck at their residence the night before the Kearney 'gassing'. He and his wife were asleep at 3 a.m. when, he said, fumes came through the bedroom window. Both experienced 'the same feeling of paralysis' and felt unwell for ninety minutes. Friends sleeping in another room were unaffected.[35] Olive Brown told police that months earlier, she too had been 'gassed'. She said that near midnight 'she had an experience similar to that related by persons during the past few days'.[36]

Police did not believe the first few gassing claims, attributing them to 'imagination',[37] yet their scepticism is not reflected in the early *Gazette* reports. These earlier few reports lent further credibility to Mrs Kearney's claims and solidified belief in the 'gasser's' reality, yet they were all based on the flimsiest of evidence. Of these subsequent gassing claims, not a single person fled their home, phoned police, told friends or relatives, or even bothered to check with a doctor! Can you imagine? Thinking you or other loved ones were sickened by poison gas and experiencing lightheadedness, limb numbness, burning lips and vomiting, what do you do? You stay in the house and go back to sleep!

In re-examining Mrs Kearney's initial report in the *Gazette*, neither she nor her sister mentioned a prowler. Mrs Kearney is quoted as saying that her sister contacted a neighbour, Mrs Earl Robertson, who called the police. The newspaper then indicated that Mr Robertson had searched the yard and neighbourhood 'but could find no trace of the prowler. Police also searched without success'. Not until Mr Kearney arrived is there mention of a prowler at the bedroom window. In the article's lead and a following reference to Mrs Kearney's parched and burned lips from 'whatever was used by the prowler', the unnamed reporter surmises that a prowler was spraying gas through the window. The 'mad gasser' was born. The *Gazette* reporter had created an imaginary chemical weapons attack by combining the first incident involving Aline Kearney's strange odour and 'paralysis', with Bert Kearney's claim of a prowler in the second incident. No one actually reported seeing the 'gasser'. A headline writer simply created the phrase. The term 'anesthetic prowler' was a media construction by the *Gazette* and quickly became a self-fulfilling prophecy as evidenced in the next four prowler reports. The *Gazette* sensationalized the events further, by suggesting that there would be more victims.[38]

FEARS ESCALATE

Between 5 and 6 September gasser reports spread beyond the *Gazette* to most Illinois newspapers. These reports quoted authorities, such as the Mattoon police commissioner and mayor and army experts, all of whom described the gasser as real. Additional gasser claims continued to be reported. Most of these reports were either alarmist or asserted the gasser's real existence. On 5 September Mrs Beulah Cordes claimed to be 'overcome' by fumes after finding a cloth on her porch and sniffing it. It was analysed at a crime laboratory where a chemical expert could detect no trace of gas, saying it must have evaporated.[39] Mattoon's mayor, E. Richardson, suggested that mustard gas could account for the numbness, while army experts from the Chicago-based Chemical Warfare Service favoured chloropicrin.[40] Richard Piper, superintendent of the Illinois Bureau of Criminal Identification and Investigation confidently proclaimed: 'The existence of the anesthetic, or whatever it is, is genuine.'[41]

The major Chicago newspapers provided coverage on 6 September. Most sent reporters to Mattoon and afforded the story considerable space. These papers had a significant Mattoon readership, undoubtedly affecting public perceptions. The *Chicago Daily Tribune* was read by 24 per cent of residents; the *Chicago Daily News* reached 20 per cent.[42] The *Chicago Herald-American* covered 5 per cent of Mattoon,[43] its audience during the 'gassings' was likely higher. In his investigation of the case, Donald Johnson of the University of Illinois said the paper's dramatic headlines and photos were often mentioned by residents.[44]

By 6 September a nightly barrage of gassing reports was overwhelming Mattoon's modest police force of two officers and eight patrolmen.[45] On 8 September about seventy people poured onto Dewitt Avenue after hearing that the gasser had been spotted nearby. When someone in the crowd detected a strange odour, others in the group were convinced that they had been 'gassed'.[46] On 10 September the *Chicago Herald-American* described the incident with its typical sensationalism, beginning its front-page account: 'Groggy as Londoners under protracted aerial blitzing, this town's bewildered citizens reeled today under repeated attacks of a mad anesthetist who has sprayed deadly nerve gas into 13 homes and has knocked out 27 known victims.'[47]

On the weekend of the 9th and 10th, the city resembled a scene from a poor 'Grade B' movie, with hundreds of citizens gathering near City Hall to hear the latest news. As a patrol car responded to a call, it was followed by a procession of vehicles with curious occupants. This prompted Police Commissioner Wright to order his officers to arrest 'chasers'.[48] Vigilante gangs roamed the streets touting clubs and guns. The Commissioner feared that a jittery resident with a gun would shoot innocent people.[49] His fears may not have been unfounded. One woman left at home, alone, loaded her husband's shotgun for protection. It went off, fortunately only blowing a hole in the wall.[50]

By the 9th, several more gassings were reported, as the *Gazette* continued to describe the affair in sensational, front-page headlines: '"Mad Gasser" Adds Six Victims! 5 Women and Boy Latest Overcome.' The most vivid gassing claim was reported that night, as sisters Frances and Maxine Smith claimed a series of attacks on their home. Frances was a school principal. They said there were suspicious noises outside their windows. The next night they claimed three 'attacks' that were published as gospel. 'The first infiltration of gas caught them in their beds. Gasping and choking, they awoke and soon felt partial paralysis grip their legs and arms. Later, while awake, the other attacks came and they saw a thin, blue smoke-like vapor spreading throughout the room. . . . Just before the gas with its "flower-like" odor came pouring into the room they heard a strange "buzzing" sound outside the house and expressed the belief that the sound probably was made by the "madman's spraying apparatus" in operation.'[51]

Separate weekend incidents resulted in two women being hospitalized for 'gassings' but they were later diagnosed as suffering anxiety attacks.[52] By Monday the 11th, ten Springfield police officers were mobilized to Mattoon. Each car had a local volunteer to assist with directions, and each officer carried a shotgun.[53] Three police officers from Urbana were also dispatched. It was also disclosed that two FBI agents had arrived to determine the type of gas the 'madman' was using 'to knock out his victims'.[54] That night a woman was so scared of a possible attack, that she was hospitalized for 'extreme mental anguish'.[55]

THE EPISODE UNRAVELS

There was a sudden shift in claims by the press and institutions of social control (i.e. police and politicians) on 11 September that described much of the recent events as 'mass hysteria'. With a small army of police on patrol, Commissioner Wright joked that they were often able to answer a call 'before the phone was back on the hook'.[56] At 11.30 a.m. Mrs Eaton Paradise told police, 'I've just been gassed.' Racing to the house, they found the culprit – a bottle of spilled nail-polish remover.[57] On the 12th, Chief Cole announced that it was all 'mass hysteria' triggered by chemicals from local factories that drifted across the city by shifting winds.[58]

On Wednesday the 13th, reporters were now describing the gasser as the 'phantom anesthetist' and 'Mattoon Will-o'-the-Wisp'. The *Gazette* reported on two more false reports overnight involving a cat on a porch and someone locked out of their car.[59] By 14 September, under a barrage of ridicule by police and the press, gassing reports in Mattoon had stopped. The *Gazette* began its account of a prowler claim the previous night by saying: 'One call! No paralyzing gas! No madman! No prowler!'[60] On the 15th, the *Gazette* reported that police in Cedar Rapids, Iowa, stated that a frantic woman telephoned, claiming that a man holding a spray gun outside her window had gassed her room. Police said 'they found no madman and no gas, but did find a billy goat tied in the yard and an odor that seemed to come from the animal'.[61]

At this point, the *Chicago Herald-American*, suddenly turned scathingly critical of gasser claims by publishing a series of interviews with a prominent Chicago psychiatrist about the 'phantom prowler', 'non-existent madman', 'wave of hysteria' and 'gasser myth', equating it to the Salem witch hysteria of 1692.[62] An editorial on the 19th in the *Decatur Herald* made fun of imaginative Mattoonites, noting that autumn was a season of odours: flowers, picnic fires, industrial wastes, and rotting Victory garden produce. 'Our neighbors in Mattoon sniffed their town into newspaper headlines from coast to coast.'[63] A *Time* reporter joked that gasser symptoms in Mattoonites consisted of temporary paralysis, nausea and 'a desire to describe their experiences in minutest detail'.[64] Other letters to the *Gazette* during late September ridiculed the episode. On the 26th, an army officer said Mattoon residents had more advanced poison gas training than his unit;[65] on the 29th another writer described the incidents as 'hysteria'.[66]

The Mattoon *Gazette* was responsible for triggering the scare, a deluge of further published dubious gassing claims contributed to the scare. Despite early reluctance, law officers and community leaders soon embraced this hypothesis – with little hard evidence – that a real gasser was prowling the community. Near the end of the episode, this process began to work in reverse, as both the press and police were soon embracing the 'mass hysteria' hypothesis. This view was given final legitimization in a series of articles in the *Chicago Herald-American* by local psychiatrist Harold Hulbert, who proclaimed the gasser to the mythical and a case of 'mass hysteria'. While certainly unusual, given the war scare context, the case of the mad gasser is not so bizarre. During the twentieth century, strange odours were the most common trigger of epidemic hysteria in both job and school settings.[67] It is a sign of our present times which are dominated by occupational safety legislation and environmental fears. Given the recent concern over chemical and biological weapons attacks by terrorists, episodes similar to the phantom anaesthetist may be set to recur.

THE PALESTINIAN POISONING HYSTERIA OF 1983

It was unthinkable. Frightening. Horrific. For several months in 1983, the world media spotlight was focused on reports that Palestinian schoolgirls may have been deliberately poisoned by Israelis. Reports of the 'poisoning' even appeared in major Israeli newspapers, further crystallizing the popular idea that Jews were behind the sinister attacks. Between March and April 1983, nearly a thousand, mostly Arab, schoolgirls in the disputed Israeli-occupied Jordan West Bank reported headaches, blurred vision, stomach aches, fainting, limb weakness, and even temporary blindness. It was eventually determined, after independent probes and a battery of medical tests, that the girls hadn't been poisoned but were suffering from anxiety.

The episode occurred amid poison gas rumours and a long-standing Palestinian mistrust of Jews. The medical complaints appeared during a fifteen-day period, coinciding with intense media publicity that poison gas was being sporadically targeted at Palestinians. The curious saga began in, and was predominantly confined to, schools in several adjacent villages in this bitterly disputed region. The case became widely known as the 'Arjenyattah Epidemic' as the incidents occurred in Arrabah, Jenin and Yattah.[68]

The Israeli military has occupied the Jordan West Bank since 1967, with their presence engendering intense hatred. While the occupation is generally viewed as temporary within the Arab world, as one observer notes, 'some tend to believe that the Israelis would do anything to perpetuate the status quo'.[69] Targeting would-be Palestinian mothers with poison, either by Israeli soldiers or civilian extremists, was a natural suspicion within this long-standing climate of fear and hatred. These circumstances acted like tissue paper, and a match was about to be struck at a school in Arrabah. The media would quickly fan those sparks into a major scare. The episode occurred in three distinct waves.

THE FIRST WAVE: ARRABAH

The first phase began on 21 March when, during a morning class at the Arrabah Girls' School, a seventeen-year-old pupil experienced dizziness and breathing difficulties including headaches and blurred vision. Soon fifteen more pupils fell ill. Some of the affected girls said that the symptoms coincided with their noticing a rotten egg-like smell from a school yard bathroom.[70] By the following day, sixty-one students and five adults had undergone hospital evaluation. A team of physicians who investigated the incident noted that the '[h]ighest rates were observed in three upper floor classes nearest the latrine from which most of the odour was reported, and lowest rates in wing [sic] most distant from the latrine'.[71]

On 22 March the *Yedi'Ot Ahronot* published a report on the mass illness at the Arrabah school and, though factually correct, the journalist implies the likely presence of poison gas in noting that the pupils 'were suddenly afflicted by an attack of blindness, headache and stomach-ache'. Also, 'blurred vision' was exaggerated and changed to 'blindness'.[72] The article also states that 'security forces had not used tear gas', seemingly suggesting and anticipating public outcry in reaction to the incident.[73]

THE SECOND WAVE: JENIN

On about 26 and 27 March, a second wave of illness reports involving similar symptoms swept through six schools in the vicinity of Jenin including the Elzahra, Burkin, Metalun, and UNRWA schools.[74] About 246 female pupils and some staff were affected. On the evening of the 27th, sixty-four residents in Jenin were rushed to local medical facilities with similar complaints when a cloud of gas was emitted from a passing car.[75]

By this time, descriptions of the episode as an attempt at genocide, appeared in the international press – even the Israeli press. Israel's *Ma'Ariv*, for example, described the episode as a mass poisoning with absolute certainty, using the sensational headlines: 'The Mysterious Poisoning Goes On: 56 High School Girls in Jenin Poisoned.' The only uncertainty was the source of the 'poison'. The report read in part: 'The mysterious poisoning of 50 students that took place last week in Arraba . . . affected 56 additional students yesterday in Jenin. Currently no definite evidence exists as to the source of the poison. Yesterday morning, 29 girl students were admitted to the hospital from Jenin High School with the following symptoms: difficulty breathing, cyanosis, and dizziness.'[76] Two days later, a report in another Israeli paper, *Ha'Aretz*, claimed that based on preliminary tests, 'nerve gas' had made the Jenin students sick.[77] While the actual cause of the symptoms was not known at the time, the *Ha'Aretz* and *Ma'Ariv* discussed the episode as a case of 'poisoning'.[78]

On 31 March, the Israeli Ministry of Health appointed psychiatrist Albert Hafez to investigate the poisoning claims. On visiting the Jenin Hospital Dr Hafez noted that the situation had a melodramatic, soap-opera-like quality as foreign journalists were swarming around, interviewing both the affected girls and hospital staff. Suddenly, an Arab girl was stretchered in and immediately enveloped in a sea of physicians and staff, pushing the frightened, bewildered mother aside. Almost instantly, an oxygen mask was forced over her face while someone else was administering an intramuscular injection. She later told doctors that her daughter was playing near their home when she experienced headache and nausea. Due to the publicity about the mass 'poisoning', the mother grew alarmed, and rushed her to hospital. Dr Hafez described a sense of the chaos at the hospital: 'While busy examining the girl amid the surrounding crowd, I became aware of a new turmoil consequent to the arrival of a new group accompanying a second patient . . . an 18-year-old girl who was quite excited and tried to throw herself off the stretcher while those escorting her tried to restrain her. As with the previous patient, the oxygen mask and intramuscular injection were used instantly. The shouting girl, the excited crowd, the first patient, and her helpless mother, together created an atmosphere of utter confusion.'[79]

THE THIRD WAVE: YATTAH

A third wave of reports occurred simultaneously on 3 April in the Tulkarem and Hebron districts, with the epicentre near a girls' school at Yattah. Students affected were attending the Beit Omar, Yattah, Neighbourhood, Nasser, and Anabtah schools.[80] When the schools were closed on 4 April, the 'outbreak' stopped. In an effort to resolve the reported poisonings, the Israeli government sent their top epidemiologist, Baruch Modan, to investigate.

Modan and his team of medical specialists soon concluded that mass hysteria was the culprit. They traced the 'outbreak' to an odorous latrine near the Arrabah school. Later that day a second, larger wave was ignited during recess when friends of the first group affected, spread rumours about their possible poisoning. During the second wave at several Jenin schools and nearby villages, the mass media and rumours were instrumental in spreading the symptoms. Part of this phase involved the sixty-four Jenin residents who were reportedly 'gassed' by a speeding car: it was concluded that the 'poison' in this case was actually thick smoke belched from a faulty exhaust system. The final wave of illness reports were, according to Modan and his investigators, triggered by the continuous spreading of poison gas rumours by the news media.[81]

Modan's report was widely viewed as biased within the Arab world, who dismissed the findings.[82] What followed was a public relations battle between the Israeli government and the Arab world, conducted through the United Nations. On 30 March the Commission on Arab Women, meeting in Tunis, Tunisia, telexed an urgent message to the UN Director-General, complaining that 'Israeli authorities' were responsible for the 'poisoning', and asking the UN 'to put a stop to this genocide and protect the life of the Palestinian people'.[83] In reaction, Israeli authorities described the poisoning claims as a propaganda campaign being fuelled by the media and pro-Palestinian politicians.[84]

In an effort to resolve the issue, investigators from the United States' National Institute for Occupational Safety and Health, and the Centers for Disease Control were invited to conduct their own independent probe, concluding that there was no evidence of a poisoning agent or that those afflicted were feigning symptoms. Their report found that the episode 'was triggered either by psychological factors, or, more probably, by the odour of low concentrations of H_2S gas [hydrogen sulphide] escaping from a latrine at the school at Arrabah. Subsequent spread was due to psychological factors operating against a background of stress, and it may have been facilitated by newspaper and radio reports.'[85] The American investigators Philip Landrigan and Bess Miller supported the findings of Modan and his team, noting that without any clear evidence to back their claims, the mass media in the region published and broadcast claims that a toxin was the likely cause.[86] The Americans took air, water and soil samples and found 'no evidence' of any toxins.[87] They also noted the curious pattern of the illness, selectively striking certain groups: 'Support for the diagnosis of psychogenic illness was provided here by the preponderance of female patients, particularly of adolescent girls. The relative sparing of infants, adolescent boys, and older adults argues against the presence of a toxin.'[88]

ATTACKING PALESTINIAN FERTILITY

Across the Arab world at this time, a popular story was circulating that a group of Jews perpetrated the poisoning in an effort to cut the

Palestinian birth rate, and hence they 'specifically targeted young girls approaching the age of marriage. The poisoning was done to harm this most fertile age group in order to limit Arab demographic growth. They even said they had found medical proof, claiming that urine tests showed a high protein level, which means that something is abnormal in the fertility system.'[89] Tests to confirm the elevated presence of the protein proved false. The Palestinian schoolgirl poisoning claims of 1983 are just one in a long list of historical claims of Jews poisoning their 'enemies'. A similar poisoning claim occurred in 1997, though the episode was devoid of mass psychogenic illness. According to Raphael Israeli, a professor of Islamic Civilization at Hebrew University: 'In 1997 the Palestinians exposed yet another Israeli "plot to suppress Arab population growth". They claimed to have tested packets of strawberry-flavored bubble gum which were found to be spiked with sex hormones and sold at low prices near schoolhouses in the West Bank and Gaza Strip. It was alleged that the gum aroused irresistible sexual appetites in women, then it sterilized them. According to Palestinian Supply Minister Abdel Aziz Shaheen, it was capable of "completely destroying the genetic system of young boys", as well.'[90]

Physicians treating the schoolgirls often interpreted their medical findings as reflective of their world view. Hence Palestinian doctors at the Jenin Hospital tended to assume that different poisons were used to sicken the girls. This assumption was made by doctors without any 'laboratory facilities at their disposal and . . . [who] had to depend solely on their clinical sense and previous experience'.[91] In sharp contrast, some Israeli doctors treating 'victims' at the country's Tel-Hashomer Hospital, were convinced that the girls were faking their symptoms as a political ploy to gain sympathizers for the Palestinian cause. To support this view, they noted that the girls tended to be hostile, aggressive and uncooperative. Some Israeli press reports also supported this 'factitious' position of events. According to Dr Hafez: 'Attracted by such a theory, reporters mobilized their resources and ingenuity to bring in evidence to confirm it. They filmed patients during doctors' rounds and alone, demonstrating the change in behavior from one situation to the other. They even tracked cars that were suspected of "recruiting" new patients and showed these films live on television.'[92]

PHANTOM ATTACK ON A RHODE ISLAND SCHOOL

The 1991 Persian Gulf War heightened fears of chemical or biological weapons attacks in parts of the Middle East. Each day, Americans were bombarded with the sight of journalists in Saudi Arabia and Israel, clutching gas masks and giving reports with air-raid sirens blaring in the background. Newspapers and television reporters warned them that Saddam Hussein had an arsenal of mobile scud missiles that were likely tipped with chemical warheads, capable of reaching Israel and Saudi Arabia, where many US troops were stationed. There were countless stories of Israelis going about their everyday business and attending the opera, with gas masks at the ready. We were shown children going off to school with gas masks. While most Americans realized that scud missiles were not a credible threat to mainland America, and that the actual threat of an Iraqi chemical weapons attack on US soil were remote at best, it was more difficult for children to assess the actual threat as described in the media. After all, the evening TV news and daily newspapers do not write for children. Ten- and eleven-year-olds live in a very different mental universe to adults. The prospect of a poison gas attack, no matter how far away, must have been disconcerting.

Then, one day, about three and a half weeks into the war, a pupil fainted at a Rhode Island elementary school. At the same time, classmates detected a strange odour in the building. A wave of anxiety swept through the school. Students began dropping like flies in the apparent belief that they were experiencing an Iraqi chemical weapons attack. In all, eighteen students and four teachers from four classrooms were stricken with dizziness, headache and nausea. The affected seventh- and eighth-graders, and the teachers, were examined at a nearby hospital emergency department where they quickly recovered. The doctors found signs of anxiety but little else. After assurance that there was nothing physically wrong with them, they were soon released.

POST-11 SEPTEMBER TERROR SCARES

The 11 September 2001 terrorist attacks in the United States, and subsequent mailing of anthrax-laced letters, generated widespread media discussion about the likelihood of further chemical or biological attacks. What followed was a wave of imaginary or pseudo-attacks. The media speculation that more attacks were imminent was a self-fulfilling prophecy fostering ever higher states of anxiety and alertness. Reminiscent of the streets of Milan in 1630, where the existence of poisoners became taken for granted, soon Americans were interpreting the most innocent events as terror-related.

On 29 September, in Washington State, harmless fumes from oil-based paints set off a bio-terrorism scare at Canyon Creek Middle School sending sixteen students to the hospital. An army of rescue personnel rushed to the scene believing a terrorist attack was under way.[93] Between 2 and 3 October a bio-terror scare swept across Manila in the Philippines when about 1,400 students from several Manila schools flooded local clinics, reporting mild flu-like symptoms: coughing, colds, mild fever. Some of the students were later confirmed as having Type A H1N1 influenza, but health authorities found that many had suffered psychogenic reactions after rumours spread among jittery parents and pupils that it was bio-terrorism. The false story spread rapidly via short text services.[94]

On 9 October, a man got into a scuffle with police and began spraying a mysterious substance in a subway station near College Park, Maryland. Many people were horrified, certain that it was a terrorist attack with chemical or biological weapons. As the man was wrestled down, rescue personnel were rushed to the scene to treat the thirty-five passengers and transit workers who began to exhibit nausea, headache and sore throats. It was later determined that the bottle contained harmless window cleaner.[95] About two weeks earlier in the Los Angeles subway, a similar incident had taken place. An unusual odour was detected and commuters became anxious fearing a terror attack. Many reported feeling ill. The system was shut down and the sick taken to local hospitals. A check of the subway system revealed no trace of chemical or biological weapons; the ill quickly recovered.[96]

The backdrop of these reports was the anthrax scare which gripped the country. It was during October that five envelopes containing the Ames strain of *Bacillus anthracis* spores were dropped into a public post box in Trenton, New Jersey. Twenty-two anthrax cases developed. Eleven were of the most serious type – inhalation – from which five people died. The remaining eleven were diagnosed with the cutaneous variety affecting the skin. All of these patients recovered following treatment with antibiotics.[97] Cable News Network reported that no less than 2,300 anthrax false alarms occurred over a two-week span in early October. It seemed as though any powdery substance someone found at work or in school prompted an evacuation, as emergency personnel, often dressed in bubble suits, would enter the building in dramatic fashion and remove the suspicious powder for testing.[98]

THE 'BIN LADEN ITCH'

The anthrax scare gave rise to what historian Elaine Showalter terms the 'Bin Laden Itch' in dozens of schools across North America. Between October 2001 and 3 June 2002 a mysterious skin rash affecting thousands of mainly primary schoolchildren was reported at widely separated locations in twenty-seven states of the United States and Canada.[99] The rashes persisted from a few hours to fourteen days, were not accompanied by other symptoms, and there was no evidence of spread from person to person.[100] After an intensive investigation by the Centers for Disease Control in Atlanta, CDC officials attributed the cause to an array of mundane culprits: bacteria, fungi, insect bites, dry skin, allergens, physical agents like fibreglass, chemical agents such as pesticides and cleaning products.[101] In a few cases, students even faked the rash by rubbing themselves with sandpaper in an effort to close the school![102] In their report, the CDC noted: 'With 53 million young people attending 117,000 schools each school day in the United States, it is expected that rashes from a wide range of causes will be observed.'[103] These skin conditions have always existed in the school system, but during the terror scare, students were paying more attention to their skin and school nurses were more likely to report such incidents. Dry skin and itching are notorious during the winter months in North America as people spend more time indoors and the air is typically dry as part of cold Canadian air masses and from heating systems.

The effects of the anthrax will continue to be felt in the form of mass psychogenic illness for years to come as hypervigilant mailroom workers redefine mundane symptoms as possible biological or chemical weapons. During May 2003, when two mail sorters at the Naperville, Illinois, City Hall experienced itching of the hands and forearms police and fire personnel rushed to the scene, locking the building down. As the facility was being searched, three more workers began to feel itchy. Four workers were evaluated at a local hospital. Physicians could find no apparent cause and there were no signs of rash or hives. Investigators scoured the building and tested for the presence of anthrax and a variety of chemicals. They even tested for the improbable – traces of itching powder. All tests were negative.[104]

THE THREAT TO OUR FUTURE?

Each age must face its own bogey men who threaten human progress. In medieval Europe, a belief in witches and werewolves resulted in the execution of tens of thousands of innocent people. During the Second World War, the doctrine of Aryan superiority spelled doom for 6 million Jews. At the dawn of the twenty-first century, the spectre and fear of terrorists haunt the landscape, filling the vacuum of evil that was once reserved for communists and drug dealers. Stereotypes of Muslims as terrorists make for easy scapegoats. We live in an age during which our very existence is in peril: ozone depletion; acid rain; nuclear waste; contamination of our food, air and water; AIDS; poverty; starvation; drug-resistant mutating viruses. These threats are not acts of God but share a common source as human creations. In the post-11 September world, these pressing concerns move to take a back seat to another human creation – exaggerated media fears over the potential use of weapons of mass destruction. These preoccupations threaten to incubate future social delusions and pseudo-terror attacks that will engender even more anxiety, disrupting routines, lowering our quality of life; diverting resources from the many more immediate social and environmental threats to our planet, and triggering new witch-hunts. As a result, the first half of the twenty-first century seems destined to be filled with episodes of mass hysteria and social delusion related to terrorism. It is our responsibility to change that destiny and rewrite the script to our own liking.

NINE

Primitive Stereotyping:
How the Media Created the
President Johnson Cult and the 'Lost'
Tasaday Tribe

Time trieth truth.

English proverb

ach year a handful of stories seem to captivate the public imagination. The year 1964 was no different as people were abuzz over news of the 'President Johnson Cult'. The tiny South Pacific island of New Hanover was thrust into the world media spotlight with news reports of a fantastic story involving the current United States President Lyndon Baines Johnson. At the time the island was part of Australian-controlled Papua New Guinea and was populated by about 7,000 natives. New Hanover is located in the Bismark Archipelago north-east of New Guinea, and is actually the largest of a small island chain that the natives inhabit. According to press accounts, government officials were arresting members of the cult for refusing to pay taxes. Instead they were collecting the money to entice President Johnson to come to the island and be their ruler.[1] During the March general election for the territory's House of Assembly, about 3,500 inhabitants refused to vote for any of the candidates on the ballot and instead wrote in 'Johnson of America'.[2] The election was a major step towards becoming a new independent country which would not happen until 16 September 1975. The elections were not exactly free, as Australian officials were dubious of New Guinea's independence movement and their capacity to rule

157

themselves without a lengthy transition period. Some expressed the idea that twenty-five or thirty years would be about right. The elections were a step towards independence, but with numerous stipulations – almost to the point of being rigged. The Assembly was to consist of forty-four openly contested positions, ten seats that had to be filled by whites, and ten candidates who could only get on the ballot with a nomination from the Australian authorities. And there was one other stipulation – Australian officials retained the right to veto any election result they felt was not in the best interests of the territory![3] Not exactly free, indeed.

Instead of focusing on the unfair nature of the elections, the Western press had a field day, depicting the natives as ignorant, misguided cultists, unhappy over not being allowed to vote for President Johnson as they were dissatisfied with the Australian-backed candidates. One sign read: 'We want to vote for the United States President in the elections because Americans are good people. Australians get out.'[4] By August of 1964, Australian officials were building a small prison on New Hanover for the non-complying cultists. At least eighty-one were under arrest.[5] By late September, events were spiralling out of control as a small, armed revolt threatened to undermine the March election process with fifty cultists brawling with government officials who had come to Lokono village when they tried to collect taxes. On 27 September, a *New York Times* report described the atmosphere as tense. 'Today a patrol of sixty armed policemen led by nine Australian officers went ashore under cover of rifle fire from three patrol boats. It found the village deserted, but a search uncovered bushknives, spears, axes and clubs. Four other villages were also found deserted.'[6] The scene is curious in that the natives, who were seemingly sowing the seeds for an armed revolt, had left their weapons behind. Even more odd, despite the build-up of weapons and threats, the natives had not killed or seriously injured a single government official.

Shortly after the March election, about $1,000 had been collected for Johnson's travel expenses,[7] and by November, when Johnson had still not come to the island, the natives reportedly pledged to exercise patience as they knew that Johnson was very busy and preoccupied with the Vietnam war. Near the end of 1964, Australian officials tried to intimidate 'tax defaulters' into paying up as native police were dispatched to New Hanover. In a show of strength, 'a coconut was shot off a tree; a smoke bomb was tossed on the beach and a young boy sent to stand in the smoke; one fleeing native was shot and wounded, though not seriously'.[8] When several hundred natives continued to defy the Local Government Council, they were jailed. In September of the following year, cultists met with a United Nations delegation, complaining that Australian officials 'had failed to keep promises of progress' and demanded that American authorities immediately take control of New Hanover.[9] At that point the group had reportedly raised $82,000 to buy Johnson's leadership.[10] Similar jailing took place in 1965 and 1966, though in diminishing numbers over time.

GAMES NATIVES PLAY

To the Western mind, and media, the Johnson cult drama was almost as pathetic as it was humorous. Just imagine, a group of unscrupulous natives thinking they could actually 'buy' Johnson as their leader. It was ridiculous. This not so complimentary image of native islanders continues to be the butt of Western humour. In 2003, the following description of the Johnson cult appeared on a website for the American Public Television System's show, *The American Experience* under events occurring during the Johnson administration. It portrays the poor New Guineans as primitive and impressionable. 'Lyndon Johnson was once worshipped as a god by followers of a "cargo cult" in Papua, New Guinea. Cargo cults are a religious phenomenon that developed when Europeans began arriving in the area, bringing with them huge amounts of material goods, which the confused native peoples thought must have been acquired from the spirit world. The people of New Hanover in Papua, New Guinea, thought so much of Lyndon Johnson that during the first House of Assembly elections there, they voted for LBJ – the feeling being that if he could lead the US, he could lead them, too, and bring to them the prosperity enjoyed in America.

159

Of course, LBJ declined to become their leader, and eventually the Johnson cult died out.'[11]

On the surface, the episode seems to be a classic example of irrational, backward thinking in a 'primitive' culture, of natives 'getting it wrong', naively misunderstanding the complex political dynamics of a Western society. This is certainly the way the Johnson cult has been portrayed in the Western media. Treatment of the native elections in *Time* and *Newsweek* magazines were typical. On 28 February 1964, an article appearing in *Time* under the banner 'Stone Age Election', claimed that the elections had revived interest in native cults. 'Cultists believe that white men do not work, that they merely write secret symbols on scraps of paper, for which they receive planeloads of "cargo" – boats, tractors, houses, cars and canned goods. After the election, cultists believe that they will inherit the white man's magic to make goods materialize without doing any work. To show faith in their belief, some have killed their pigs in sacrificial offerings; others have hacked airstrips out of the bush for the planes that will bring in the cargo.'[12]

If this picture of the Johnson movement painted by *Time* is not very complimentary, an account in *Newsweek* of 9 March, was even less so. The article's title, 'Don't Eat the Candidate', conveys the tone. 'In the coastal town of Port Moresby, burly Papuan tribesmen thrust hibiscus blossoms in their hair and danced to the polls in carnival spirit. In the snow-crested mountains of the interior, helicopters dropped teams among the murderous Kukukuku warriors and the wild Nembi people – who promised not to eat any candidates.'[13]

On 22 June 1964, *Newsweek* published another article, 'What Price LBJ?' in which it tried to account for the origin of the cult. 'Almost from the moment a U.S. Air Force geodetic survey team landed on tiny New Hanover island . . . Bos Malik became the Big Man on the atoll. If the Americans needed vegetables or other goods and services, Bos was right there with prompt delivery; and in return for services rendered, he received cigarettes, Hershey bars, and other delights of the American way of life. . . . But then one day a few months ago, the Americans told Bos that they were leaving. He was shattered. "Don't worry kid", said one of the Americans. "There's plenty more where this came from. The man to talk to is Lyndon Baines Johnson, President of the U.S.A." . . . This gave Bos an idea. Bring President Johnson to the island and back would come the American goods.'

From the moment the *New York Times* first began describing the elections on 9 February, New Guinea voters in the New Ireland–New Hanover election were described as cultists whose activities were revived by the election fever. Australian Director of Native Affairs, J.K. McCarthy, was quoted as saying, 'Electoral officers come in to enroll voters. Political education teams arrive with tape recorders and movie projectors to explain voting techniques. Candidates harangue big meetings. The native concludes that something very important is about to happen.'[14] Judging from the remaining *Times* election coverage through the rest of 1964, the Australians were having a tough time trying to educate the New Guineans and bring them into the fold of the twentieth century. For instance, on 28 September the *Times* reported that the 'President Johnson cultists', 'typical of cults in the South Pacific islands, are a result of misunderstandings about foreigners' wealth and possessions. The people believe that the white man intercepts goods intended for them.'[15]

Based on these and other popular press accounts of the strange happenings off New Guinea, it was clear to readers that the simplistic natives had completely misunderstood the Western political mind. How silly it was for these savages with few morals to actually think that they could 'buy' Johnson's influence. Time and again the Johnson cultists were portrayed as 'cargo cultists', naively waiting for American freighters to dock, unload their cargo of US goods and revolutionize their lives. This was an ethnocentric assumption being made thousands of miles away in editorial offices. No effort was made to hire an anthropologist to actually go to the islands and view the cultists through the eyes of the natives. If they had, it would have almost certainly resulted in the projection of a radically different native image. When, in 1964, anthropologist Dorothy Billings of the University of Wichita decided to study the cult as part of her doctorate, she immediately became suspicious when Australian authorities refused her permission to study the group. When she finally did go, she found that the natives were far more sophisticated than they were being portrayed in the media.

The *New York Times* articles on the 1964 New Hanover election troubles are conspicuous in that they were without bylines, and portrayed the natives as irrational cultists. Billings and a companion, Nic Peterson, were the first anthropologists to go to New Hanover and study the cult. She says media reports on the cults had been simply taken from the Australian government, which had a vested interest in the election outcome and winning the war of public opinion by portraying the locals as backward: anyone acting in such an irrational manner was certainly not capable of self-rule. There was no effort to understand the events 'from the native's point of view'. In fact, during the mid-'60s the Australian authorities were keeping Westerners *out* of New Hanover. Billings was refused entry for nearly eighteen months before finally going in on her own. She now believes officials did not want outsiders to see just how poorly the New Hanoverians had been treated under the Australian administration. The Australians controlled what was being reported – and the rest of the world's media simply bought into the idea of the Johnson cult. Why were they so willing? The answer is simple – the images the Australians wanted depicted conformed with popular stereotypes of 'primitive' New Guineans. A local political event was being portrayed by the Australian government, then dispatched to the mainstream Western media, as a bizarre cult, in order to justify their continued political domination. According to Billings, acts of resistance and defiance were being portrayed as acts of craziness and irrationality.

EXOTIC POLITICAL THEATRE

The news media often portrays native peoples as simplistic caricatures and stereotypes while poking fun at their 'strange' customs and beliefs. In a twist of irony, the New Hanoverians may have had the last laugh. Once press reports of these strange goings-on had first captured Billings's attention and she decided to study the Johnson cult, she conducted fieldwork on the island, visiting numerous times from February 1967. Having gained a deep knowledge and understanding of the native's political understanding and conduct codes, she says the Johnson cult has been misportrayed through the Western media lens. Billings contends that the Johnson saga is an illustration of a complex native symbol system and that the affair was actually a form of political performance intended to embarrass the unpopular Australian government.[16] 'What made me understand that this was street theater was that when (locals) told me about buying LBJ they would laugh . . . [knowing] the Australians would be embarrassed. It was a way of expressing a demand. People who resist oppression are often thought to be crazy.'[17]

The episode corresponded with the beginnings of a separatist movement across the region as natives began voicing their desire for independence from Australian control of Papua New Guinea. During an early phase of the independence movement, a national House of Assembly was created, and on New Hanover many locals tried to elect Johnson. When Australian officials told natives that Johnson was not a candidate, some collected money for Johnson's plane ticket.[18] But how did the Americans get dragged into the drama? Billings says that in this ad-libbed drama, the Americans were already 'backstage' as they were fondly remembered on the island from the Second World War. The natives did not want cargo, but independence in the spirit of America. At its core, the cult embodied the islanders' notion of shaming. 'In the vote for Johnson, the people shamed the Australian administration for not having done a better job of developing New Hanover, while pretending that they were just following Australian orders to vote. . . .' Such 'double plays' were a common part of New Hanover life including having large public feasts for someone deemed as stingy as a way to shame them. 'Everyone knew, of course, that the gesture was one of contempt and mockery', but it was hard to prove it. Just as the islanders laughed when they told Billings of these acts of satiric generosity, she says 'they laughed when they told me about the look on the faces of the Australian patrol officers when the Lavongais [natives] innocently voted for Johnson and then quickly disappeared into the bush'.[19]

Every culture has its unique conduct codes, and the New Hanoverians were no different. They are very theatrical and enjoy play-acting. Billings observes that the New Hanover natives have a complex system of game-playing and the Johnson cult appears to have been enjoyed by the natives as a test of wits. The one exception was the jailings which were not part of the game. Billings notes that the New Hanoverians 'enjoy dramatic quarrels both as participants and as spectators'.[20] Even though participants may win or lose, the act of playing 'implies a kind of equality and intimacy between the parties. A display of anger seems to promote intimacy . . . [and] New Hanoverians seem to feel that you cannot trust a person until you have seen his anger – then you know him and are at ease. Provoking a quarrel is also a way of gaining attention.'[21] To the arrogant Western mind, such a realization was almost unthinkable in 1964.

Yet if the media had consulted with anthropologists in 1964, they may have received a different view of the Johnsonites – even from their armchairs – if the Australians had not let them go to the islands. The movement, while uniquely New Hanoverian, was part of a pattern that had been observed by anthropologists since the early part of the century. Journalists are expected to be instant experts on every topic. With the exception of reporters at a relatively small number of major newspapers or magazines, few have the time to devote to in-depth coverage of a politically insignificant group of natives in the middle of the Pacific. It's quickly on to the next story. And even so, why bother with the story, it's just a bunch of ignorant natives anyhow.[22] As a result, the misunderstanding of the Johnson cult has endured for four decades.

WILD MAN 'MADNESS' AS THEATRE IN NEW GUINEA

In the mid-1960s, anthropologists had been observing for decades a curious pattern of behaviour in New Guinea that involved similar forms of complex performance and political theatre. In parts of the Highlands, natives will on occasion suddenly appear deranged to outsiders, engaging in pseudo-aggression, bluffing and play-acting.

Dubbed the 'wild man' behaviour,[23] it has often been the subject of Western mislabelling as 'crazy', by outsiders unfamiliar with the conduct code.[24]

One form of 'wild man' acting is known as *negi-negi* among the Guramumba.[25] The 'wild man' often brandishes a weapon and appears to enter a state of uncontrollable rage against people and property. When he 'regains his senses', claims of amnesia and spirit possession deflect the attribution of blame. Those affected are typically young males who are socially and/or politically weak, grow impatient and feel aggrieved by excessive dowry stipulations from relatives of the betrothed. Performances allow for a re-negotiation of marriage compensation terms, explaining the 'disproportion between the injury threatened and actually inflicted',[26] and why natives appear composed and casual during episodes. 'Outbursts' have a distinctly soap-opera-like atmosphere. Anthropologist P.L. Newman remarks that people come from nearby villages just to watch the spectacle, and while 'spectators are prone to keep their distance because of the potential danger', they 'obviously enjoy the instances when the wild man turns on the group and chases one after another of them in erratic, and seemingly comic pursuit . . . the community can be regarded as an audience to a performance'.[27]

Australian anthropologist Marie Reay observes that among the Kuma, 'wild man' episodes never result in death or serious injury, despite threatening behaviour.[28] During October 1954, Reay was visiting the southern Wahgi Valley in the western Highlands of Papua New Guinea, when she observed an outbreak of 'mushroom madness' (known as *Komugi Taï* to the locals) after natives began eating a fungus called *nonda*.[29] Although the Kuma people eat this fungus all year, on occasion during the late dry season it appears to have hallucinogenic properties. Reay observed that 11 males and 19 females, out of a village of 313, began acting crazy. The men ran amok, decorating themselves, grabbing bows and arrows or spears, chasing people around and threatening to kill them. Curiously, many young adults and children seemed to react to the goings-on as a game, as they 'dodged behind houses and peeped out, calling the men to incite them to further violence'.[30] Women affected remained in their huts, often exhibiting fits of giggling – recounting both real and fantasized sexual escapades. Many of the women had delusions they were not married. In one case, a woman claimed a man had raped her when he obviously hadn't – only to begin flirting with him. The chaos ended after two days.

Reay suggested that the episode was an 'opportunity for social catharsis' and offered a brief chance each year to engage in behaviour that was ordinarily proscribed.[31] The *Komugi Taï*, whatever its stimulus, is highly ritualized and appears to offer natives the temporary opportunity to breach customs and mores, especially married women who are forbidden to have extramarital sexual affairs, but whose husbands regularly engage in such behaviour as part of a culture which favours males. Reay observes: 'The women feel like dancing; normally they are not permitted to dance, but they are encouraged to do so now. The behaviour of women is a symbolic regression to the . . . sexual freedom of their earlier years.' During episodes, single women encourage men to dance with them, at which point, they attempt to seduce them. In Kuma society, there is a double standard when it comes to sexual affairs. While wives are required to stay faithful to their husbands, 'he is able to enjoy a variety of sexual experience. . . . Many men go with unmarried girls and turn to their wives only when they desire children. Women frequently voice their resentment at this difference. . . .'[32]

Perplexed at what she had observed Reay wanted to find out if it was the fungus that had made the Kuma act so strangely. In 1963, two botanists, Roger Heim of France and American R. Gordon Wasson of Harvard, went to the region, met Reay, and together they gathered samples of the *nonda* mushrooms that she had identified as being consumed during the 'madness'. They later determined that the 'mushrooms – or at least most of them – do not seem to cause physiological effects leading to madness'.[33] As a result of these findings, Reay speculated that the episode was caused by 'collective hysteria'.[34] While there has been subsequent speculation that other mushrooms or nicotine poisoning from chewing tobacco leaves may account for some of this behaviour,[35] this is far from conclusive.

It also fails to explain many conspicuous acts during such temporary 'madness', including why no one is ever killed or seriously hurt.

LATAH AS THEATRE IN MALAYSIA[36]

Several hundred miles north-west of New Guinea, I (co-author Robert Bartholomew) encountered a similar display of what could be described as ritualized theatre in Malaysia and Indonesia called *latah*. In many respects this is similar to the 'wild man' acting.[37] On the surface, it seems bizarre and crazy. When startled, a few ordinarily shy, stolid Malay women seemingly go temporarily mad, shouting out vulgarities and making obscene gestures, often with outrageous sexual connotations. Some will follow their 'teaser's' every command. After the episode, which rarely lasts more than a few minutes, the woman claims amnesia and is not held accountable for her actions. Since the late nineteenth century when *latah* was first recorded by colonizing Europeans, psychiatrists and physicians have assumed it is a mental disorder reflecting the unique racial and cultural make-up of the area. Most psychiatry textbooks continue to label it as such.

But when I travelled to Malaysia and began studying *latah* among my Malay wife's relatives, I soon realized that something was amiss. What I was seeing didn't make sense. One day at a wedding party, my wife's elderly aunt Sembok was startled on purpose by her uncle. She behaved like a robot from a grade B movie, and I couldn't believe my eyes. Over the next ten minutes, Sembok began following her uncle's every command. At times she would lift her sarong in a sexually suggestive manner, blurting out the most foul obscenities. Before it was over, she had been made to dance, cry like a baby, even partially disrobe. As the drama began, people from the wedding quickly gathered around this spectacle. Other family members even joined in teasing their beloved aunt. Yet it made no sense. In Malay society, elders are treated with the utmost respect and dignity. Why would relatives humiliate and degrade their poor elderly aunt in such a cruel fashion? In Malaysia, there are many stories of persons in a *latah* state, hurting – even killing – bystanders during these 'fits'. However, the crowd seemed to relish the display, and put their young children in front of the crowd so they could get a good look – just a few feet from this 'mad woman'. The paradoxes continued a few days later when I saw Sembok cradling a small newborn baby! I was stunned. Here was a woman who, upon being accidentally or intentionally startled, was supposedly sent into temporary fits of madness during which she was dropping and throwing objects. I later found out that Sembok made a habit of attending weddings and would inevitably end up being 'startled' into 'fits'. I discovered a curious pattern. Most severe *latahs* were Malay, female, elderly, and were living reclusive lives after having lost their husbands to death or divorce. As Canadian anthropologist Michael Kenny has suggested, *latah* is not a mental disorder at all. It is a learned role – a way for lonely, depressed Malay women to attract attention.

Latah may be a local idiom that has been 'mistranslated' by outsiders – Western scientists and observers who fail to appreciate the significance of its cultural context and meaning. *Latah* seems to be the Eastern equivalent of a foreigner observing the occasional antics of North American major league baseball managers disputing umpiring decisions. Managers are renowned for kicking dirt on umpires, tossing bats, gloves and other equipment onto the field, and knocking over water coolers. Among their most dramatic actions is appearing to be about to push or strike an umpire, only to be held back by fellow players, and placing their nose as close as possible to the umpire's face without touching. In reality, just lightly bumping an umpire would result in automatic ejection and fine, and striking an umpire, especially with the intent to do serious harm – would likely result in a lifelong ban. Parents and children in Canada and the United States typically relish these displays. Neither are children shielded by their parents during these outbursts nor do they refuse to return to the ballpark fearful that the manager might, in his 'uncontrollable' rage, strike a fan. Why this doesn't occur is only obvious to those intimately familiar with baseball tradition and protocol. Many fans actually attend games hoping to see such displays by managers which serve a variety of purposes depending on the circumstances. There is a common folk belief in baseball that managers need to occasionally dispute a close call in order to get the next close call to go in your favour. Other times he may be releasing frustration during a losing streak or trying to 'fire up' the team by getting deliberately 'kicked out' of a game. Sometimes a manager appears to be genuinely upset. Other times he will rush onto the field to argue a close call that is being disputed by one of his star players in order to protect him from being thrown out. In baseball circles this is known as 'protecting a player'.

On other occasions, the manager uses the opportunity of a 'blown call' to engage in farce by playing to the crowd and offering his glasses to the umpire or pointing to a spot outside the foul line, implying that a ball ruled to have fallen in fair territory, was actually foul. Managers are among the oldest and wisest team members and know full well that an umpire almost never reverses his decision. Like *latah*, his actions are symbolic. One could imagine a psychiatrist on vacation in North America, with no knowledge of baseball, watching these managerial displays and perceiving them literally at face value as a transient culture-specific syndrome affecting managers, triggered by the stress of a close umpiring decision.[38] Nothing could be further from the truth – and to get at the truth we must understand the context and meaning of the displays. This has not occurred because the knowledge of baseball has been exported to much of the world through US-dominated mass communications: television, movies, films, and the disproportionate influence of North American psychiatrists in writing the infamous *Diagnostic and Statistical Manual of Mental Disorders* – the 'Bible' of the world psychiatric community.

Lesson: the world is far more complex than the mass media, in its superficial money-driven quest to report and inform, is capable of describing. While we cannot expect the media to do a perfect job in reporting cultural differences, they must do a better job than at present. Far from being abnormal or irrational, *latah*, 'wild man' and Johnson cultists are forms of theatrics that highlight the remarkable, adaptive, creative capacity of the human mind, that has unfortunately been oversimplified and misclassified using Western standards of what passes for normal. The media's portrayal of the

Johnson cult is a form of modern-day colonialism that justifies the suspicion of foreigners as somehow inferior or second rate. They perpetrate the myth that non-Western peoples are prone to irrationality, when in fact their behaviour is the rational outcome of unfamiliar belief systems that are a testament to human imagination and creativity in adapting to change. The media must be better educated and sensitive to non-Western ways.

We need to be concerned when Western values and norms have become the world's reporting yardstick. Most of the world's population resides outside North America and Europe. The prevalence of such intellectual arrogance continues to perpetuate Western journalistic imperialism whereby global human values and norms are evaluated by Western standards. The media should report what both sides have to say on an issue and refrain from making value judgements. Of course, this is an impossibility. Due to their social and cultural conditioning, it's impossible to be completely objective. But journalists need to be educated in history and culture. Deviance is relative. When a behaviour is labelled as 'bizarre' and 'exotic', they should ask: 'By whose social or cultural standard?' We should try to view events through the eyes of those being reported on.

The world is not black and white – though ingrained social and cultural traditions often make it appear that way. Even scientists, for all of their specialized knowledge and expertise, are no less susceptible than the man or woman on the street, to superimposing their social and cultural beliefs onto their evaluations of human behaviour. Humans cannot tolerate ambiguity, and sociocultural patterns provide local psychic stability. Over multiple generations people grow accustomed to certain views or practices which become institutionalized as normal, right, proper and moral. Over time, what comes to be accepted as right or wrong, good or bad, legal or illegal, varies greatly and includes altruism and philanthropy, Nazism and cannibalism. It is something we cannot change simply because we don't like it, no more than we can or should cut off our external sex organs just because a particular conduct code dictates so. If this sounds outlandish, it was just one hundred years ago that psychiatrists advocated clitorectomy and castration for chronic masturbators. Today masturbation is viewed as perfectly normal and healthy. It wasn't fifty years ago that prominent psychoanalysts viewed prostitution as a mental disturbance. How times change.

When you use a Western standard – which is biased towards Europe and North America – to judge the rationality of the rest of the world's people, you're going to make mistakes. The unconventional becomes redefined as bizarre, the exotic is looked upon as strange; diversity is viewed as perversity; creativity is mistaken for eccentricity; devoutness as fanaticism; and the unusual is redefined as deviant with its negative connotations. The present system is too prone to interpreter bias, popular culture, professional fad and diagnostic fashion. How then do we address these issues? To begin with, all researchers must possess a thorough knowledge and understanding of the ethnographic record. To put a 'primitive' label on the unfamiliar or distasteful is to deprive non-Western peoples of their cultural heritage, ignoring and censoring the enormously rich ethnographic record.

THE NOBLE TASADAY

Instead of ridiculing natives for their 'strange', unfamiliar ways, as happened with the Johnson cult, the other extreme is media glorification of antiquated, grandiose stereotypes of the 'primitive'. No case better exemplifies this than the sad, convoluted saga of the Tasaday. By some accounts, you'd think journalists had found the Garden of Eden. In early June 1971, Philippine officials announced a startling discovery. It was billed by some as the anthropological find of the century. We were told that during a government survey of native groups, agents had stumbled across a 'stone age' tribe living in a remote part of the southern island of Mindanao. The tribe had reportedly been cut off from outside contact for between 400 to perhaps as many as 2,000 years.

On 11 July, the *New York Times* reported on the find in which a Philippine official was quoted as saying the tribe had no knowledge of sugar, salt, tobacco, corn and rice. Even more startling, the Tasaday had no knowledge of the ocean or use of pottery.[39] If this wasn't remarkable enough, there were more surprises. That autumn, the *Times* published another article, by someone with the ironic name of John Noble Wilford, quoting Philippine officials who called for the creation of a sanctuary, warning that the Tasaday faced extermination from loggers and diseases. More revelations seeped out. It was disclosed that they were strictly hunter-gatherers, being without any knowledge of agriculture or metal. The tribespeople were described as 'friendly' but 'reluctant to talk about other groups of their tribe that might be elsewhere in the forest'.[40] *Time* magazine reported on the 'Lost Tribe of the Tasaday', noting that 'The Tasaday are a timid people, wary of strangers . . . [and] like to stand in the rain and let the water drips course down their bodies. And they enjoy the music of the *kubing* . . . made from bamboo. . . .'[41]

The Tasaday quickly became the media darlings of the civilized world, grabbing headlines during the rest of 1971 and into '72. Another *Times* article in April '72, describes them as 'a friendly, peaceful people'.[42] Four months later they graced the August cover of *National Geographic*. The article with the sexist title, 'Stone Age Cavemen of Mindanao', gushed with superlatives.[43] One caption to a picture of a father and son read: 'In naked innocence, a Tasaday boy toys with a bright bloom plucked from the wilds of a primeval Eden.'[44] It was stated that 'The Tasadays do not look on their stone tools as weapons, and have no word in their vocabulary for war.'[45] It was one of the lengthiest articles ever in the illustrious history of the magazine.

In 1975, journalist John Nance published his romanticized bestseller, *The Gentle Tasaday: A Stone Age People in the Philippine Rain Forest*. Nance, worried about outside 'contamination' from the civilized world, lauded their innocence. He wrote that the Tasaday were an important model 'for their more sophisticated fellow man. Although we could not or would not emulate them and may never extract new principles of behavior from them, we could treasure them as reminders of what was humanly possible; as inspiring emblems of social peace and harmony, of, simply, love.' Nance's descriptions of the Tasaday as innocent and angelic, untainted by civilization, was highly simplistic.

In reading Nance, one could be forgiven for thinking they were reading about life in a 1960s hippy commune. 'Their love was everywhere – for each other, for their forest, for us – for life.'[46] Manuel Elizalde, a Harvard-educated sociologist-millionaire who had been put in charge of protecting the Tasaday, once said something curious to Nance. 'For God's sake, enjoy these people. Quit trying to figure them out.'[47] It was as if Elizalde did not want the 'lost tribe' closely scrutinized. Early on in his dealings with him, even before the Tasaday issue, Nance had found Elizalde to be a publicity hound. While initially sceptical of his motives, overwhelmed by the Tasaday's charm, Elizalde's companionship, and the excitement of being part of a big story, Nance didn't seem to catch the implication of Elizalde's statement. There were red flags popping up everywhere but where were the tough media questions of Philippine officials or anthropologists who were only briefly allowed to study the Tasaday? Too infatuated by a good story and in love with the Tasaday, the media treated them with kid gloves. It was as if a doe-eyed teeny-bopper were trying to conduct an exposé on 'The Beatles'.

One red flag popped up early. Elizalde hand-picked nine scientists to camp with him near the Tasaday cave and study the tribe in March 1972. Over the next several months, Elizalde allowed numerous visits by celebrities, reporters, politicians and documentary-makers, although, oddly enough, he refused access to many qualified scientists, especially anthropologists. If he was intent on limiting cultural contamination by restricting access to other scientists, why let in amateurs? By one estimate, for every one scientist allowed in, eleven non-scientists were let in – everyone from schoolchildren to Italian actress Gina Lollobrigida and American aviation pioneer Charles Lindbergh.[48] Then Elizalde announced that the Tasaday land would be set aside as a special sanctuary, and by mid-December, on the orders of President Ferdinand Marcos, access to the tribe was forbidden on penalty of imprisonment. The Tasaday were off-limits, yet we still knew little about their world.

In 1986, the deception quickly unravelled. Amid the political turmoil and confusion that took place as support for the Marcos government crumbled, Swiss reporter Oswald Iten slipped into the sanctuary to check on the Tasaday. What he found was stunning. The 'stone age' tribe were wearing Western T-shirts and blue jeans; some admitted to faking the whole thing at Elizalde's prompting.[49] Iten had surprised the group – no one knew he was coming. Upon learning of Elizalde's departure from the country, they admitted that they were poor farmers who had lived near the caves, and Elizalde had promised them assistance for their cooperation. Iten says, 'It was not a matter of paying *actors* for a role in a difficult-to-learn Stone Age play. It was easy to get a few local tribesmen to exchange their shabby clothes for orchid leaves and have them sit around in caves or gather food (as they normally would) in the forest, all the while smuggling rice into the camp to fill their bellies.'[50] Elizalde was able to maintain the deception for a brief period by strictly controlling who came in and out, and for how long, through use of his helicopter. Most of the communication with the native population was conducted by the same interpreter.

About a week after Iten left to file his story, German reporters from *Stern* magazine arrived at the caves, only to find a very different picture. This time the 'tribe' had been warned by the journalists' guide, Dafal, who insisted on first visiting the Tasaday alone to tell them of the impending visit by outsiders. When the reporters arrived, the caves were teeming with Tasaday, but this time they were in their 'cavemen' outfits with leaves covering their private parts and looking very much as they had fourteen years earlier. The *Stern* team was unaware of Iten's recent visit, but they sensed that something was amiss. Beneath their G-strings, some of the 'lost tribe' 'were wearing colored underpants' while some women had 'orchid leaf brassieres'. There were many other inconsistencies. Most of the tribe was said to be out on their nightly hunting expeditions yet their caves were barren of any food, and the Tasaday that remained were totally reliant on the journalists' provisions. Suspiciously, when the reporters tried to leave, they were kidnapped and later released for a sizeable ransom. In the video shot by the Germans, the kidnappers spoke the Tasaday language fluently.[51]

RED FLAGS AND COLOUR BLINDNESS

With hindsight, so many obvious questions needed answering, yet no one was asking. If they were a 'lost tribe' having been isolated for up to 2,000 years, how come outsiders were able to communicate with them, admittedly with some difficulty? With such a small group – twenty-six in all – and none over the age of thirty, there were unanswered questions about the adequacy of their breeding population, diet, and tools. Anthropologists Richard Lee and Gerald Berreman note these red flags – all with 20/20 hindsight – yet reporters and scientists were blind to them prior to 1986.[52]

While supposedly living in the caves for hundreds of years – generation upon generation – they were barren of artefacts and even basic remnants of everyday Tasaday life. While it has been argued that the Tasaday routinely swept the floor clean with their crude brooms, they supposedly never had brooms until their introduction by Dafal. In fact, no buried artefacts or rubbish heaps have ever been found. This would be a situation unprecedented in human history. What stone tools they did make were of poor design and construction, being made of soft pebbles. Anthropologist Gerald Berreman was astonished by their crude construction, calling them 'amateurish tools such as seventh graders might be expected to invent in response to a classroom project'.[53] About the only task they were good for was cracking nuts – which can easily be done by picking up any old stone. Photographs were taken of more finely crafted 'heirloom tools', but later these important artefacts were conveniently lost.

It is also a stretch of credulity to believe that, before Dafal's arrival, the Tasday failed to hunt or even raise food. There is also the question of how they managed to get sufficient nutrition to sustain themselves. Several scientists were never able to account for their remarkable ability to survive on such a paltry diet. On the one hand, the Tasaday and their ancestors were so inept as to wander the same tiny area of the jungle for up to 2,000 years and locate just one type of edible tuber, when at least seven other edible varieties were plentiful throughout the area. On the other hand, we are asked to believe that this is the same group that adapted so quickly to Western life that in the course of just fifteen years, they had comfortably adjusted to their new life, donning jeans, puffing on cigarettes and living in houses. No, friends, something is seriously amiss.

Most incredible of all, the Tasaday were just a few miles – a three-hour walk – from the ocean and its virtually endless supply of food and resources. Claiming that they had been neither aware of the ocean nor had a word for it, defies belief. Over the course of several hundred years, one would think that someone would have been curious enough to have ventured the few miles needed to discover the ocean. Farming villages were also just a few miles away, yet remained undiscovered. One would think they would have seen the smoke and been curious, or that the farmers would have come into regular contact with the Tasaday, no matter how bashful, over the course of hundreds of years. Like so many other aspects of the Tasaday's strange world, such behaviour is unique in the annals of human history.

When 'discovered' in 1971, the Tasaday supposedly told Elizalde that they were one of two other kin groups living in the jungle, yet not a single member of these mysterious bands have ever been found, while there is agreement among population experts that the small number of tribe members found in 1971, twenty-six, were inadequate to maintain their numbers without outside breeding.

Then there is the bizarre episode of the 'missing boy'. One day a Tasaday boy who had always been with the 'tribe', was gone, another boy of similar age and height appearing in his place. In *The Gentle Tasaday*, Nance was baffled by the event. 'What had happened to him? Had he joined another group? Run away? Died? Been traded?'[54] Gerald Berreman has a more plausible explanation that is more consistent with the facts, an explanation that never crossed Nance's naive mind. 'I would guess that in dispatching people into the forest to pose as cavemen for the occasional batch of visitors one boy chanced to be unavailable or disinclined, and another of similar age and description seemed to whomever rounded up the cast to be a suitable substitute. Little boys, they probably reasoned, look pretty much alike to strangers.'[55]

176

While some scientists questioned whether the Tasaday were an authentic Stone Age tribe and wondered if the various claims may have been exaggerated during the early initial excitement,[56] no one prior to 1986 publicly suspected a hoax. Carlos Fernandez and Frank Lynch, for instance, wrote cautiously of their findings, implying that further ethnographic investigation was required to confirm the scant research: 'Preliminary linguistic evidence suggests that the Tasaday have been isolated from their nearest non-forest neighbours for 600 years or more. This conclusion, like the report in general, is tentative.'[57] In this report, Fernandez and Lynch had accurately contended that the Tasaday were not a 'discovery' or a lost or completely isolated tribe, 'since they were always in contact with neighbouring tribes'.[58] Yet the media was fixated on the 'lost tribe' story, and that's what they created.

In fairness to the investigating scientists, there was insufficient time to conduct a thorough analysis of the Tasaday claims – a huge red flag. In fact, the scientist who had been allowed longest access to the Tasaday was probably least likely to uncover the deception, an ethnobotanist named Douglas Yen, being more focused on plants than people. Of the few scientists who were allowed to visit the Tasaday, none spent more than two weeks with the 'tribe', and most were there for no more than four days. During these visits, very little time was available for study as visitation hours were limited and access to the tribespeople at night was forbidden. This frustrating state of affairs fostered disillusionment among the three primary investigators – Robert Fox, Frank Lynch and David Baradas, who left the project.[59]

After the hoax claims were made public in 1986, a surprising outcome was the reaction in some media quarters. In the wake of the persuasive evidence compiled by Iten, most media outlets quickly reported the story. But not all. When Iten, an accomplished journalist with a PhD in anthropology, first got wind of a possible hoax, he contacted *National Geographic*, but they telegrammed back saying they 'had no interest whatsoever in a follow-up story about the Tasaday, nor did it want to look at any of my field material'.[60] Later, in its 1988 centennial issue, after having been silent on the subject ever since the hoax claims hit the press, the *National Geographic* had to say something about the affair. After all, it had been widely discussed as one of the major anthropological finds of the century. In devoting an entire page to the Tasaday, they are described as 'arguably the most primitive people to survive into the 20th century'. It then went on to make the outrageous claim that recent hoax claims 'have been largely discredited'. What evidence did the magazine use to support this assertion? None.[61] What's puzzling is why, given the importance of the Tasaday, such a prestigious publication did not themselves send someone to visit them and try to ascertain at first hand what really had happened. This was a huge story and the subject of a major anthropological debate. *National Geographic* built its reputation on sending people into the field and steering clear of armchair research. One is left with the distinct impression that the powers that be (or were) at *National Geographic*, were embarrassed at having accepted the Tasaday claims on such meagre scientific evidence, and as often happens in scientific debates, began defending their original position despite mounting evidence to the contrary. Such acts seem based more on wishful thinking than any compelling evidence. At best, *National Geographic* officials exercised poor judgement in assessing the affair.

Iten notes that from the onset of their 'discovery', the Tasaday were at the centre of a media circus, with journalists shamelessly shedding their objectivity and integrity in order to court Elizalde's favour and take the helicopter ride back to the 'Stone Age'. The anthropological discovery of the century had turned into a mass media debacle. Everyone wanted so much to believe. A peaceful Stone Age tribe living in blissful harmony with themselves and nature: it was a perfect distraction for a weary American nation struggling to cope with widespread civil unrest and the unpopular Vietnam war. We wanted so much to believe this image that we created our own Garden of Eden. Perhaps we expect too much from journalists. Reporters are born with an 'original sin' of sorts. It's called objectivity. Blinded by culture, country, and ideology, they can never achieve true objectivity. Yet, it didn't take a rocket scientist to see the red flags. They were everywhere. Very little scientific study was actually done. Too many stipulations were put on the media. Journalists need to be more forceful in applying basic rules of evidence, and more aware of the world's diverse cultural traditions. Armed with this knowledge, it should have been clear that something was amiss, and that a deeper investigation was in order.

TEN

Protecting Ourselves from Media Manipulation

The new electronic independence re-creates the world in the image of a global village.

Marshall McLuhan[1]

In 1905, Spanish-born American philosopher George Santayana uttered the immortal words: 'Those who cannot remember the past are condemned to repeat it.' His sage warning went unheeded throughout the twentieth century which endured two devastating world wars, a global depression, countless political upheavals and financial scandals, a nuclear stand-off, and hundreds of bloody regional conflicts. The truth is, history does repeat itself. People do make the same mistakes. It's part of the human condition. As such, media manipulation will continue to occur on many levels, most notably in the form of deliberate hoaxes, inadvertent scares and biased reporting. The relatively small number of elite humans who are involved in creating or airing television and radio programmes or publishing newspapers, magazines or websites, must be responsible for their actions and held accountable when they *wilfully* engage in perpetrating malicious hoaxes. The present legal systems in Europe and America are well equipped to deal with such crimes. And make no mistake – they are crimes. While a relatively few number of spectacular hoaxes get the most publicity and interest, the greater threat is quietly lurking in the background in the form of subtle bias – both conscious and subconscious. Ultimately, it is our responsibility to educate ourselves in the history of media distortions and delusions in order to reduce their impact.

180

THE WAR OF THE WORLDS

While outright hoaxes are uncommon, they are too frequent for comfort. Take the *War of the Worlds* adaptations. There have been seven such scares since 1938, averaging more than one per decade. Each of theses scares was no coincidence. They happened because they were allowed to happen. Each was scripted to be plausible, with the inclusion of local names and places incorporated into the script. The quality of the acting and impersonations were such as to be believable. Each of these so-called 'panic' broadcasts was preceded by disclaimers. The case of WKBW in Buffalo is an extreme example. Fearing possible FCC repercussions, station officials warned listeners and local authorities for three weeks prior to the broadcast as hundreds of press releases were mailed to every police, fire and emergency response agency across eight counties in western New York, and parts of Ontario province in Canada.[2] What programme director Jeff Kaye did is known as 'cya' in the business world – 'cover your ass'. He covered it well. That he went to such lengths to do so suggests that he knew the power of the media and the risk they were taking by using live news bulletins of a supposed local disaster. The *Buffalo Evening News* even published a story on the upcoming drama. It appeared in the regular TV and radio listings. Yet even this extraordinary effort was not enough to eliminate the significant anxiety generated by the broadcast. Obviously, disclaimers don't work. They are rendered impotent by the live bulletins with local news reporters that listeners have grown to know and trust over the years.

So what's the solution? Should something be done to reduce the likelihood of more scares being triggered by future, realistic adaptations on this or other themes? Similar events seem inevitable if the history of the twentieth century is any indicator. After each of these broadcasts, there were knee-jerk reactions to impose stricter rules and regulations. At first glance, it would seem that we face future media hoaxes that, unlike *War of the Worlds*, have the potential to cause panic and social chaos on an unprecedented scale. This is especially so given the tensions that pervade the world in the early twenty-first century involving the fear of 'terror' attacks. What would happen if someone created another adaptation of the Welles drama, but instead of Martians, the invaders were terrorists bent on mayhem and destruction? How would people react? Do we risk having the streets of New York or Los Angeles looking like Quito in 1949, as riots broke out across the city when an angry mob surrounded and torched the building housing the radio station which broadcast a play describing an approaching Martian invasion? The offices of the city's oldest newspaper were destroyed, up to fifteen lives were lost and scores of residents were injured; damage totals were in the hundreds of thousands of dollars. Could something like this happen today? Only someone with an ignorance of history would answer 'No'.

What can be done to prevent future Quito-like outbreaks from happening again? Since we know that disclaimers don't work for a percentage of listeners, perhaps we can strike a balance between creativity and responsibility. Would it be that stifling to require that in the future no radio station, under any circumstances, be allowed to knowingly broadcast news reports that appear real, when in fact they are not – be they in a commercial, contest, comedy hour or drama. The loss of artistic licence is a small price to pay for our continued peace of mind in a world that continues to grow ever smaller with advances in technology. On the other hand, if we want to maintain our present freedoms, living with this risk may be the occasional price we pay for freedom and creativity on our airwaves. There are those who believe that radio hoaxes such as *War of the Worlds* offer a silver lining since they don't seem to have had any serious, negative long-term consequences. According to Justin Levine: 'People should be reminded now and then that it can be dangerous to be too reliant on the media.' He also sees a second function, to keep people on guard against media bias. 'Hoaxes for entertainment purposes can remind people to scrutinize the news in order to help defend against the biased editor or reporter who deliberately slants information in order to advance an ideological agenda. In other words, the up front and obvious nature of exposed hoaxes can serve as useful training in getting media consumers to think about disinformation which often operates on a much more subtle and subconscious level.[3]

DO WE NEED PROTECTION FROM SHOWS LIKE *GHOSTWATCH*?

Shows such as *Ghostwatch* present their own challenges. The best we can say is that it did not appear to be a malicious attempt to cause anxiety and mental trauma. Not every viewer is well-informed or sophisticated enough to figure out the fictitious nature of such programmes. Many children across Britain were unduly alarmed as two popular children's TV hosts were involved in the drama. Without a doubt, the programme caused emotional distress for thousands of British children as evidenced by the flood of parental complaints. There were even documented cases of post-traumatic stress disorder and at least one suicide. On the one hand, we need the viewers to know that certain realistic TV broadcasts are not authentic but dramatizations. But then we have the problem of people tuning in late, overlooking the disclaimer, or, alternatively, of ruining the ambience and suspense by inserting disclaimers. So how should we address the issue?

As advances in technology and mass communications continue to shrink the size of our global village, we are seeing a world where syndication is a growing concern. Never in the history of our planet can so many viewers or listeners be tuned to the same programme at the same time. What if *Ghostwatch* had been shown around the world through syndication? Many viewers may have already been familiar with its hosts from watching syndicated British TV shows, and trusted them. What if, in 1938, the *War of the Worlds* drama could have been heard around the world simultaneously? Herein lies the problem – in the future, we may have media-generated scares that are not simply limited to a single country or region. The potential chaos and disruption to everyday lives is enormous and would have to be paid for in billions of dollars in lost work and anxiety. Because of cultural differences, we could have scenarios whereby a programme broadcast simultaneously might significantly affect the inhabitants of one country but not another owing to

183

pre-existing beliefs about the topic under discussion. For instance, a realistic radio or TV programme claiming that tiny thumb-sized fairies were running about causing havoc and destruction is not likely to be taken seriously in most places. Yet, in a few parts of the world, it very well could cause mass social disruption. The populations of Malaysia and Indonesia in Southeast Asia have strong folk beliefs about the existence of tiny fairy creatures. Such a broadcast could resonate with listeners and cause anxiety and panic. There are numerous sightings of various fairy people in these countries each year. Much of their populations are certain they exist and fear them.[4] The point is, we live in a complex world. Perhaps the solution is to have worldwide media guidelines that can be agreed upon, such as placing the letter 'D' in the corner of the TV screen to indicate that the programme is a dramatization and not real. There is a need for such a system. From the longhouses of Borneo to the deserts of Mongolia, more and more remote peoples around the world have access to satellite dishes.

On the other hand, we live in a very different world from that of Orson Welles in 1938. Unlike in the 1930s, national news outlets are much more interconnected today, making the likelihood of a nationwide *War of the Worlds*-style hoax tougher to pull off.[5] Levine states: 'Most people would realize that a national catastrophe would be covered live by several media outlets simultaneously. If they heard something unusual on one station, they would eventually switch over to other sources to see if they too had interrupted their regular programming. If only one station was reporting on the phenomenon, it would likely raise suspicion. This kind of mentality in news coverage and listener scrutiny didn't exist in the 1930s because electronic news reporting was too new.'[6]

THE REAL THREAT: MEDIA MISINFORMATION

Newspaper and magazine-generated misinformation pose less of an immediate concern for creating anxiety and panic. For one thing, they lack the immediacy of radio and television. Unlike the Central Park Zoo hoax of 1874, with today's widespread availability of

184

telephone, radio, television and the internet, such claims would be readily dismissed if they were to happen again. The real threat from the print media, and this is true for every form of media – is the slow perpetration of myths and stereotypes as they relate to social and cultural assumptions about the world. In certain cases such as the Tasaday hoax and the invention of the 'Johnson cult', journalists and news agencies must guard against self-delusion and complacency. These events were created by Western arrogance in not bothering to closely check the facts. The result was to reproduce pre-existing stereotypes about native peoples. With the Tasaday, journalists wanted to believe the myth of a 'Stone Age' tribe without a translatable word for war, so much so that they deluded themselves, temporarily suspending their critical judgement. The Australian government's portrayal of the 'Johnson' tax protest movement as primitive, irrational 'cargo cultists', fits with Western stereotypes of these natives. We did not send journalists there to get the real story, we simply believed what the Australian authorities were 'feeding' us.

Journalists from around the globe must become more aware and sensitive to the vast array of beliefs, values and norms on our planet, and truly strive to report factual information to the best of their ability, regardless of which 'side' they are on. There is but one side, that of humanity. It is not a journalist's job to instil value judgements, yet it happens every day. We need to report both sides of issues. We need to move beyond reporting 'stock' stories that make every soldier on 'our' side a hero and 'theirs' a terrorist. In the war on ignorance, there are no heroes or terrorists; everyone is a loser when misinformation is propagated. There are different points of view – points that need to be heard on both sides in order to promote a better global understanding. If we are to survive as a human race, hearing those voices and understanding each other's world view will be essential for our continued survival on this planet. And while we all know that objectivity is ultimately unattainable, it is worth striving for.

Episodes such as the great 'kissing bug' scare of 1899, the Halley's Comet panic of 1910, and the terrorism scare of 2001, were based

185

on real threats that were exaggerated by the media. The best defence against such occurrences is a good education. There *were* kissing bugs; there *was* a comet containing poison gas approaching Earth; there *were* and *are* people intent on unleashing a chemical or biological attack on the United States or Europe. But in reality, the risk of any of these events was highly unlikely and not supported by the available evidence. Yet, during each episode, the media seemed to report worst-case scenarios as likelihoods. Yes, there are insects called 'kissing bugs' and they can cause death; however, such bites in North America are uncommon and sickness and death are *extremely* rare. The real danger is from South American kissing bugs; their North American cousins are relatively harmless. As it turned out, when bug experts had time to examine the various specimens that were turned in as 'kissing bugs' that had supposedly caused serious swelling, the culprits were a variety of common bugs – everything *but* kissing bugs! Yes, Halley's Comet's tail passed through our atmosphere but it was clear that the amount of deadly cyanogen gas in the tail was minuscule. Several papers, including the *New York Times*, gave prominence to the rogue views of a handful of astronomers, causing unnecessary alarm. A good education would have also been the best defence against the 'Moon Hoax' of 1835. As Edgar Allen Poe noted at the time, there were many tell-tale flaws in the science of the stories appearing in the *Sun*, which clearly could not have been true.

OUR FUTURE GLOBAL VILLAGE

Like nuclear energy, the mass media has the potential to effect change for the improvement of humanity. It makes the world a better place by educating and informing. Yet both are double-edged swords that must be wielded with great care. Nuclear power without regulation is a recipe for Armageddon. Mass media freedoms are essential for the future prosperity of humanity. The malicious, deliberate reporting of fictitious events in order to wreak havoc – be it in the form of hoaxes, dramas or publicity stunts – is sufficiently addressed in the existing legal systems of most countries.

We don't need more rules and regulations. What we do need are journalists who are thoroughly schooled in human diversity, cross-cultural differences, and neutral political allegiance. Such tutoring will certainly not eliminate our prejudices, but should heighten reporter awareness of their nationalistic biases, reducing the capacity for skewed reporting and self-delusion. Such awareness might have reduced or eliminated the media misportrayal of the Johnson cult, the Tasaday hoax and the one-sided reporting on the Iraq war. A well-educated and informed public offers our best defence against media hoaxing.

Notes

Chapter One

1. Young, E., cited in Roberts, K.L. (compiler) (1940), *Hoyt's New Cyclopedia of Practical Quotations*. New York: Funk & Wagnalls, p. 67.
2. O'Brien, Frank M. (1918), *The Story of the* Sun. New York: George H. Doran.
3. Evans, David S. (1981), 'The Great Moon Hoax – I'. *Sky and Telescope*, September: 196–8.
4. 'CELESTIAL DISCOVERIES', *Sun* (New York), 21 August 1835: 2.
5. Schudson, Michael (1981), *Discovering the News*. New York: Basic Books, p. 15.
6. Hallett, Vicky (2002), 'Extra! Extra! Life on Moon! (Creation of Tabloid Journalism)', *US News & World Report*, 26 August: 53.
7. The quotations from the original text are taken from Mitchell, S.A. (1900), 'The Moon Hoax', *Popular Astronomy* 8(5): 256–67, where it is substantially reprinted. Unless otherwise indicated, this is the principal source of the account.
8. 'Great Astronomical Discoveries Lately Made by Sir John Herschel, L.L.D, F.R.S, &c. At The Cape of Good Hope', *Sun* (New York), 25 August 1835: 1.
9. O'Brien (1918), op. cit., p. 72.
10. 'Great Astronomical Discoveries Lately Made by Sir John Herschel . . .', op. cit., 26 August 1835.
11. 'Great Astronomical Discoveries Lately Made by Sir John Herschel . . .', op. cit., 27 August 1835.
12. 'Great Astronomical Discoveries Lately Made by Sir John Herschel . . .', op. cit., 28 August 1835.
13. 'Great Astronomical Discoveries Lately Made by Sir John Herschel . . .', op. cit., 28 August 1835.
14. 'Great Astronomical Discoveries Lately Made by Sir John Herschel . . .', op. cit., 29 August 1835.
15. 'Great Astronomical Discoveries Lately Made by Sir John Herschel . . .', op. cit., 31 August 1835.
16. 'Great Astronomical Discoveries Lately Made by Sir John Herschel . . .', op. cit., 31 August 1835.
17. Evans, David S. (1981), 'The Great Moon Hoax – II', *Sky and Telescope*, October: 308–11, see p. 310; O'Brien (1918), op. cit., p. 85.

18. Hallett (2002), op. cit.

19. Bulgatz, Joseph (1992), *Ponzi Schemes, Invaders from Mars and More Extraordinary Popular Delusions and the Madness of Crowds*. New York: Harmony Books, p. 150.

20. Bulgatz, op. cit., p. 150.

21. Martineau, Harriet, *Retrospect of Western Travel*, quoted by MacDougall, Curtis (1940), *Hoaxes*. New York: Macmillan, p. 230.

22. Poe, Edgar Allan (1848), 'Richard Adams Locke', unpublished manuscript intended for publication in literary America. Poe abandoned the manuscript for uncertain reasons. Source: The Edgar Allen Poe Society of Baltimore, Maryland. Accessed 1 October 2003 at: http://www.eapoe.org/works/index.htm.

23. Poe (1848), op. cit.

24. Anonymous (1853), 'Locke Among the Moonlings', *Southern Quarterly Review* 24: 510–14, see p. 502.

25. Quotations from these various newspapers can be found in Locke, Richard Adams (1859), *A Discovery that the Moon has a Vast Population of Human Beings*. New York: pp. 60–1; O'Brien (1918), op. cit., pp. 75–6.

26. Museum of Hoaxes internet website: www.museumofhoaxes.com/moonhoax.

27. O'Brien (1918), op. cit., pp. 82–3.

28. Museum of Hoaxes, op. cit.

29. Anonymous (1853), op. cit., p. 504.

30. Crowe, Michael J.T. (1986), *The Extraterrestrial Life Debate 1750–1900*. Cambridge: Cambridge University Press, pp. 202–15.

31. Hering, Daniel W. (1924), *Foibles and Fallacies of Science*. London: Routledge, p. 202.

32. Hering (1924), op. cit., p. 205.

33. Museum of Hoaxes, op. cit.

34. Hallett (2002), op. cit.

35. Poe, Edgar Allan (1844), 'Doings of Gotham – Letter IV'. *The Columbia Spy* (Columbia, Pennsylvania), 8 June 1844; accessed online from the Edgar Allan Poe Society of Baltimore: http://www.eapoe.org/works/misc/gothamb4.htm.

36. Poe (1844), op. cit.

Chapter Two

1. Thomas, William Isaac (1932), *The Child in America*. New York: Alfred Knopf, p. 572.

2. Littmann, Mark, and Yeomans, Donald K. (1985), *Comet Halley: Once in a Lifetime*. Washington, DC: American Chemical Society, p. 27.

3. Halley's Comet takes a different orbit during every fly-by. For one thing, it loses mass every time it passes near the Sun and produces a tail. The

changing positions of the planets, especially Jupiter and Saturn, also create variations as they alter the comet's trajectory. Its appearance has varied from 74.4 years between 1835 and 1910, to as long as 79.6 years from AD 451 to 530. See Lipanovic, Zeljko, 'Comets'. Accessed 4 August 2003 at: http://www.geocities.com/zlipanov/comets/comets.html.

4. Yeomans, Donald K. (1991), *Comets: A Chronological History of Observation, Science, Myth, and Folklore*. New York: John Wiley, p. 207.
5. Littmann and Yeomans (1985), op. cit., p. 37.
6. Littmann and Yeomans (1985), op. cit., pp. 38–9; Burnham, Robert (2000), *Great Comets*. Cambridge: Cambridge University Press, p. 72.
7. 'Science Web: Explorations in Science and Technology', accessed 4 August 2003 at: http://www.scienceweb.org/comet.html.
8. Shuman, James, and Galdrikian, Edward (2003), *Historical Outline of American Journalism*. The Journalism Education Association of Northern California. Accessed 31 July 2003 at: http://www.jeanc.org/histoutline.html.
9. Mott, Frank Luther (1965). *American Journalism: A History: 1690–1960*. New York: Macmillan, p. 600.
10. Burnham (2000), op. cit., p. 183.
11. Asimov, Isaac (1985), *Asimov's Guide to Halley's Comet*. New York: Walker and Company, p. 59.
12. Burnham (2000), op. cit., pp. 62, 65–6, 70–2, 184; Brown, Peter Lancaster (1985), *Halley and His Comet*. New York: Blandford Press, pp. 123–4.
13. Burnham (2000), op. cit., p. 184.
14. 'Comet's Poisonous Tail. Yerkes Observatory Finds Cyanogen in Spectrum of Halley's Comet'. *New York Times*, 7 February 1910, p. 1.
15. 'Comet's Poisonous Tail', op. cit.
16. Flaste, Richard, Noble, Holcomb, Sullivan, Walter, and Wilford, John Noble (1985), *The New York Times Guide to the Return of Halley's Comet*. New York: Times Books, p. 68.
17. 'No Danger From Comet', *New York Times*, 10 February 1910, p. 1.
18. 'Poison in the Tail of a Comet' [Editorial], *New York Times*, 11 February 1910, p. 10.
19. Asimov (1985), op. cit., p. 59.
20. Burnham (2000), op. cit., p. 184.
21. 'Discuss Halley's Comet', *Washington Post*, 6 February 1910, p. 15.
22. 'Discuss Halley's Comet', op. cit.
23. 'Comet Quits its Path', *Washington Post*, 11 May 1910, p. 1.
24. McAdam, D.J. (1910), 'The Menace in the Skies: I. The Case for the Comet', *Harper's Weekly* 54: 11–12 (14 May), see p. 12.
25. Jacoby, Harold (1910), 'The Menace in the Skies: II. The Case for the Earth', *Harper's Weekly* 54: 12, 30 (14 May), see p. 12.
26. 'Comet on its Way', *Washington Post*, 17 May 1910, p. 3.

27. Klein, Jerry (1960), 'When Halley's Comet Bemused the World', *New York Times Magazine* (8 May): 45, 57, 60, 62, see p. 57.
28. Klein (1960), op. cit., p. 57.
29. Klein (1960), op. cit., p. 45.
30. Klein (1960), op. cit., p. 45.
31. 'Ephemeris of Halley's Comet', *Scientific American* 102: 143 (12 February 1910); 'Measures of Halley's Comet', *Scientific American* 102: 162 (19 February 1910); Lynch, J.K. (1910), 'Halley's Comet – A Model of its Orbit', *Scientific American* 102: 359 (30 April).
32. Russell, Morris (1910), 'Halley's Comet and its Brightness', *Scientific American* 102: 317–18 (16 April), see p. 318.
33. 'The Comet to be Good in Passing', *Glens Falls Daily Times* (Glens Falls, New York), 16 May 1910, p. 1.
34. Harpur, Brian (1985), *The Official Halley's Comet Book*. London: Hodder & Stoughton, pp. 44, 46.
35. Harpur (1985), op. cit., p. 51; Flaste et al. (1985), op. cit., p. 75.
36. Flaste et al. (1985), op. cit., p. 75.
37. Harpur (1985), op. cit., pp. 49–50.
38. Harpur (1985), op. cit., p. 56.
39. Harpur (1985), op. cit., p. 57; Littmann and Yeomans (1985), op. cit., pp. 48–50.
40. Littmann and Yeomans (1985), op. cit., p. 51.
41. Littmann and Yeomans (1985), op. cit., p. 41.
42. *Washington Post*, 23 May 1910: 1.
43. Littmann and Yeomans (1985), op. cit., p. 41.
44. 'Some Driven to Suicide', *New York Times*, 19 February 1910: 1.
45. 'Misses Comet; Takes Life', *Washington Post*, 20 May 1910: 5.
46. Harpur (1985), op. cit., p. 43.
47. Dinsmore, Alter (1956), 'Comets and People', *Griffith Observer* 20 (7): 82. Published by the Griffith Observatory, 2800 East Observatory Road, Los Angeles, California.
48. Harpur (1985), op. cit., pp. 51–2.
49. Flaste et al. (1985), op. cit., pp. 63–4.
50. 'Pills for Comet Ills . . . Comet Scare in New York Trolley Car . . .', *Washington Post*, 17 May 1910: 3.
51. Flaste et al. (1985), op. cit., p. 63.
52. Flaste et al. (1985), op. cit., p. 63.
53. Sagan, Carl (1985), *Cosmos*. New York: Ballantine Books, p. 140.
54. 'Mysterious Missile Falls', *New York Times*, 19 February 1910: 1.
55. 'Thunder Scares Boston', *New York Times*, 19 February 1910: 1.
56. Moore, Patrick, and Mason, John (1984), *The Return of Halley's Comet*. New York: W.W. Norton, p. 71; Flaste et al. (1985), p. 61.

57. Huestis, David, 'Stardust Memories: Frank E. Seagrave and Halley's Comet'. Published by Skyscrapers, Inc., Amateur Astronomical Society of Rhode Island. Accessed 1 August 2003 at:
http://www.theskyscrapers.org/contentmgr/showdetails.php/id/471.

58. Gropman, Donald (1985), *Comet Fever*. New York: Simon & Schuster, p. 123.

59. 'Southern Negroes in a Comet Frenzy', *New York Times*, 19 February 1910: 1.

60. 'Comet Jerusalem's Omen', *Washington Post*, 11 May 1910: 1.

61. 'Miners Refuse to Work', *New York Times*, 19 February 1910: 1.

62. 'Miners Refuse to Work', op. cit., p. 1.

63. Littmann and Yeomans (1985), op. cit., p. 43; Flaste et al. (1985), op. cit., p. 58.

64. 'Comet Watcher Gets Wet', *Washington Post*, 20 May 1910: 5.

65. Harpur (1985), op. cit., pp. 54–5.

66. Sagan, Carl, and Druyan, Ann (1985), *Comet*. New York: Random House, p. 140.

67. 'Pope Not Impressed by Halley's Comet', *New York Times*, 29 May 1910: 2.

68. 'Parisians Feared Comet Would Kill', *New York Times*, 22 May 1910: 3.

69. Harpur (1985), op. cit., pp. 48–9.

70. 'Miners Refuse to Work', op. cit., p. 1.

71. Sagan and Druyan, op, cit., p. 140.

72. 'Night Services in Russia', *New York Times*, 19 February 1910: 1.

73. 'Alarm on the Rand', *New York Times*, 19 February 1910: 1.

74. Flaste et al. (1985), op. cit., p. 80.

75. 'Porto Ricans Confess', *New York Times*, 19 February 1910: 1.

76. 'Mexicans Pray, Then Dance', *New York Times*, 19 February 1910: 1.

77. Gropman (1985), op. cit., pp. 128–9.

78. 'Berlin Comet Picnics', *New York Times*, 19 February 1910: 1.

79. 'Rush to Alpine Heights', *New York Times*, 19 February 1910: 1.

80. Gropman (1985), op. cit., pp. 119–20.

81. 'Fear in Constantinople', *New York Times*, 20 May 1910: 2.

82. Flaste et al. (1985), op. cit., p. 75.

83. Jaroff, Leon (1997), 'The Man Who Spread the Myth', *Time* (14 April) 149 (15): 46; Genoni, Thomas C. Jr (1997), 'Art Bell, Heaven's Gate, and Journalistic Integrity' (UFO trailing the Comet Hale-Bopp myth perpetrated by radio talk show host Art Bell), *The Skeptical Inquirer* 21 (4): 22–3.

84. Locke, Michelle (1997), *South Bend Tribune*, 31 March: 1.

85. Hoffmann, Bill, and Burke, Cathy (1997), *Heaven's Gate: Cult Suicide in San Diego*. New York: HarperCollins.

86. Steel, Ronald (1997), 'Ordinary People. Heaven's Gate Suicides', *New Republic* 216 (16): 25 (21 April).

87. Flaste et al. (1985), op. cit., p. 68.

Chapter Three

1. Brady, Frank (1989), *Citizen Welles: A Biography of Orson Welles*. New York: Charles Scribner's Sons, p. 168.
2. Cantril, Hadley, Gaudet, Hazel, and Herzog, Herta (1940), *The Invasion From Mars: A Study in the Psychology of Panic*. New Jersey: Princeton University Press, p. 4.
3. Cantril et al. (1940), op. cit., p. 5.
4. Cantril et al. (1940), op. cit., p. 6.
5. Cantril et al. (1940), op. cit., pp. 6–11.
6. Uncut version of the original broadcast of Orson Welles's radio adaptation of H.G. Wells's novel, *The War of the Worlds*. Distributed by Metacom Incorporated.
7. Cantril et al. (1940), op. cit., pp. 18–19.
8. Cantril et al. (1940), op. cit., p. 30.
9. Cantril et al. (1940), op. cit., p. 31.
10. Brady (1989), op. cit., pp. 169–70.
11. Leaming, Barbara (1986), *Orson Welles: A Biography*. New York: Penguin, p. 198.
12. Leaming (1986), op. cit., p. 193. See also Johnston, Alva, and Smith, Fred (2002), 'How to Raise a Child: The Education of Orson Welles, Who Didn't Need it', pp. 11–23, in *Orson Welles Interviews* (Mark W. Estrin, editor). Jackson, Mississippi: University of Mississippi Press, p. 14; Brady (1989), op cit., pp. 169–70.
13. Cantril et al. (1940), op. cit., p. 77.
14. 'FCC to Scan Script of "War" Broadcast', *New York Times*, 1 November 1938: L26.
15. Welles, Orson and Bogdanovich, Peter (1992), *This Is Orson Welles*. New York: HarperCollins. The book, edited by Jonathan Rosenbaum, comprises revealing interviews between Welles and his close friend Peter Bogdanovich over a fifteen-year period, and was published after Welles's death in 1985, pp. 18–19.
16. Brady (1989), op. cit., p. 167.
17. No title. *New York Times*, 31 October 1938: 4.
18. Cantril et al. (1940), op. cit., pp. 42–3.
19. 'Radio Listeners in Panic, Taking War Drama as Fact'. *New York Times*, 31 October 1938: 4.
20. Houseman, John (1948), 'The Men From Mars', *Harper's Magazine* (December): 74–82; Cantril et al. (1940), op. cit., p. 54.
21. 'Hoax Spreads Terror Here', *Trenton Evening Times*, 31 October 1938: 1.
22. Marvin, Scott (1975), 'The Halloween Radio Spoof that Shook a Nation', *Parade* (29 October): 4–5.
23. Hoax Spreads Terror Here', op. cit., p. 1.

24. 'Hoax Spreads Terror Here', op. cit., p. 1.

25. 'Radio Listeners in Panic, Taking War Drama as Fact', op. cit., p. 4.

26. 'Boo!' *Time,* 7 November 1938: 40.

27. 'Scare is Nation-wide', *New York Times,* 31 October 1938: 4.

28. 'Geologists at Princeton Hunt "Meteor" in Vain', *New York Times,* 31 October 1938: 4.

29. Photocopy of the actual police log. Accessed at: http://www.war-ofthe-worlds.co.uk/.

30. 'Scare is Nation-wide', op. cit.

31. 'Nasty Monsters from Mars Give Radio Listeners Uneasy Moments', *Nebraska State Journal,* 31 October 1938: 1.

32. 'Scare is Nation-wide', op. cit.

33. 'Scare is Nation-wide', op. cit.

34. 'Women Faint as Lights Go Out at Concrete', *Seattle Post-Intelligencer,* 31 October 1938: 1; 'Radio "Invasion" Throws Listeners into Hysteria', *Seattle Post-Intelligencer,* 31 October 1938: 1, 2.

35. 'Scare is Nation-wide', op. cit.

36. 'Hoax Spreads Terror Here', op. cit., p. 1.

37. Markush, R.E. (1973), 'Mental Epidemics: A Review of the Old to Prepare for the New', *Public Health Reviews* 2: 353–442, see p. 379.

38. Scott (1975), op. cit., p. 5.

39. 'Scare is Nation-wide', op. cit.

40. 'Radio War Drama Creates a Panic', *New York Times,* 31 October 1938: 4.

41. 'Hoax Spreads Terror Here', op. cit., p. 1.

42. Cantril et al. (1940), op. cit., p. 181.

43. Cantril et al. (1940), op. cit., p. 55.

44. Cantril et al. (1940), op. cit., p. 93.

45. Cantril et al. (1940), op. cit., p. 93.

46. 'Even Author H.G. Wells Was Deeply Perturbed', *Trenton Evening News,* 31 October 1938: 1.

47. 'Mars Monsters Broadcast Will Not Be Repeated. Perpetrators of the Innovation Regret Causing of Public Alarm', Associated Press report, 1 November 1938. Accessed 8 August 2003 at: http://www.war-of-the-worlds.org/Radio/Newspapers/Nov01/No-Repeat.html.

48. 'Probe on as Protests Mark Program that Spread Panic', *Trenton Evening Times,* 31 October 1938: 2.

49. 'Probe on as Protests Mark Program that Spread Panic', op. cit., p. 2.

50. Levine, Justin (1999), 'History and Analysis of the Federal Communications Commission's Response to Radio Broadcast Hoaxes', *Federal Communications Law Journal* 52 (2): 274–320, see p. 280.

51. Levine (1999), op. cit., p. 280.

52. Levine (1999), op. cit., p. 286.

53. Levine (1999), op. cit., p. 286.

54. 'Canada to Take No Action', *Report from the Canadian Press Association*, 31 October 1938.

55. Cantril et al. (1940), op. cit., pp. 55–8.

56. Milio, James, Peltier, Melissa Jo, and Hufnail, Mark (producers) (1998), 'Martian Mania: The True Story of the War of the Worlds' (hosted by James Cameron). First aired on the Science Fiction Channel, USA, 30 October.

57. Bainbridge, William (1987), 'Collective Behavior and Social Movements', pp. 544–76, in Rodney Stark (ed.), *Sociology*. Belmont, California: Wadsworth.

58. Miller (1985), op. cit., p. 100; Naremore, James (1978), *The Magic World of Orson Welles*. New York: Oxford University Press.

59. Miller (1985), op. cit., p. 107.

60. Goode, Erich (1992), *Collective Behavior*. New York: Harcourt Brace Jovanovich, p. 315.

61. Brady (1989), op. cit., p. 176; Crook, Timothy, 'The Psychological Impact of Radio'. Accessed at http://www.irdp.co.uk/hoax.html.

62. Higham, Charles (1985), *Orson Welles: The Rise and Fall of an American Genius*. New York: St Martin's Press, p. 128.

63. 'Boo!' *Time*, 7 November 1938: 40.

64. Levine (1999), op. cit., p. 278.

65. Crook, op. cit.

66. Levine (1999), op. cit., p. 278.

67. Higham (1985), op. cit., p. 128.

68. Letter from Keay Davidson to Robert Bartholomew dated 12 December 2002. Davidson is the science writer for the *San Francisco Chronicle*.

69. Michell, John, and Rickard, Robert (2000), *Unexplained Phenomena: A Rough Guide Special*. Shorts Gardens, London: Rough Guides, p. 104.

70. Transcript of remarks by Senator Christopher J. Dodd, Vice Chair, 'Committee on the Year 2000 (Y2K) Technology Problem' before the National Press Club, Wednesday, 8 September 1999. Full transcript available at http://www.senate.gov/~y2k/speeches/dodd 990908.htm.

71. Callow, Simon (1996), *Orson Welles: The Road to Xanadu*. New York: Viking, p. 400.

72. Cantril et al. (1940), op. cit., p. 160. Italics in original.

73. Levine (1999), op. cit., p. 275.

74. Levine (1999), op. cit., p. 275.

75. Fettmann, Eric (1988), '"The Martians Have Landed!" In Radio Show 60 Years Ago, America Lost its Innocence', *New York Post*, 28 October 1988: 41.

76. Leaming (1986), op. cit., p. 198

77. Welles and Bogdanovich (1985), op. cit., p. 20.

Chapter Four

1. 'Those Men from Mars', *Newsweek,* 27 November 1944, p. 89.
2. 'Those Men from Mars', op. cit.
3. Bulgatz (1992), op. cit., p. 137.
4. 'Those Men from Mars', op. cit.
5. 'Those Men from Mars', op. cit.
6. 'Mars Raiders Caused Quito Panic; Mob Burns Radio Plant, Kills 15', *New York Times*, 14 February 1949: 1, 7. Quote appears on p. 1.
7. 'Mars Raiders Caused Quito Panic . . .', op. cit.
8. 'Mars Raiders Caused Quito Panic . . .', op. cit.
9. 'Wolf, Wolf', *Newsweek* 33 (8), 21 February 1949, p. 44.
10. 'Martians and Wild Animals', *Time* (21 February 1949), p. 46.
11. 'Invasion From Mars', *The Times* (London) 14 February 1949: 4; Anonymous, 'When You Say That, Smile', *Commonweal* XLIX, no. 20, pp. 483–4.
12. 'Two Officials Indicted', *The Times* (London), 15 February 1949: 4. Associated Press report.
13. 'Jittery World', *Portland Press Herald* (Portland, Maine), 15 February 1949.
14. 'Two Officials Indicted', op. cit.
15. 'Mars Raiders Caused Quito Panic . . .', op. cit.
16. 'Mars Raiders Caused Quito Panic . . .', op. cit.
17. Tovar, Enrique (1996), 'The Martians Cause Panic', *La Nación*, 3 March 1996.
18. '20 Dead in Quito Riot', *New York Times*, 15 February 1949: 5; Anonymous (1949), 'Quito Holds 3 for "Mars" Script', *New York Times*, 16 February: 15; '"Mars Invasion" Radio Program Costs 15 Lives', *Gettysburg Times* (Gettysburg, Pennsylvania), 15 February 1949.
19. 'Two Officials Indicted', op. cit.
20. 'Quito Holds 3 for "Mars" Script', op. cit.
21. Personal communication from Robert Koshinski to Robert Bartholomew dated 29 December 2002, containing a description of the 1968 WKBW broadcast based on interviews with station personnel and having heard the original airing in 1968. Mr Koshinski's information was originally published in the newsletter of the Buffalo Radio Pioneers. It is entitled: 'WKBW and the War of the Worlds'.
22. Telephone interview between Jefferson Kaye and Robert Bartholomew on 31 December 2002.
23. Telephone interview with Jefferson Kaye, op. cit.
24. Koshinski, op. cit.
25. Telephone interview with Jefferson Kaye, op. cit.
26. Koshinski, op. cit.; telephone interview with John Zach, op. cit.
27. Excerpt from WKBW's 1971 *War of the Worlds* radio broadcast, slightly modified by Jefferson Kaye from the original 1968 broadcast.

Notes

28. Recording of the original 1968 *War of the Worlds* broadcast on WKBW, op. cit.
29. Koshinski, op. cit.
30. Telephone interview with Jefferson Kaye, op. cit.
31. Telephone interview with Jefferson Kaye, op. cit.
32. Untitled. *Buffalo Evening News*, 1 November 1968: 34.
33. Telephone interview with Jefferson Kaye, op. cit.
34. Telephone interview with Jefferson Kaye, op. cit.
35. Holmsten, Brian, and Lubertozzi, Alex (eds) (2001), *The Complete War of the Worlds: Mars' Invasion of Earth from Orson Wells to H.G. Wells.* Naperville, Illinois: Sourcebooks Inc., p. 77.
36. Koshinski, op. cit.
37. Telephone interview with Jefferson Kaye, op. cit.
38. Telephone interview with Jefferson Kaye, op. cit.; telephone interview with John Zach, op. cit.
39. Schlaerth, J. Don (1968), 'Airwaves go Spooky in Halloween Spirit', *Buffalo Evening News*, 31 October 1968: 50.
40. Excerpt from WKBW's 1971 *War of the Worlds* radio broadcast, slightly modified by Jefferson Kaye from the original 1968 broadcast.
41. Telephone interview with Jefferson Kaye, op. cit.
42. Koshinski, op. cit.
43. Telephone interview between Holland Cooke and Robert Bartholomew on 2 January 2003. Mr Cook is a talk radio consultant living in Block Island, Rhode Island. Holland Cooke is his stage name; his real name is Robert Cooke.
44. Reid, David (1974), '"Halloween Hoax" Broadcast by WPRO is Studied by FCC', *Evening Journal-Bulletin* (Providence, Rhode Island), 31 October 1974: B8.
45. Levine (1999), op. cit., p. 288.
46. 'Broadcast Jams Police Switchboards', *Evening Journal-Bulletin* (Providence, Rhode Island), 31 October 1974: A1.
47. Levine (1999), op. cit., p. 288.
48. 'Broadcast Jams Police Switchboards', op. cit.
49. Levine (1999), op. cit., p. 288.
50. 'Broadcast Jams Police Switchboards', op. cit.
51. Reid (1974), op. cit.
52. Reid (1974), op. cit., B8; 'Broadcast Jams Police Switchboards', op. cit.
53. 'Broadcast Jams Police Switchboards', op. cit.
54. Reid (1974), op. cit.
55. Levine (1999), op. cit., p. 289.
56. Levine (1999), op. cit., p. 288.
57. Telephone interview with Holland Cooke, op. cit.
58. Telephone interview with Holland Cooke, op. cit.

59. 'Radio Hoaxes Must Carry Warnings' [Editorial], *Evening Journal-Bulletin* (Providence, Rhode Island), 3 November 1974: F16.

60. 'A 50th Anniversary Recreation', *Post-Star* (Glens Falls, New York), 31 October 1988: 2.

61. 'Revised Welles' Show Panics Area in Portugal', *Arizona Daily Star* (Tucson), 31 October 1988.

62. Dispatch in French from l'Agence France Presse, 31 October 1988.

63. Knox, Richard A. (1930), *Essays in Satire*. New York: E.P. Dutton, p. 285.

64. 'Britain is Alarmed by Burlesque Radio "News" of Revolt in London and Bombing of Commons', *New York Times*, 18 January 1926: 3.

65. Knox, Ronald A. (1950), *Enthusiasm: A Chapter in the History of Religion*. London: Oxford University Press.

66. Cantril et al. (1940), op. cit., xi-xii; 'Britain is Alarmed by Burlesque Radio "News" . . .' op. cit., p. 3.

67. Knox (1930), op. cit., p. 281.

68. 'We Are Safe from Such Jesting', *New York Times*, 19 January 1926: 26.

Chapter Five

1. Tripp, Rhoda Thomas (compiler) (1970), *The International Thesaurus of Quotations*. New York: Thomas Y. Crowell, p. 445.

2. Sifakis, Carl (1993), *Hoaxes and Scams: A Compendium of Deceptions, Ruses and Swindles*. New York: Facts on File, p. 283.

3. Sifakis (1993), op. cit., p. 283.

4. 'Practical Jokes' [Editorial], *New York Times*, 10 November 1874: 4.

5. 'Practical Jokes', op. cit., p. 4.

6. Figures were for 2002, obtained from the Seattle Biomedical Research Institute, 4 Nickerson Street, Suite 200, Seattle, Washington. Refer to: http://www.sbri.org/Mission/disease/Chagas.asp.

7. Eaton, Eric (2003), 'Amazing Assassins'. Missouri Conservationist online 64 (6) (June 2003). Accessed 14 July 2003 at: http://www.conservation.state.mo.us/conmag/2003/06/50.htm.

8. Howard, Leland O. (1899). 'Spider Bites and "Kissing Bugs"', *Popular Science Monthly* 56 (November): 31–42, see p. 34.

9. McElhone, James F. (1899), 'Bite of a Strange Bug', *Washington Post*, 20 June.

10. Howard (1899), op. cit., p. 34.

11. *The Audubon County Journal* (Exira, Iowa), 20 July 1899. Accessed at http://metc.net/jwalker/calendar/humannature.html.

12. 'More "Kissing Bug" Victims', *New York Times*, 2 July 1899: 2.

13. '"Kissing Bugs" at Seaside', *New York Times*, 4 July 1899: 1.

14. '"Victims" of "Kissing Bug"', *New York Times*, 11 July 1899: 4.

15. 'The Kissing Bug at Newport', *New York Times*, 20 July 1899: 7.

16. Howard (1899), op. cit., p. 34. Italics in original.
17. W.J.F. (1899). [Editorial] *Entomological News* 10 (September): 205–6.
18. 'Captured a Kissing Bug', *Fort Wayne Evening Sentinel* (Indiana), 19 July 1899.
19. 'The Kissing Bug', *Brooklyn Eagle*, 17 July 1899.
20. 'The Kissing Bug', op. cit.
21. Murray-Aaron, Eugene (1899), 'The Kissing Bug Scare', *Scientific American* (new series) 81 (22 July): 54.
22. 'Weird Tales of Kissing Bug', *Chicago Daily Tribune*, 11 July 1899: 2.
23. 'Latest in Kissing Bugs', *Brooklyn Eagle*, 14 July 1899: 1.
24. 'Bug Kissed His Toe', *Fort Wayne News* (Indiana), 21 July 1899.
25. 'Caught a "Kissing Bug"', *Trenton Times* (New Jersey), 11 July 1899.
26. 'Died of a Kissing Bug's Bite', *Naugatuck Daily News* (Naugatuck, Connecticut), 19 July 1899.
27. 'The Kissing Bug', *Fort Wayne Sentinel* (Indiana), 13 July 1899, citing the *Washington Star*.
28. Howard (1899), op. cit., p. 34.
29. Gloyne, Harold F. (1950), 'Tarantism: Mass Hysterical Reaction to Spider Bite in the Middle Ages', *American Imago* 7: 29–42, see p. 29.
30. Sigerist, Henry E. (1943), *Civilization and Disease*. Ithaca, New York: Cornell University Press, pp. 218–19.
31. Gloyne (1950), op. cit., p. 35.
32. Bartholomew, Robert E. (2000). *Exotic Deviance: Medicalizing Cultural Idioms – From Strangeness to Illness*. Boulder, CO: University Press of Colorado, p. 149.
33. Bartholomew (2000), op. cit., p. 149.
34. Australian Museum, online at: http://www.amonline.net.au/factsheets/wolf_spiders.htm. Accessed 3 March 2003.
35. Bartholomew (2000), op. cit., pp. 133–4.
36. Mora, George (1963), 'A Historical and Socio-Psychiatric Appraisal of Tarantism', *Bulletin of the History of Medicine* 37: 417–39, see p. 430. While tarantism may be both ritual and hysteria, Robert Bartholomew argues that it may be more of the former than the latter. See Bartholomew (2000), op. cit., pp. 127, 132–9, 142, 146, 149, 151.
37. Volk, Stephen (2003), 'Faking It: Ghostwatch', *Fortean Times* 166 (January).
38. Simons, D., and Silveira, W.R. (1994), 'Post-Traumatic Stress Disorder in Children after Television Programmes', *British Medical Journal* 308 (6925): 389–90.
39. Harrison, Kristen (1999), 'Tales from the Screen: Enduring Fright Reactions to Scary Media'. Republished from *Media Psychology* (Spring). Accessed 17 August 2003 at: http://www.media-awareness.ca/english/resources/research_documents/reports/violence/upload/34411_1.pdf, p. 8.
40. Harrison (1999), op. cit., p. 10.

41. Rickard, Robert (1992), 'Whatever Possessed Parkinson?', *Fortean Times* 67: 38–41.
42. Volk (2003), op. cit.
43. Newman, Kim (2003), 'Kim Newman on Ghostwatch'. A review for the British Film Institute. Accessed 17 August 2003 at: http://www.bfi.org.uk/videocat/more/ghostwatch/newman.html.
44. Green, Earl (1984), 'Without Warning'. Accessed 17 August 2003 at: http://www.thelogbook.com/movies/withoutw.html
45. Newman, op. cit.
46. Volk (2003), op. cit.
47. Rickard (1992), op. cit., p. 40.
48. Rickard (1992), op. cit., p. 40.
49. Martinez, Yleana (1993), 'A Long, Tall Texas Tale', *American Journalism Review* 15 (4): 11 (May).
50. Martinez (1993), op. cit.
51. Martinez (1993), op. cit.
52. Martinez (1993), op. cit.
53. Saint-Hilaire, Auguste de (1847), 'On the Minhocão of the Goyanes', *American Journal of Science* 2: 4; Heuvelmans, Bernard (1995), *On the Track of Unknown Animals*. London: Kegan Paul; 'Minhocão'. Accessed 23 August 2003 at: http://www.fortunecity.com/roswell/siren/552/souam_minhocao.html.

Chapter Six

1. Tripp, Rhoda Thomas (compiler) (1970), *International Thesaurus of Quotations*. New York: Thomas Y. Crowell, p. 216.
2. Cobb, Chris (1999), 'The Aftermath of Coke's Belgian Waffle', *Public Relations Antics* (September), p. 1. Accessed 20 August at: http://www.levick.com/media/news/news.49.pdf; Goddard, Sarah (1999), 'No Long-term Health Consequences Expected: Illnesses Spur Coke Recall', *Business Insurance* (21 June): 25.
3. Nemery, B., Fischler, B., Boogaerts, M., Lison, D., and Willems, J. (2002), 'The Coca-Cola Incident in Belgium, June 1999', *Food and Chemical Toxicology* 40: 1657–67, see pp. 1657–8; Gallay, A., and Demarest, S. (1999), *Case Control Study among Schoolchildren on the Incident Related to Complaints Following the Consumption of Coca-Cola Company Products, Belgium, 1999*. Scientific Institute of Public Health, Epidemiology Unit (November). Accessed 10 April 2002 at: http://www.iph.fgov.be/epidemio/epien/cocacola.htm
4. Casert, Raf (1999), 'Belgian Students Back at School as Coke Sickness Still Unexplained', Associated Press, 29 June.
5. Nemery et al. (2002), p. 1658.

6. Nemery et al. (2002), p. 1659.

7. Nemery et al. (2002), pp. 1659–60.

8. Nemery, B., Fischler, B., Boogaerts, M., and Lison, D. (1999), 'Dioxins, Coca-Cola, and Mass Sociogenic Illness in Belgium', *Lancet* 354 (9172): 77 (3 July).

9. Nemery et al. (1999), op. cit.

10. Nemery et al. (1999), op. cit.

11. 'Het Coca-Cola incident juni 1999 in België. Evaluatie van de gebeurtenissen, discussie, besluit en aanbevelingen.' Ad hoc Werkgroep van de Hoge Gezondheidsraad. Ministerie van Volksgezondheid, Brussels, March 2000. Accessed 10 April 2003 at: http://www.health.fgov.be/CSH_HGR/Nederlands/Advies/Coca-colaNl.htm

12. Anonymous (1999), 'Coke adds life, but cannot always explain it' [Editorial], *Lancet* 354 (9174): 173 (17 July); Leith, Scott (2002), 'Three Years after Recall, Coke Sales in Belgium at Their Best'. *Atlanta Journal-Constitution*, 26 August 2002.

13. 'Het Coca-Cola incident juni 1999 in België', op. cit.

14. Nemery et al. (2002), p. 1662.

15. Roughton Jr., Bert (1999), 'Coke Crisis Latest Scare in Europe's Food Hysteria', Cox News Service report issued 11 July.

16. Nemery et al. (2002), p. 1665.

17. Bernard, A., and Fierens, S. (2002), 'The Belgian PCB/Dioxin Incident: A Critical Review of Health Risks Evaluations', *International Journal of Toxicology* 21 (5): 333–40.

18. Schepens, P.J., Covaci, A., Jorens, P.G., Hens, L., Scharpe, S., and van Larebeke, N. (2001), 'Surprising Findings Following a Belgian food Contamination with Polychlorobiphenyls and Dioxins', *Environmental Health Perspectives* 109 (2): 101–3; van Larebeke, N., Hens, L., Schepens, P., Covaci, A., Baeyens, J., Everaert, K., Bernheim, J.L., Vlietinck, R., and De Poorter, G. (2001), 'The Belgian PCB and Dioxin Incident of January–June 1999: Exposure Data and Potential Impact on Health', *Environmental Health Perspectives* 109 (3): 265–73; Bester, K., de Vos, P., Le Guern, L., Harbeck, S., Hendrickx, F., Kramer, G.N., Linsinger, T., Mertens, I., Schimmel, H., Sejeroe-Olsen, B., Pauwels, J., De Poorter, G., Rimkus. G.G., and Schlabach, M. (2001), 'Preparation and Certification of a Reference Material on PCBs in Pig Fat and its Application in Quality Control in Monitoring Laboratories during the Belgian "PCB-Crisis"', *Chemosphere* 44 (4): 529–37.

19. Nemery et al. (2002), p. 1659.

20. Ridgway, Thomas (2002), *Mad Cow Disease: Bovine Spongiform Encephalopathy*. New York: Rosen, pp. 5–6.

21. NewScientist.com. 'Timeline: The Rise and Rise of BSE'. Accessed at: http://www.new scientist.com/hottopics/bse/bsetimeline.jsp.

22. Ridgway (2002), op. cit., p. 7.

23. Noble, Kate (2003), 'Whatever Happened to Mad Cow Disease?', *Time International* 162 (4): 44 (28 July).
24. Ratzan, Scott C. (1997), 'Don't be Cowed by this Disease', *Wall Street Journal*, 11 May. Accessed 4 November 2003 at:
    http://www.junkscience.com/news/madcow.html.
25. Ratzan (1997), op. cit.
26. Ridgway (2002), op. cit., pp. 14–20.

Chapter Seven

1. Robbins, Rossell Hope (1959), *The Encyclopedia of Witchcraft and Demonology.* New York: Crown Publishers, p. 180; Goode, Erich (2001), *Deviant Behavior* (6th edn). Upper Saddle River, New Jersey: Prentice-Hall, pp. 344–5.
2. Occasionally it is translated from Latin as 'The Witch Hammer', 'Hammer Against Witches' or 'Hexenhammer'.
3. Sprenger, Jakob and Kramer, Heinrich (1928 [1486]), *Malleus Maleficarum.* Translated into English by Montague Summers. London: Rodker.
4. Lea, Henry Charles (1957), *Materials Towards a History of Witchcraft.* New York: Thomas Yoseloff, 1957, vol. 1, pp. 260–416.
5. Lea (1957), op. cit., p. 339.
6. Lea (1957), op. cit., p. 336.
7. Lea (1957), op. cit., p. 338.
8. Robbins (1959), op. cit., p. 338.
9. Lea (1957), op. cit., p. 347.
10. Sprenger and Kramer (1928 [1486]), op. cit., p. 197.
11. Sprenger and Kramer (1928 [1486]), op. cit., p. 1.
12. Cohn, Norman (1974), *Europe's Inner Demons.* London: Chatto-Heinemann for Sussex University Press, pp. 211, 217.
13. Robbins (1959), op. cit., p. 180.
14. Bass, Ellen, and Davis, Laura (1988), *The Courage to Heal: A Guide for Women Survivors of Child Sexual Abuse.* New York: Harper & Row; Davis, Laura (1990), *The Courage to Heal Workbook.* New York: Harper & Row.
15. 'The Courage to Heal Debunked', online at: www.stopbadtherapy.com; Sheaffer, Robert, book review, *The Courage to Heal*, online at: www.menweb.org.
16. Davis (1990), op. cit., p. 340
17. False Memory Syndrome Foundation (1997), *Frequently Asked Questions.* Brochure published by the False Memory Syndrome Foundation, 3401 Market Street, Suite 130, Philadelphia, Pennsylvania, USA.
18. Pendergrast, Mark (1995), *Victims of Memory: Incest Accusations and Shattered Lives.* Hinesburg, Vermont: Upper Access, Inc., pp. 43–5.
19. Pendergrast (1995), op. cit., pp. 46–7.

20. Bass and Davis (1988), op. cit.

21. Pendergrast (1995), op. cit., p. 51.

22. Eberle, Paul, and Eberle, Shirley (1993), *The Abuse of Innocence*. Buffalo, New York: Prometheus Books.

23. Eberle and Eberle (1993), op. cit., p. 202.

24. Loftus, Elizabeth, and Ketcham, Katherine (1994), *The Myth of Repressed Memory: False Memories and Allegations of Sexual Abuse*. New York: St Martin's Press, p. 142.

25. Loftus and Ketcham (1994), op. cit., p. 49; Pendergrast (1995), op. cit., p. 49.

26. Pendergrast (1995), op. cit., p. 49.

27. Loftus and Ketcham (1994), op. cit., p. 143.

28. Coon, Dennis (2000), *Introduction to Psychology: Exploration and Application* (8th edn). Pacific Grove, California: Brooks/Cole Publishing, p. 343.

29. Campbell, Terence W. (1998), *Smoke and Mirrors: The Devastating Effect of False Sexual Abuse Claims*. New York: Plenum Press.

30. Loftus and Ketcham (1994), op. cit., p. 153.

31. Loftus and Ketcham (1994), op. cit., pp. 153–4.

32. Loftus and Ketcham (1994), op. cit., p. 156.

33. Loftus and Ketcham (1994), op. cit., pp. 158–64.

34. '"I Tawt I Taw" a Bunny Wabbit at Disneyland: New Evidence Shows False Memories Can Be Created', *Science Daily* News Release, University of Washington, 12 June 2001. Accessed at: http://www.sciencedaily.com/releases/2001/06/010612065657.htm.

35. Bass and Davis (1988), op. cit., p. 17.

36. Victor, J.S. (1993), *Satanic Panic: The Creation of a Contemporary Legend*. Chicago, IL: Open Court; Victor, J.S. (1991), 'The Dynamics of Rumor-Panics about Satanic Cults', pp. 221–36, in James Richardson, J. Best and D. Bromley (eds), *The Satanism Scare*. New York: Aldine de Gruyter; Hicks, R. (1990), 'Police Pursuit of Satanic Crime Part II: The Satanic Conspiracy and Urban Legends', *Skeptical Inquirer* 14: 378–89; Victor, J.S. (1989), 'A Rumor-Panic about a Dangerous Satanic Cult in Western New York', *New York Folklore* 15: 23–49.

37. Smith, Michelle, and Pazder, L. (1980), *Michelle Remembers*. New York: Congdon & Latte.

38. Pendergrast (1995), op. cit., p. 49.

39. Pendergrast (1995), op. cit., p. 49.

40. Alexander, David (1990), 'Giving the Devil More Than His Due', *Humanist* 50 (2): 5–14 (March/April). Accessed at: http://users.cybercity.dk/~ccc44406/smwane/Devildue.htm.

41. Victor, Jeffrey S. (1998), 'Social Construction of Satanic Ritual Abuse and the Creation of False Memories', pp. 191–216, in *Believed-In Imaginings: The Narrative Construction of Reality* (edited by Joseph de Rivera and

Theodore R. Sarbin). Washington, DC: American Psychological Association, p. 200.

42. Victor (1998), op. cit., p. 201.
43. Victor (1998), op. cit., pp. 201–2.
44. Victor (1998), op. cit., p. 203.
45. Victor (1998), op. cit., p. 203.
46. Victor (1998), op. cit., pp. 204–5.
47. Victor (1998), op. cit., p. 206.
48. Victor (1998), op. cit., p. 206.
49. Victor (1998), op. cit., p. 206.
50. Victor, Jeffrey S. (1992), 'The Search for Scapegoat Deviants', *Humanist* (September/October): 10–13.
51. Victor (1992), op. cit., p. 11.
52. Victor (1992), op. cit., p. 13.
53. Aldridge-Morris, Ray (1989), *Multiple Personality: An Exercise in Deception*. Hove and London: Lawrence Erlbaum, pp. 43, 108–9.
54. Ofshe, Richard, and Watters, Ethan (1995), *Making Monsters*. London: André Deutsch, p. xi.
55. Hewlett, Jennifer (1998), 'Kentucky Art Teacher was "Sybil", Scholar Confirms', Knight Ridder newspapers report, 23 December.
56. Bass and Davis (1988), op. cit., pp. 35, 37.
57. McHugh, Paul R. (1992), 'Psychiatric Misadventures', *American Scholar* 61: 4: 497 (Autumn).
58. Spanos, Nicholas P. (1996), *Multiple Identities and False Memories*. Washington, DC: American Psychological Association, p. 9.
59. Bliss, Eugene L. (1986), *Multiple Personality, Allied Disorders, and Hypnosis*. New York: Oxford University Press, p. 136.
60. S. Mulhern quoted in Spanos (1996), op. cit., p. 271.
61. Spanos (1996), op. cit., p. 108.
62. Alan E. Siegel quoted in Cohn (1974), op. cit., p. 440.
63. Freud, Sigmund (1955 [1893–95]), 'The Psychotherapy of Hysteria', in *Studies on Hysteria*, Collected Works, vol. 2. London: Hogarth Press, p. 279. Original publication in German.
64. Putnam quoted in Kluft, Richard P. (1985) (ed.), *Childhood Antecedents of Multiple Personality*. Washington, DC: American Psychiatric Press, p. ix.
65. August Piper Jr, cited in Cohen (1974), op. cit., p. 161.
66. Ofshe and Watters (1995), op. cit., p. 16.
67. Bliss (1996), op. cit., pp. 122, 124.
68. Jack Leggett, quoted in Acocella, Joan (1999), *Creating Hysteria*. San Francisco: Jossey-Bass, p. 116.
69. Pendergrast (1995), op. cit., p. 140.
70. See among others Loftus and Ketcham (1994), op. cit.; Ofshe and Watters

(1995), op. cit.; Pendergrast (1995), op. cit.; Spanos (1996), op. cit.; Victor (1993).
71. Bass and Davis (1988), op. cit., p. 22.
72. Acocella (1999), op. cit., pp. 8, 23.
73. Acocella (1999), op. cit., pp. 20–2.
74. Ofshe and Watters (1995), op. cit., p. 172.
75. Paul R. McHugh, quoted in Acocella (1999), op. cit., p. 25.

Chapter Eight

1. http://www.giga-usa.com/gigaweb1/quotes2/qutopfearx001.htm
2. *The New Collins Dictionary and Thesaurus*. London: William Collins & Sons, p. 1037.
3. Mackay, Charles (1852), *Memoirs of Extraordinary Popular Delusions and the Madness of Crowds*, vol. 2. London: Office of the National Illustrated Library, p. 264.
4. Manzoni, Alessandro (1909), *I Promessi Sposi* (The Betrothed). Published in Eliot, Charles W. (ed.), Harvard Classics, vol. XXI. New York: P.F. Collier & Son Company, 1909, p. 534.
5. Manzoni (1909), op. cit., p. 535.
6. Manzoni (1909), op. cit., p. 535.
7. Manzoni (1909), op. cit., p. 535.
8. Manzoni (1909), op. cit., p. 536.
9. Manzoni (1909), op. cit., p. 537.
10. Manzoni (1909), op. cit., p. 541.
11. Manzoni (1909), op. cit., p. 542.
12. Mackay (1852), op. cit., p. 264.
13. Johnson, Donald Max (1945), 'The "Phantom Anesthetist" of Mattoon: A Field Study of Mass Hysteria', *Journal of Abnormal Psychology* 40: 175–86.
14. Lindley, E.K. (1943), 'Thoughts on the Use of Gas in Warfare', *Newsweek* 22: 24 (20 December); Sanders, V. (1945), 'Our Army's Defense Against Poison Gas', *Popular Science* 146: 106–11 (February); Scott, E.W. (1944), 'Role of the Public Health Laboratory in Gas Defense', *American Journal of Public Health* 34: 275–8 (March).
15. Marshall, J. (1943), 'We are Ready with Gas if the Axis Turns on the Gas', *Collier's* 112: 21 (7 August).
16. Brown, F.J. (1968), *Chemical Warfare: A Study in Restraints*. Princeton, New Jersey: Princeton University Press, p. 244.
17. Taylor, L.B. and Taylor, C.L. (1985), *Chemical and Biological Warfare*. New York: Franklin Watts, pp. 23–38.
18. Brown (1968), op. cit., p. 104.

19. Kenworthy, J.M. (1930), *New Wars; New Weapons*. London: E. Matthews & Marrot; Hart, L. (1933), *The British Way of War*. New York: Macmillan; Lefebure, V. (1931), *Scientific Disarmament*. London: Mundamus; Duffield, M. (1931), *King Legion*. New York: Jonathan Cape and Harrison Smith.

20. *Ibid.*, p. 1.

21. For a partial bibliography, see Fradkin, Elvira K. (1934), *The Air Menace and the Answer*. New York: Macmillan, pp. 321–2.

22. Cantril et al. (1940), op. cit., p. 160.

23. Harris, R. and Paxman, J. (1991), *A Higher Form of Killing: The Secret Story of Chemical and Biological Warfare*. New York: Noonday Press, p. 108.

24. Anonymous (1934), The *New York Times* Index., op. cit.

25. Roosevelt, F.D. (1943), 'Statement on Poison Gas', *Current History* 4: 405 (August); Lindley, E.K. (1943), 'Thoughts on the Use of Gas in Warfare', *Newsweek* 22: 24 (20 December); Marshall, J. (1943), 'We are Ready with Gas if the Axis Turns on the Gas', *Collier's* 112: 21 (7 August); Scott, E.W. (1944), 'Role of the Public Health Laboratory in Gas Defense', *American Journal of Public Health* 34: 275–8 (March); Wood, J.R. (1944), 'Chemical Warfare: A Chemical and Toxicological Review', *American Journal of Public Health* 34: 455–60 (May); Sanders, V. (1945), 'Our Army's Defense Against Poison Gas', *Popular Science* 146: 106–11 (February).

26. Anonymous (1944), 'Should the US Use Gas?', *Time* 42: 15 (3 January).

27. Cousins, N. (1944), 'The Poison Gas Boys' [Editorial], *Saturday Review of Literature* (22 January), p. 12.

28. 'Hunt Escaped Nazi Here', *Daily Journal-Gazette*, 31 August 1944: 12. Wilhelm Zeigler was not taken into custody until the night of the first 'gassing'. He was arrested by police at a Peoria, Illinois, tavern. 'Nazi Prisoner Caught', *Daily Journal-Gazette*, 2 September 1944: 1.

29. 'Two Homes Entered', *Daily Journal-Gazette*, 31 August 1944: 12; 'Robbery Wave Continues', *Daily Journal-Gazette*, 1 September 1944: 6.

30. Reconstruction of the initial 'attack' on Mrs Kearney is taken from the following sources which include first-hand interviews by Mattoon police and Chicago psychiatrist Harold S. Hulbert. 'Anesthetic Prowler on Loose', *Daily Journal-Gazette*, 2 September 1944: 1; 'Show How They Were Gassed', *Chicago Herald-American*, 10 September 1944: 10; Alley, E., 'Illness of First Gas "Victim" Blamed for Wave of Hysteria in Mattoon', *Chicago Herald-American*, 17 September 1944: 3; 'Chicago Psychiatrist Analyzes Mattoon Gas Hysteria', *Chicago Herald-American*, 17 September 1944: 3; Johnson (1945), op. cit.

31. 'Anesthetic Prowler on Loose', op. cit., p. 1.

32. '. . . Seen by Kearney . . .', *Daily Journal-Gazette*, 2 September 1944, p. 1.

33. Johnson (1945), op. cit., p. 180.

34. 'Mattoon's Phantom "Suggestive" Fear', *Chicago Herald-American*, 21 September 1944: 2.

35. '"Anesthetic Prowler" Covers City', *Daily Journal-Gazette*, 5 September 1944: 1.
36. '"Anesthetic Prowler" Covers City', op. cit.
37. 'Mattoon's Mad Anesthetist' [Editorial], *Daily Journal-Gazette*, 8 September 1944: 2.
38. Ladendorf and Bartholomew (2002), op. cit.
39. '"Mad Gasser" Adds Six Victims! 5 Women and Boy Latest Overcome', *Daily Journal-Gazette*, 9 September 1944: 1.
40. 'Safety Agent to Aid Police in "Gas" Case', *Daily Journal-Gazette*, 6 September 1944: 6.
41. 'Chemists Trace Mattoon Mad Man's "Gardenia Gas"', *News-Gazetteer* (Champaign, IL), 9 September 1944: 3; 'Mattoon Gets Jitters from Gas Attacks', *Chicago Herald-American*, 10 September 1944: 1. '"Chasers" to be Arrested', *Daily Journal-Gazette*, 11 September 1944: 1; 'Sidelights of "Mad Gasser's" Strange Case', *Daily Journal-Gazette*, 12 September 1944: 4; 'Safety Agent to Aid Police in "Gas" Case', *Daily Journal-Gazette*, 6 September 1944: 6.
42. Johnson (1945), op. cit., p. 181.
43. Johnson (1945), op. cit., p. 181.
44. Johnson (1945), op. cit., p. 181.
45. Ballenger, C., 'Mattoon's Gas Fiend Attacks Girl, 11, in Home', *Chicago Daily Tribune*, 9 September 1944: 10.
46. 'Mattoon Gets Jitters from Gas Attacks', op. cit.
47. 'Mattoon Gets Jitters from Gas Attacks', op. cit.; '"Chasers" to be Arrested', *Daily Journal-Gazette*, 11 September 1944: 1; 'Sidelights of "Mad Gasser's" Strange Case', *Daily Journal-Gazette*, 12 September 1944: 4.
48. '"Chasers" to be Arrested', *Daily Journal-Gazette*, 11 September 1944: 1.
49. 'To All Citizens of Mattoon', *Daily Journal-Gazette*, 11 September 1944: 1.
50. 'Sidelights of "Mad Gasser's" Strange Case', *Daily Journal-Gazette*, 12 September 1944: 4.
51. '"Mad Gasser" Adds Six Victims! . . .', op. cit., p. 1.
52. '. . . Two Women Believed Victims Examined at Hospital', *Daily Journal-Gazette*, 11 September 1944: 1.
53. 'Many Prowler Reports . . .', op. cit., p. 1.
54. Ballenger, C., 'FBI at Mattoon as Gas Prowler Attacks 5 More', *Chicago Daily Tribune*, 10 September 1944: 15; 'Many Prowler Reports . . .', op. cit., p. 1.
55. '"Mad Gasser" Case Limited to 4 Suspects', *Daily Journal-Gazette*, 12 September 1944: 1.
56. Johnson (1945), op. cit., p. 177.
57. Erickson, G., 'Mad Gasser Called Myth', *Chicago Herald-American*, 13 September 1944: 1.
58. '"Gasser" Case Mistake', *Daily Journal-Gazette*, 12 September 1944: 4; 'Police Chief Says Sprayer Tales Hoax', *Illinois State Journal*, 13 September 1944: 1; '. . . Cole Amplifies Statement', *Daily Journal-Gazette*, 13 September 1944: 1.

59. '. . . Police get Two False Alarms During Night . . .', *Daily Journal-Gazette*, 13 September 1944: 1.

60. 'No Gas, Not Even Madman Seen During Night', *Daily Journal-Gazette*, 15 September 1944: 6.

61. 'No Gas, Not Even Madman Seen During Night', op. cit., p. 6.

62. 'Debunk Mattoon Gas Scare', *Chicago Herald-American*, 13 September 1944: 4; Erickson (1944), op. cit., p. 1; Alley, E. 'Illness of First Gas "Victim" Blamed for Wave of Hysteria in Mattoon', *Chicago Herald-American*, 17 September 1944: 3; 'Chicago Psychiatrist Analyzes Mattoon Gas Hysteria', *Chicago Herald-American*, 17 September 1944: 3; 'Study Terror in Mattoon', *Chicago Herald-American*, 18 September 1944: 1; Alley, E., 'Credulity Seat of Mattoon's Terror', *Chicago Herald-American*, 20 September 1944: 4; 'Mattoon's Phantom "Suggestive" Fear', *Chicago Herald-American*, 21 September 1944: 2.

63. 'The "Perfumed City" Speaks' [Editorial], *Daily Journal-Gazette*, 20 September 1944: 2.

64. Anonymous (1944), 'At Night in Mattoon', *Time*, 18 September, p. 23; 'Letter to the Editor', *Daily Journal-Gazette*, 26 September 1944: 2.

65. 'Letter to the Editor', op. cit., p. 2.

66. 'Letter to the Editor', op. cit., p. 2.

67. Bartholomew, Robert E., and Sirois, Francois (1996), 'Epidemic Hysteria in Schools: An International and Historical Overview', *Educational Studies* 22 (3): 285–311; Bartholomew, Robert E., and Sirois, Francois (2000), 'Occupational Mass Psychogenic Illness: A Transcultural Perspective', *Transcultural Psychiatry* 37 (4): 495–524.

68. Modan, Baruch, Tirosh, Moshe, Weissenberg, Emil, Acker, Cilla, Swartz, T.A., Coston, Corina, Donagi, Alexander, Revach, Moshe, and Vettorazzi, Gaston (1983), 'The Arjenyattah Epidemic', *Lancet* ii: 1472–4.

69. Hafez, A. (1985), 'The Role of the Press and the Medical Community in an Epidemic of Mysterious Gas Poisoning in the Jordan West Bank', *American Journal of Psychiatry* 142: 833–7, see pp. 834–5.

70. Modan et al. (1983), op. cit., p. 1472.

71. Modan et al. (1983), op. cit., p. 1472.

72. Hafez (1985), op. cit., p. 834.

73. Hafez (1985), op. cit., p. 834.

74. Modan et al. (1983), op. cit., pp. 1472–3.

75. Modan et al. (1983), op. cit., p. 1472.

76. Hafez (1985), op. cit., p. 834.

77. Hafez (1985), op. cit., p. 834.

78. Hafez (1985), op. cit., p. 834.

79. Hafez (1985), op. cit., p. 834.

80. Modan et al. (1983), op. cit., pp. 1472–3.

81. Modan et al. (1983), op. cit., p. 1473.

82. Modan et al. (1983), op. cit.

83. Report issued by the United Nations Educational Scientific and Cultural Organization (UNESCO) Executive Board, 13 June 1983 (116th Session) 116 EX/16 Add., Paris, 9 June 1983, Item 5.1.5 of the agenda: 'Implementation of 21 C/Resolution 14.1 Concerning Educational and Cultural Institutions in the Occupied Arab Territories: Report of the Director-General. Accessed at: http://domino.un.org/UNISPAL.NSF/0/1198eaeac7114c0585256970005642d8? Open Document.

84. Report issued by UNESCO Executive Board, 13 June 1983, op. cit.

85. Landrigan, Philip J. and Miller, Bess (1983), 'The Arjenyattah Epidemic: Home Interview Data and Toxicological Aspects', *Lancet* ii: 1474–6, see p. 1475.

86. Landrigan et al. (1983), op. cit., p. 1474.

87. Landrigan et al. (1983), op. cit., p. 1475.

88. Landrigan et al. (1983), op. cit., p. 1475.

89. Israeli, Raphael (2002), 'Poison: The Use of Blood Libel in the War Against Israel', *Jerusalem Letter* (no. 476), 15 April 2002, p. 2 of 6. Accessed at: http://www.jcpa.org/jl/vp476.htm.

90. Israeli, Raphael (2002), op. cit., p. 4 of 6.

91. Hafez (1985), op. cit., p. 836.

92. Hafez (1985), op. cit., p. 837.

93. Durbin, K. and Vogt, T. (2001), 'Fumes . . .', *Columbian*, 29 September 2001.

94. Villanueva, R.L., Payumo, M.C., and Lema, K. (2001), 'Flu Scare Sweeps Schools', *Business World* (Philippines), 3 October 2001, p. 12.

95. Lellman, L. (2001), 'Suspicious Incident Forces Subway's Closing', *Rutland Daily Herald*, 10 October, p. A3.

96. Becerra, H. and Malnic, E., 'Complaints of Dizziness Shut Down Subway', *Los Angeles Times*, 27 September 2001.

97. Center for Disease Control (2001), 'Update: Investigation of Bioterrorism-Related Anthrax – Connecticut, 2001', *Morbidity and Mortality Weekly Report*, 7 December: 50 (48), 1077–79. Accessed at: http://www.cdc.gov/od/oc/media/pressrel/r020313.htm.

98. CNN (2001), 'Special report live with Aaron Brown'. Atlanta, Georgia, 16 October 10–11p.m.

99. No authors listed (2002), 'Update: Rashes Among Schoolchildren – 27 States, October 4, 2001–June 3, 2002', *Morbidity and Mortality Weekly Report* (Center for Disease Control, Atlanta) (2002), 51 (24): 524–52) (21 June), posted on the CDC website without specific page numbers at: http://www.cdc.gov/mmwr/preview/mmwrhtml/mm5108a1.htm; no authors listed (2002), 'Rashes Among Schoolchildren – 14 States, October 4, 2001–February 27, 2002', *Morbidity and Mortality Weekly Report* (Center for Disease Control, Atlanta) 51 (8): 161–4 (1 March), posted on the CDC website without specific page

numbers at:
http://www.cdc.gov/mmwr/preview/mmwrhtml/mm5108a1.htm.

100. *Ibid.*
101. 'Rashes Among Schoolchildren – 14 States, October 4, 2001–February 27, 2002', op. cit.
102. Bartholomew, Robert E. and Radford, Benjamin (2002), 'Rash of Mysterious Rashes may be Linked to Mass Hysteria', *Skeptical Inquirer* 26 (3): 8.
103. 'Rashes Among Schoolchildren – 14 States, October 4, 2001–February 27, 2002', op. cit.
104. Rozek, Daniel (2003), 'Unexplained Itching Strikes Naperville Workers', *Chicago Sun-Times*, 24 May 2003.

Chapter Nine

1. '"President Johnson Cult" Getting New Guinea Jail', *New York Times*, 23 August 1964: 49.
2. Billings, Dorothy K. (1969), 'The Johnson Cult of New Hanover', *Oceania* 40 (1): 13–19, see p. 13.
3. Cotlow, Lewis (1966), *In Search of the Primitive*. Boston: Little, Brown and Company, p. 370.
4. 'New Guinea Cult Ends Efforts to "Buy" Johnson', *New York Times*, 9 February 1964: 15.
5. '"Johnson" Cultists Jailed; Evaded New Guinea Tax', *New York Times*, 3 August, p. 3; '64 Lyndon Johnson Cultists Arrested by Australians'. 9 August 1964: 46; '"President Johnson Cult" Getting New Guinea Jail', op. cit., p. 49.
6. 'President Johnson Cultists Vacate New Guinea Areas', *New York Times*, 28 September 1964: 29.
7. Billings (1969), op. cit., p. 13.
8. Billings (1969), op. cit., p. 14.
9. 'Johnson Cultists Jeer American in U.N. Group', *New York Times*, 4 April 1965: 5.
10. 'Johnson Cultists Jeer American in U.N. Group', op. cit.
11. 'The Presidents: LBJ'. Accessed 16 July 2003 at:
   http://www.pbs.org/wgbh/amex/presidents/nf/teach/john/johndk.html.
12. 'Stone Age Election', *Time* 83: 40 (28 February 1964).
13. 'Don't Eat the Candidate', *Newsweek* 63: 40 (9 March 1964).
14. 'New Guinea Cult Ends Efforts to "Buy" Johnson', op. cit.
15. 'President Johnson Cultists Vacate New Guinea Areas', op. cit.
16. Billings, Dorothy K. (2002), *Cargo Cult as Theater: Political Performance in the Pacific*. Lanham, Maryland: Lexington Books.
17. Geiszler-Jones, Amy (2002), 'Billings Studies Pacific "Cult"', *Inside Witchita State University* (online edition), 6 November 2002. Accessed at:

http://www.wichita.edu/insidewsu.

18. Geiszler-Jones (2002), op. cit.
19. Billings (1969), op. cit., p. 169.
20. Billings (1969), op. cit., p. 17.
21. Billings (1969), op. cit., p. 17. For a more detailed discussion of this performance, see Billings (2002).
22. My thanks to Dorothy Billings whom I interviewed by phone concerning her research, 6 August 2003.
23. Clarke, W.C. (1973), 'Temporary Madness as Theatre: Wild-Man Behaviour in New Guinea', *Oceania* 43 (3): 198–214; Newman, P. L. (1964), '"Wild Man" Behavior in a New Guinea Highlands Community', *American Anthropologist* 66: 1–19.
24. Bartholomew, Robert E. (2000), *Exotic Deviance: Medicalizing Cultural Idioms – From Strangeness to Illness*. Boulder, Colorado: University Press of Colorado.
25. Newman (1964), op. cit., p. 7.
26. Littlewood, R. and Lipsedge, M. (1985), 'Culture-bound Syndromes', pp. 105–42, in K. Granville-Grossman (ed.), *Recent Advances in Clinical Psychiatry*. London: Churchill Livingstone, p. 119.
27. Newman, op. cit.
28. Reay, M. (1965), 'Mushroom Madness and Collective Hysteria', *Australian Territories* 5 (1): 18–28, see p. 26.
29. Reay, Marie (1960), '"Mushroom Madness" in the New Guinea Highlands', *Oceania* 31 (2): 137–9.
30. Reay (1960), op. cit., p. 138.
31. Reay (1960), op. cit., p. 139.
32. Reay (1960), op. cit., p. 139.
33. Heim, R. and Wasson, R.G. (1965), 'The "Mushroom Madness" of the Kuma', *Botanical Museum Leaflets*, Harvard University 21 (1): 1–36, see p. 20.
34. Reay (1965), op. cit., 5: 22–4.
35. 'Boletus Manicus'. Accessed 5 June 2003 at: http://www.entheogen.com/boletusm.html; Thomas, Benjamin (2002), '"Mushroom Madness" in the Papua New Guinea Highlands: A Case of Nicotine Poisoning?', *Journal of Psychoactive Drugs* 34 (3): 321–3; Reay, Marie (1977), 'Ritual Madness Observed: A Discarded Pattern of Fate in Papua New Guinea', *Journal of Pacific History* 12: 55–79.
36. Excerpted and modified from Bartholomew, Robert E. (1999), 'Rejoinder to Invited Replies by Drs Ronald Simons, Michael G. Kenny and Robert L. Winzeler on "The Conspicuous Absence of a Single Case of *Latah*-Related Death or Serious Injury"', *Transcultural Psychiatry* 36 (3): 393–7.
37. Bartholomew, Robert E. (1999), 'The Conspicuous Absence of a Single Case of *Latah*-Related Death or Serious Injury', *Transcultural Psychiatry* 36 (3):

369–76; Bartholomew, R.E. (1997), 'The Medicalization of the Exotic: *Latah* as a Colonialism-Bound Syndrome', *Deviant Behavior* 18: 47–75; Bartholomew, R.E. (1994), 'Disease, Disorder or Deception? *Latah* as Habit in a Malay Extended Family', *Journal of Nervous and Mental Disease* 182: 331–8.

38. This paragraph is a modified version which was published in Bartholomew, Robert E. (1999), 'Rejoinder'.

39. 'Jungle Find', *New York Times*, 11 July 1971, section IV, p. 3.

40. Wilford, John Noble (1971), 'Stone-Age Tribe in Philippines is Imperiled', *New York Times*, 17 October 1971, section IV, p. 64.

41. 'Lost Tribe of the Tasaday', *Time*, 18 October, pp. 58, 60.

42. 'Manila Gives Land to Cave Dwellers', *New York Times*, 7 April 1972: 2.

43. MacLeish, Kenneth, and Launois, John (1972), 'The Tasadays: Stone Age Cavemen of Mindanao', *National Geographic* 142 (2): 219–9.

44. MacLeish and Launois (1972), op. cit., pp. 218–19.

45. MacLeish and Launois (1972), op. cit., p. 226.

46. Nance (1975), op. cit., p. 447.

47. Nance (1975), op. cit., p. 447.

48. Iten, Oswald (1992), 'The "Tasaday" and the Press', pp. 40–58 in *The Tasaday Controversy: Assessing the Evidence* (edited by Thomas N. Headland), a Special Publication of the American Anthropological Association, no. 28, Scholarly Series. Washington, DC: American Anthropological Association, p. 50.

49. Iten, Oswald (1986), 'Die Tasaday: Ein Philippinischer Steinzeit Schwindel', *Neue Zurcher Zeitung* (Zurich), 12–13 April: 77–9.

50. Iten (1992), op. cit., p. 47.

51. Iten (1992), op. cit., pp. 40–1.

52. Berreman, Gerald D. (1992), 'The Tasaday: Stone Age Survivors or Space Age Fakes?', pp. 21–39 in *The Tasaday Controversy: Assessing the Evidence* (edited by Thomas N. Headland), a Special Publication of the American Anthropological Association, no. 28, Scholarly Series. Washington, DC: American Anthropological Association. Marshall, E. (1989), 'Anthropologists Debate Tasaday Hoax Evidence', *Science* 246: 1113–14, see p. 1114.

53. Berreman (1992), op. cit., p. 33.

54. Nance (1975), op. cit., p. 287.

55. Berreman (1992), op. cit., p. 34.

56. Elizalde, Manuel Jr, and Fox, Robert A. (1971), *The Tasaday Forest People: A Data Paper on a Newly Discovered Food-Gathering and Stone-Tool-Using Manobo Group in the Mountains of South Catabato, Mindanao. Philippines*. Washington, DC: Smithsonian Institution, Center for Short-Lived Phenomena; Llamzon, Teodoro A. (1971), 'The Tasaday Language So Far', *Philippine Journal of Linguistics* 2 (2): 1–30; Lynch, Frank, and

Llamzon, Teodoro A. (1971), 'The B'lit Manobo and the Tasaday', *Philippine Sociological Review* 19 (1–2): 91–2.

57. Fernandez, Carlos II, and Lynch, Frank (1984), 'The Tasaday: Cave-Dwelling Food Gatherers of South Cotabato, Minanao', pp. 231–78, in A.A. Yengoyann and P.Q. Makil (eds), *Philippine Society and the Individual: Selected Essays of Frank Lynch, 1949–1976*. Ann Arbor: University of Michigan, Center for South and Southeast Asian Studies, Michigan Papers in South and Southeast Asia no. 24, p. 231.

58. Dumont, Jean-Paul (1988), 'The Tasaday, Which and Whose? Toward the Political Economy of an Ethnographic Sign', *Cultural Anthropology* 3 (3): 261–75, see p. 262.

59. Moses, Judith (1990), Letter, *Anthropology Today* 6 (1): 22.

60. Iten (1992), op. cit., p. 51.

61. McCarry, Charles (1988), 'Three Men Who Made the Magazine', *National Geographic* 174 (3): 287–316.

Chapter Ten

1. Cited in Jones, A. (ed.), *Chambers Dictionary of Quotations*. New York: New York, p. 635.

2. Telephone interview with Jefferson Kaye, op. cit.; telephone interview with John Zach, op. cit.

3. Robert Bartholomew interview with Justin Levine, 26 November 2003.

4. Bartholomew, Robert E. and Jamaludin, Ahmad (2000), 'Contemporary Malaysian Encounters with Fairies and Aliens', *Australian Folklore* 15: 178–98 (August); Bartholomew, Robert E., Jamaludin, Ahmad, and Ryan, J.S. (2000), 'Perspectives on the Recently Reported Malaysian Extraterrestrial Encounters', *Australian Folklore* 15: 199 (August).

5. Interview with Justin Levine, op. cit.

6. Interview with Justin Levine, op. cit.

Index